THE CAMPAIGN IN GERMAN SOUTH WEST AFRICA
1914 - 1915

THE CAMPAIGN IN GERMAN SOUTH WEST AFRICA
1914 - 1915

By
BRIGADIER-GENERAL J. J. COLLYER
C.B., C.M.G., D.S.O.

*Formerly Chief of the General Staff
Union Defence Forces*

The Naval & Military Press Ltd

Published by

The Naval & Military Press Ltd
Unit 5 Riverside, Brambleside
Bellbrook Industrial Estate
Uckfield, East Sussex
TN22 1QQ England

Tel: +44 (0)1825 749494

www.naval-military-press.com
www.nmarchive.com

In reprinting in facsimile from the original, any imperfections are inevitably reproduced and the quality may fall short of modern type and cartographic standards.

♦ PREFACE ♦

> *We learn wisdom from failure much more than from success. We often discover what will do by finding out what will not do; and probably he who never made a mistake never made a discovery.*

THE ABOVE WORDS indicate one, and perhaps the most forcible, of several motives which have prompted the writing of the record which follows.

The campaign in German South West Africa in 1914-15—incidentally the only land campaign undertaken, planned and brought to a conclusion by the military forces of any Dominion of the British Empire entirely on its own responsibility in the Great War—was the first, and remains at this date, the only, campaign in which the military forces of the Union of South Africa have been employed on active service in such numbers as proved to be necessary.

That there were many mistakes, as well as successes, stands to reason, if for no other cause than that, excepting a very small nucleus of regular troops, citizen forces were employed throughout.

The Citizen Force established under the Defence Act proved to be numerically far short of the total strength required, and expansion—unforeseen and unprovided for—had to be effected.

If this volume should catch the eye and engage the attention of any trained professional soldier, he is asked to realise—before dismissing the comments and criticisms as quite elementary and perhaps superfluous—that the mistakes *were* made, and unless remembered and guarded against, will in all probability be made again in similar circumstances. Should such an emergency as that of 1914 again face South Africa, great expansion of her regularly maintained forces will become an immediate necessity.

A second object is to record the operation of a strategy based on a national system of tactics.

In the event of serious attack by a stronger nation, South Africa will have to supplement an inferiority in respect of *all* modern appliances of war by employing to the full, as she has done before, every single advantage which may accrue from a national system of defence based on any special aptitude of her citizen soldiers for war in the terrain in which they will have to fight.

Weak nations have constantly sought aid from the physical features of their country and a system of defence which takes full advantage of such natural support.

Finally, the writer has endeavoured to give some idea of the characteristics and methods of a great South African soldier whose example should always prove an inspiration to his fellow countrymen.

It would seem desirable that some explanation should be offered of the comparatively brief record of the operations in the south and south-east of German South West Africa after the arrival of General Botha at SWAKOPMUND.

Though these operations, except as regards the transport difficulty, exercised slight influence strategically on the decisive campaign in the north, the work done by the troops engaged in them in country practically the counterpart of that northward, and facing physical difficulties as formidable as they were in other parts of the country, suffers in no way when compared with that elsewhere. It is therefore a matter for much regret that little record of them exists.

The omission to prepare any plans for military operations anywhere before war broke out (this defect is fully dealt with in the text) and the failure, except in the case of General Botha's operations, to keep full records or furnish periodical dispatches to Defence Headquarters are the main causes of the meagre account of the southern operations.

Presumably the official historian suffered also from this paucity of information, for in his account of 50 pages he has not been able to devote more than two full pages, and a few lines on two others, to the operations of the Southern and Eastern Forces.

To the same cause must be attributed the form of the record which follows.

It admittedly lacks the regular and precise form which is of much value to the student and which is a feature of studies of campaigns for the compilation of which full records kept on regular and identical lines throughout the forces engaged are available.

Where comment or criticism is offered it is to be understood as the expression of the writer's opinion.

In each case the facts upon which that opinion is based are given, and, with access to the facts, a reader is enabled to pay only such attention as he may feel disposed to accord to the writer's views and is in a position to form his own.

J. J. COLLYER.

October, 1936.

♦ LIST OF MAPS ♦

	Facing Page
Map of South West Africa (*Frontispiece*)	1
Lines of Communication of Opposing Forces	24
Dispositions and Movements in Connection with Action at Sandfontein	32
Action at Sandfontein	40
Situation on Arrival of General Botha at Swakopmund	56
Movement of General Botha's Force from Swakopmund	57
Engagements at Riet, Pforte and Jakalswater	65
Plan of Action at Gibeon Station	88
McKenzie's March to Gibeon	89
General Situation on General Botha's Second Advance	97
General Botha's Movements Against Karibib and Windhoek	104
Strategic Result of General Botha's Five Days Operations	105
General Botha's Movements in the Final Advance	128
Movements of Night, June 30-July 1, 1915, and Action at Otavifontein, 1 July, 1915	137
Final Movements Leading to Surrender	145
Strategical Positions: 26 September, 1914, and End of March, 1915	160

♦ ♦

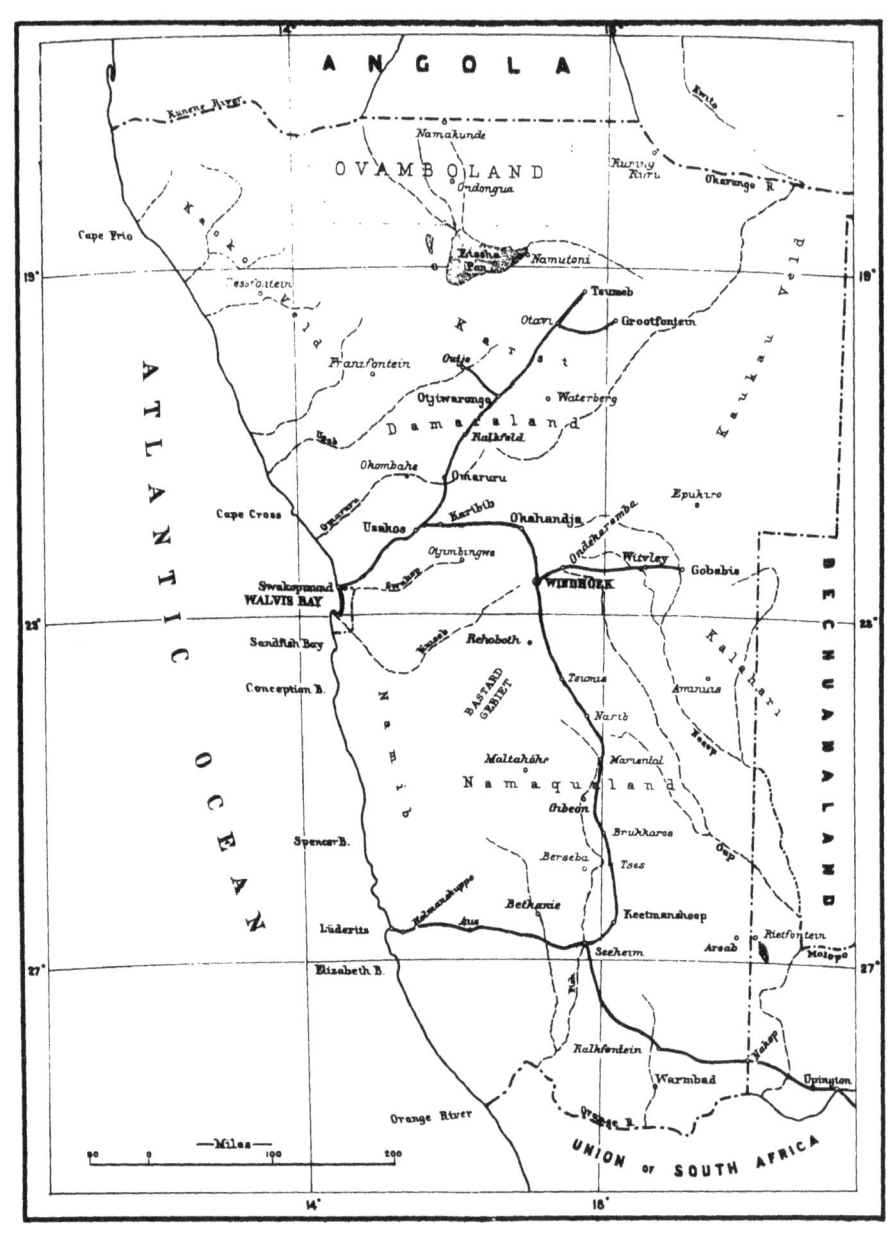

SOUTH WEST AFRICA

CHAPTER I

THE WORLD WAR of 1914-18 gave rise to many minor campaigns and among them was one which alone was planned, conducted and brought to a successful conclusion by a self-governing Dominion of the British Empire.

This was the expedition undertaken by the Government of the Union of South Africa against the neighbouring Territory of German South West Africa.

Apart from any general interest it may possess, the campaign has a special interest for South Africa, as it was the first occasion of the employment on active service of the then recently formed Union Defence Forces which came into being as united forces on the passage of the South Africa Defence Act through the Union Parliament in 1912.

As might be expected, the test of war revealed at once the weaknesses and the strength of those forces in the most practical way.

South Africa, always a strategic point of great importance, has now become almost indispensable to any scheme of Empire defence since the appearance of a European Power on the continent of Africa within striking distance of British territory as the occupant, by right of conquest, of Ethiopia.

This occupation constitutes a potential menace to the Suez Canal, and the alternative route to the East by the Cape of Good Hope has an enhanced value.

In 1914 the maintenance of the naval base at SIMONSTOWN and the free passage of such sinews of war as gold, wool and maize were considerations which could not be ignored.

In that year, immediately bordering on the territory of the Union, lay the German Imperial Protectorate of German South West Africa.

The first visit from the Cape into GREAT NAMAQUALAND, the southern half of this Protectorate (the scene of the operations which will be described), was made in 1685 by Governor van der Stel. From that date the territory was occasionally visited by other travellers.

Moravian missionaries were the first settlers in the country of the Griquas in 1799 and afterwards made their way into GREAT NAMAQUALAND. They were followed by the missionaries of other societies.

The Campaign in German South West Africa, 1914-1915

Of these the most active proved to be the Rhenish Missionary Society which established its first station at BETHANY in 1842.

Though they regarded the country as then being under British protection and influence, they maintained close intercourse with Germany and eventually influenced the policy of the German Government in the crisis of 1884.

The country became known, in spite of its inhospitable nature in many of its parts, as well adapted for cattle raising in the interior uplands.

The pioneers and missionaries were followed by the traders and the usual consequences of their activities ensued.

The lives and properties of the settlers were endangered, traders were killed and dwellings burnt by the natives, and both British and German subjects were living in insecurity.

In 1867 the Governor of the Cape Colony, Sir Philip Wodehouse, urged the British Government to extend its authority over the south-west coast up to just north of SWAKOPMUND and WINDHOEK, but the latter refused to take action fearing the extension of responsibility without prospect of adequate material return.

Both the Cape Government and the Germans, however, were anxious that some stable administration of the territory should be assured, and in 1868 the Rhenish Missionary Society urged the intervention of Great Britain and asked for a commissioner and some troops. " In the last two years ", they said, " the prestige of the British name has been lost in the above-mentioned lands which adjoin Cape Colony."

The intervention on behalf of French missionaries in Basutoland was quoted and it was suggested that the British Government would be well advised to adopt similar measures in Damaraland and, it was added prophetically, " the Namaqua-Hereroland coast might be of greater importance than Basutoland for the further development of South Africa."

Beyond aiding to conclude a peace between the tribes of the country, then engaged in fighting among themselves, the British Government did nothing.

In 1875 the Cape Parliament, bowing to public opinion, passed a resolution that the limits of the Cape Colony should be extended so as to acquire Walvis Bay and as much of the country adjacent to it as might be found expedient.

A Commissioner, Mr. Palgrave, was sent to the tribes north of the Orange River in the next year, 1876, to explain to them

The Campaign in German South West Africa, 1914-1915

" the benefit they would derive from colonial rule and government ".

German merchants were by this time active in the country and owned many fine stores.

Samuel Maherero, Paramount Chief of the Hereros, asked that " someone should be sent to rule us and be the head of our country ".

Several petty chiefs submitted similar requests and Europeans expressed their view that it was urgently necessary that " this country be placed under British rule and protection ".

Sir Bartle Frere, Governor at the Cape, on receipt of this practically unanimous request for intervention, strongly advised the annexation of the coast up to the Portuguese border. He significantly represented that, in spite of German readiness to agree to a British protectorate, the German Government were really anxious to secure an entry into the country.

These representations were virtually ignored and the only action taken by the British Government was the annexation of Walvis Bay and 40 miles of coast to a depth of 20 miles on 12th March, 1878.

For the next six years, in spite of warnings from Sir Bartle Frere and others, a policy of hesitation and vacillation was pursued by British and Cape Government alike, and in 1883 Heinrich Vogelsang, the agent of a Herr Lüderitz, a Bremen merchant, obtained a cession of 215 square miles at ANGRA PEQUENA (now LUDERITZBUCHT) from a chief, Joseph Frederick, and there hoisted the German flag in the territory of the first German Colony.

In October, 1884, a German protectorate was recognised over Great Namaqualand, and a year later a similar recognition in the case of Damaraland became effective.

German South West Africa became the possession of a great military nation on the border of what was to be the Union of South Africa.

For fuller detail of the different steps in the events described above, the reader is referred to " The Germans and Africa ", by Evans Lewin, from which the information has been taken.

Twelve years before the outbreak of the Great War in 1914 the Anglo-Boer War of 1899-1902 had terminated, and in order that the events which occurred in the Union after the decision of its Government to attack the Germans on its borders may be rightly appreciated, it is necessary that the political situation

The Campaign in German South West Africa, 1914-1915

after the conclusion of peace in South Africa in 1902 should be made clear.

The war, fought between Great Britain and the two Republics, the South African Republic in the Transvaal and the Orange Free State, in alliance, inevitably left an aftermath of inflamed and bitter feeling, for it drew into its orbit Afrikaans-speaking and English-speaking South Africans on opposite sides often in the conditions of the bitterest of all war, civil war.

The struggle represented the culmination of differences, misunderstanding and resentment on both sides over more than a century, too often fanned to heat by party political action.

The defeat of the Republics entailed the total loss of their independence and, so far as the individual burghers were concerned, in most cases of all their wordly goods. Severe measures, judged by those in authority to be necessary to end the war, though many who had to give effect to them and to face the prospect of living alongside the sufferers were dubious as to the need and occasionally even the justice of them, tended further to produce feelings of hatred and strong resentment.

That Afrikaans-speaking South Africans and those of British descent should find it possible at all to fight beside each other as comrades after the experience of 12 years earlier, as they did in German South West Africa, is surprising enough.

That it was found possible may be largely attributed to the courage and political sagacity of Sir Henry Campbell-Bannerman, the Prime Minister of Great Britain, who restored the territory of the two republics to the control of their former peoples by the grant of responsible government to the Transvaal and Orange Free State in 1906, and to the fundamental humanity and common sense of either race.

Four years later, in 1910, the Union of South Africa was established with General Louis Botha as its first Prime Minister, with a Cabinet composed of Afrikaans- and English-speaking colleagues.

Striking as the co-operation was, however, it may be well supposed that the utmost care had often to be exercised to avoid easily hurt susceptibilities and racial pride, particularly in the pressure and strain of active service. The situation was at times delicate, calling for much forbearance and tact on either side.

In such circumstances it was hardly to be wondered at that some of the former soldiers of the Republics who had never forgotten nor forgiven the loss of their independence should view any semblance of real co-operation with the power that they regarded as responsible for that loss with repugnance.

Mindful rather of the differences of the past than of the possibilities of the present, they hailed the entry of Great Britain into the World War as a heaven-sent opportunity for an effort to regain the complete independence which they considered they had lost.

It is almost more surprising that only some 11,000 in all—many of them, as those who took part in the operations in the Union are well aware, under complete misapprehension—should have taken up arms, as it will be seen they did, against the Government.

The German Government were, of course, well aware of the military advantage of such a diversion as the Rebellion, and probably supposed, and certainly hoped, that it would prove to be a far more decisive and general movement than it did.

The extent to which any citizens of the Union had been suborned will never be known, but it would be idle to pretend that arrangements for rebellion had not been made with the enemy across the Union border some time before the declaration of war.

The co-operation of the Boers against England had been regarded by the Germans as practical politics as far back as 1880 when, just after the recall of Sir Bartle Frere from the Cape of Good Hope, Ernst von Weber, in an article in the " Geographische Nachrichten ", wrote:—

"A new empire, possibly more valuable and more brilliant than even the Indian Empire, awaits, in the newly-discovered Central Africa, that Power which shall possess sufficient courage, strength and intelligence to acquire it.

. . . .

In South East Africa we Germans have quite a peculiar interest, for here dwell a splendid race of people allied to us by speech and habits. The Boers or farmers there are the descendants of former Dutch Settlers; and they are, as I most emphatically maintain, our kinsmen and brethren; so-called Low-Germans to be sure, but none the less of right Teutonic blood . . . and one may speak of a nation of Afrikaanders or Low-German Africans, which forms one sympathetic race from Table Mountain to the Limpopo. This is a fact which would be of great importance in any possible future rising of the Boers having for its object the formation of a Dutch African confederation. . . .

For the sake of sure and certain protection from the greed of annexation of the hateful English Government, the Boers would gladly have placed themselves under the German Government in the form of two protected states, with as far as possible their own free self-government."

While the extent of the help which Afrikaans-speaking citizens of the Union were prepared to give to their German neighbours in the event of a quarrel with Great Britain was probably much overestimated in Germany, there was disaffection to some extent in the Union as will be seen.

Almost immediately after the outbreak of war in 1914, the Union Government offered to take upon itself all the obligations for the fulfilment of which a military garrison was maintained in South Africa by the British Government which accepted the offer on August 6 and at once began preparations for the evacuation of its forces to Europe.

Since the termination of the Anglo-Boer War in 1902 a military garrison, of considerable dimensions at first, but which had undergone successive reductions in strength, had been maintained by the British Government in South Africa. The defence of the Cape Peninsula had, of course, been its concern since 1815.

In spite of the satisfactory political situation, the unreadiness of the newly-formed Union Defence Forces, referred to in more detail on page 30, and the lack of trained specialist troops for coast defence, had precluded the earlier entire withdrawal of Imperial troops.

On August 10 the Ministers of the Union further pledged themselves to dispatch a military expedition against the enemy forces in German South West Africa in order to secure the seaports of that territory and the powerful wireless installation at WINDHOEK.

The presence of the German Asiatic Naval Squadron in southern latitudes made it necessary to deny to it bases on the coast of South West Africa and to deprive it of facilities for wireless communication, and the British Government had asked the Union Government to undertake the task of seizing the bases and destroying the means of communication which the Secretary of State for the Colonies described as " a great and urgent Imperial service ".

The Campaign in German South West Africa, 1914-1915

The first objectives of the military forces of the Union, then, were the wireless installation at WINDHOEK, in the north of Germany territory, and the sea bases on its coast.

There were two ports, SWAKOPMUND, close to WALVIS BAY, in the north, and LUDERITZUCHT (formerly ANGRA PEQUENA), rather more than 50 miles north of the mouth of the Orange River, to the south.

The former was an open roadstead, and the Germans had built a long jetty from the shore for the landing of cargo from the steamers by lighters. This jetty was damaged and the local wireless station put out of action by naval bombardment shortly after the commencement of hostilities.

LUDERITZBUCHT, though not to be compared with the excellent natural harbour at WALVIS BAY, was a useful port, and became the objective of the first military force which left the Union by sea.

It is now necessary to appreciate the nature of the task to which the Union Government had put its hand, and first to consider the field of the coming operations.

The largest part of South West Africa is a plateau of an average altitude of 3,500 feet above sea-level. It has a very limited rainfall and the temperature varies greatly.

Along the railway from WINDHOEK to KARIBIB northwards there is a narrow belt, broadening out in the same direction to OUTJO and GROOTFONTEIN, which receives more rain.

Water is very scarce and is only obtainable from under the surface and in well-known localities, a fact which, as far as watering any considerable force goes, strictly limits possible lines of advance by an invading force and greatly aids the defence.

To the west the plateau falls rapidly to sea-level, forming a barren and waterless desert belt to the coast from 40 to 100 miles wide. This belt is devoid of any kind of sustenance for man and beast.

At the time of the campaign there were no made roads, and the country was extremely difficult for any kind of transport.

Beyond the edge of the desert some grass begins to show itself and the grass veld, such as it is, continues inland where it is broken by highlands of considerable altitude—about 5,000 feet in the neighbourhood of WINDHOEK and still higher further north.

The Campaign in German South West Africa, 1914-1915

To the south, in Great Namaqualand, the country is of a poorer quality, but the highlands are continued to the borders of the Cape Province at altitudes ranging from 2,000 to 3,000 feet.

The considerable heights make the temperature cold in the winter, when the thermometer frequently drops appreciably below freezing point.

To the east of South West Africa lies the Kalahari Desert, an absolutely sterile waste, presenting no opportunities for agriculture or pasturage.

A terrain presenting many disadvantages to an invading force, but served by a climate which is wonderfully healthy for human beings and animals alike.

CHAPTER II

WITHOUT A KNOWLEDGE of the special characteristics of the soldiers of the two white races in South Africa and of the nature and composition of the forces in which they served, a proper estimate of what they achieved in the German South West African campaign is impossible.

For this knowledge it is necessary to go back to the Anglo-Boer War of 1899-1902.

The history of the many events which, in the course of 100 years, led up to this trial of strength is recorded in many extant works, and it is by a comparison of the military methods of each of the combatants in the struggle that a true conception of the military characteristics of the South African soldier of twelve years later may best be arrived at.

In 1899 the bulk of the forces opposed to those of the South African Republic and the Orange Free State were furnished from the British regular army reinforced to some extent by small detachments from the Colonies and a substantial number of local irregular units drawn chiefly from the English-speaking population of the Cape Colony and Natal.

These Colonial troops were in some measure not unlike the burghers of the Republics, notably in their self-reliance, independence of spirit, knowledge of local conditions and tactical sense.

The British Army had not taken part in any great war since that in the Crimea in 1854-56, and its experience of active service in the second half of the 19th century, though continuous and varied, had been largely gained against savage enemies.

In any case, it had not been pitted against the highly trained, armed, organised and disciplined army of a Great Power.

Thus large numbers of its officers, non-commissioned officers and rank and file had participated in a considerable amount of fighting on active service, but against weaker and, as a rule, poorly armed adversaries who, though in greatly superior strength, rarely inflicted any heavy casualties except when a lapse or carelessness on the part of their opponents gave them an opening.

In consequence, while the British Army had much experience

of overcoming very severe physical difficulties, and, as a result of this experience, was adept in matters of supply and transport in most trying conditions, it lacked any real scientific staff system and a general staff (or thinking department) was non-existent.

There was no system of selecting staff officers nor was any opportunity afforded of training them.

In the words of the " Times History of the War in South Africa ":—

" Englishmen who would not dream of sending a crew to Henley Regatta whose members had never rowed together before were quite content that a General's Staff should be hastily improvised at the last moment from officers scraped together from every corner."

And again:

" Nowhere was there any definite preparation for war, nowhere any conception that war was the one end and object for which armies exist."

Making due allowance for local difficulties and conditions, these words might have been truthfully written of the Union Defence Forces in 1914.

One serious result of the absence of a General Staff was that no systematic and continuous examination of future conditions or theatres of war had been maintained, and the British Army had adhered to a rigid formal type of tactics, and, when faced with the conditions in South Africa early in the Anglo-Boer War, was tactically inflexible and its soldiers were quite incapable of adapting themselves to circumstances of which they had been previously ignorant.

They were no match for their straight-shooting, invisible, highly mobile enemies.

Great traditions, fine discipline, stubborn bravery and keen *esprit de corps* were shorn of all their great military value except as the stimulus of an example of how to take punishment and accept defeat, and greater resources and efficient supply and transport arrangements did nothing to compensate for the want of competent direction and sound tactical training.

After the war the Esher Committee for the reconstitution of the War Office in 1904 instituted great reforms.

The General and Administrative Staffs were separated—though the complete separation usual on the Continent of Europe was not effected—fighting commanders were relieved of routine business work, and perhaps it is not too much to say that it is

The Campaign in German South West Africa, 1914-1915

to the early defeats and disasters to British arms in South Africa at the end of last century that the Empire owes the General Staff and highly-trained professional army which saved the situation on the Western European front in 1914.

In addition to the defects which have been mentioned, the consistently satisfactory result of all the campaigns—with a notable exception, also in South Africa, in 1880-81—in which the British Army had been engaged with a relatively insignificant casualty list had naturally produced a feeling of superiority with a not unusual tendency to underrate an opponent.

Certain it is that both the magnitude of the task and the calibre of the enemy were seriously misunderstood by the British nation and War Office in 1899, though a plain warning had been given at MAJUBA 18 years before.

The military forces of the two Republics in 1899 were the product of the conditions of life of the burghers in the ranks and of their predecessors.

The idea, widely prevalent in Great Britain just before the war, that the Boers were simply bodies of farmers with rifles who would put up a brave, but short and ineffectual resistance against the soldiers of a disciplined army, was woefully mistaken.

The Boer was essentially a fighting man and the organisation and tactics of the commandos in which he served reflected a truly national system of defence.

It is impossible here to examine all the causes which prompted the different treks which finally took the Boers up to the Transvaal—as has been mentioned, they are fully recorded in history—but it may be broadly stated that a thoroughly independent spirit, impatient of the restraint and formality of life in the settled centres, urged the Boer to remove himself from the restrictions imported from the older countries and to take up his abode in fresh places where he was entirely independent of others and largely left to his own devices.

In the early days he lived remote from his fellow men in uncivilised country where he maintained himself and his family in the midst of native tribes by his own efforts, relying upon his astuteness and gun for his protection and often upon the latter for his food.

In such circumstances every bullet had to find its billet and he could afford to waste no single shot.

The habit of careful approach to a good fire position whence the quarry might be dealt with at a disadvantage and with

The Campaign in German South West Africa, 1914-1915

certainty, and without warning of the approach of its attacker, became second nature. This fact explains both the Boer tactics and the implicit reliance of their exponents on the rifle as their sole weapon. It also accounts largely for the omission in later years to estimate properly the role of artillery as a means of support and attack.

These tactics and their effect were clearly revealed in 1880-81 at BRONKHORSTSPRUIT, where in ten mintes a British force lost 66 per cent. of its strength, at LAING'S NEK and INGOGO, and finally at MAJUBA, where 200 Boers scaled the mountain held by more than twice that number of regular soldiers, whom they routed with a loss of 50 per cent., their own casualties amounting to two.

Had an efficient staff system existed in the British Army from 1880 to 1899, these striking lessons would have been recorded and taken to heart and most likely not repeated, as they were twenty years later. There was, however, no such system and the warning was totally ignored.

General de Wet once said that " a Boer without his horse is only half a man ", and it was the horse that completed the equipment of the Burghers of 1899 for the successes which they achieved in the Anglo-Boer War.

They were of course fine horsemen, and though an extraordinary notion to the contrary sometimes finds expression, admirable horsemasters. Their horses, trained to stand when their riders dismounted to fire—an advantage which did away with the horseholders usual in trained armies, and swelled the firing line accordingly—hardy and handy and moving at a pace which combined the maximum speed with the minimum physical demand on the riders, or their mounts, together with a frugal mode of life, conferred on the commandos their extraordinary mobility.

As rifle fire was the sole method of inflicting loss upon his enemy upon which the Boer mounted rifleman relied, anything like shock tactics, involving close contact with his foe, was entirely opposed to his scheme of fighting. Accordingly he always kept a way of retreat in his mind to enable him to abandon a position when danger of being surrounded became apparent. His retirement was to another position where, secure from encirclement, he once more awaited a favourable chance of getting his advancing enemy under an effective rifle fire.

The Campaign in German South West Africa, 1914-1915

The "Boer Mounted Charge" resorted to in the later stages of the Anglo-Boer War was usually a rapid advance in mass to gain a closer fire position before having recourse once more to the rifle.

A reluctance to push home an attack, of which there were several remarkable instances in the larger battles of the war, was emphatically not due to want of courage, for in this respect the burgher was the equal of any other soldier.

It was chiefly the consequence of the view that, having repulsed the enemy and having inflicted heavy loss upon him, it was merely stupid to give him any chance of retaliating in kind.

It follows that many tactical successes fell short of full result and that opportunities against an enemy who had been driven off in confusion and with heavy loss were allowed to slip by.

In the early days a common danger was met by a concentration of scattered burghers who elected a leader, usually of some age and whose standing was assured, and this was the genesis of the commando system, later improved and regularised under organisation.

This system was in operation at the outbreak of the Anglo-Boer War, all burghers of from sixteen to sixty years of age being liable for military service.

The main defects of the system were:—

The election of officers which at the outset of hostilities gave to the Republican Armies leaders who were past the age at which vigorous action may be reasonably looked for, and at a time when bold leading would have enormously enhanced their success.

Lack of discipline, for the same self reliance that gave the burger no inconsiderable degree of his tactical value made him fret at any kind of interference with his freedom of action.

Finally, the armies of the South African Republic and Orange Free State were not under one undivided command and were without any staff system.

The faults and failures on either side from 1899 to 1902 were almost all traceable to the weak points which have been described as in either military system.

On the date of Union, eight years after the conclusion of the Peace of Vereeniging, when the Colonies of the Cape and Natal and the two former Republics of the Transvaal and Orange Free State became the four Provinces of the Union of South

The Campaign in German South West Africa, 1914-1915

Africa, the following military forces and arrangements for their supervision were in existence.

In the Cape Colony there was a small permanent force, varying from 1,000 to 750 strong, the Cape Mounted Riflemen, organised on a military basis and mainly stationed in or close to the Native Territories of the Transkei with a large strength at UMTATA. It furnished the means of training some officers selected for staff work in regimental duty.

There was a permanent command of all the Cape Colonial Forces—permanent and volunteer—exercised by a Commandant-General, who was also the Commanding Officer of the Cape Mounted Riflemen, assisted by one or two staff officers.

The bulk of the Cape Forces—some 3,000 all told—was composed of volunteer regiments. Several of these had long traditions and had served in local campaigns and kaffir wars.

The militia force of Natal differed from the Cape Volunteer Force in no essential respect, either as regards strength or composition. It had its regiments of good record.

The Transvaal Volunteer Force was of much more recent origin, but in other respects much the same as the other two. It had come into existence after the Anglo-Boer War and was practically entirely composed of English-speaking citizens of the Transvaal.

In each of these provinces there was a command of the Forces by a Commandant-General (as has been explained) in the Cape, by an officer similarly styled in Natal and by an Inspector of Volunteers in the Transvaal, in each instance aided by one or two staff officers.

Until after Union no force was provided for in the Orange Free State.

A very small number of officers were trained in any of the Colonies for staff work, though some of those who held staff appointments had had experience of staff work in the field and here and there one or two had attended the Staff College at Camberley for a year.

The volunteer forces exhibited the advantages and the defects inherent in such a system.

Principal among the former was a strong element of keen officers and non-commissioned officers as well as a small proportion of the rank and file who, impelled by an active sense of duty and responsibility, gave up time and leisure, and often money, to consistent efforts to become proficient in their military duties.

The Campaign in German South West Africa, 1914-1915

This useful nucleus was, however, only a nucleus, and all Volunteer Commanding Officers had to contend with the difficult problem arising out of the existence of a large number of volunteers in the ranks who merely did the least amount of training demanded for regulation " efficiency " and attended the minimum number of drills to earn the capitation grant for their corps, and the by no means inconsiderable quantity of those who failed to do even this.

The training of all the three forces was based as far as possible on that of the British Army at that time.

The main defect of such a system is that it is impossible to produce a uniform and satisfactory degree of efficiency in a force which contains a certain percentage of interested members who take every opportunity of learning, while the larger proportion attain a mere paper efficiency, and an appreciable number fail to do anything at all.

The Defence Act of 1912 showed recognition of the unsatisfactory features of a Volunteer System and, except for the retention of some of the older colonial volunteer regiments to the extent of perpetuating their former titles under certain conditions, abandoned that system altogether.

The first and main line of defence of the Union became the Active Citizen Force, and all members of this force were compelled by law to undergo such continuous and non-continuous training as it was considered would produce an adequate return for the expenditure of public money in the shape of practical efficiency. Penalties for failure to undergo this training were made enforceable by the civil courts on the application of the military authorities.

By the end of 1913 the Active Citizen Force was composed of units of all arms in which the best personnel of the old Volunteer Regiments was incorporated with the addition of those citizens of seventeen to twenty-one years of age who entered under the new conditions.

The latter provided for voluntary entry for four years' peace training and service by all citizens of from seventeen to twenty-one years of age (both inclusive) up to the strength of the establishments. If the voluntary entries should fall short of the number required, any shortage was to be made good by the enforcement of the ballot in the case of citizens of twenty-one who had registered, as compelled to do by law, but had not entered voluntarily.

The Campaign in German South West Africa, 1914-1915

The first year's registration, in January, 1913, produced 44,193 voluntary entries (out of a total of 64,000 liable for service), a figure much in excess of the total establishment of 30,000.

The Active Citizen Force was thus filled by voluntary effort in the first year of its existence and contained the pick of the experienced volunteers and young manhood of the country.

It was this force which formed the original personnel and backbone of the units from South Africa which rendered such good service overseas in Europe and East Africa.

It furnished a proportion of the mounted units (especially from Natal) and the great bulk of the infantry and departmental units which took part in the campaign in German South West Africa.

There were, however, many South Africans with experience of active service, who did not belong to the Active Citizen Force but were anxious to bear their part in the first campaign of the Union Forces, and additional specially raised regiments gave them their opportunity of doing so.

The Transvaal and Free State, in addition, were a most valuable source of supply of mounted troops in the burghers, experienced veterans of the war of twelve years earlier, who, though over the age for the Active Citizen Force, were hardy and resourceful horsemen peculiarly well suited for a campaign of hard marching and rapid movements.

Twenty thousand of the thirty thousand troops employed to suppress the Rebellion were drawn from these burghers.

The mounted troops which served under General Botha in the north of German South West Africa and under General Smuts in the south were chiefly from this last-named quarter and were organised for the expedition on a basis and in formations specially suited to their traditional mode of fighting which will be described in detail later.

Individually they probably represented the mounted rifleman at his best.

Before the Rebellion in October, 1914, the whole burgher organisation had lain dormant since it left the field in May, 1902, on the conclusion of the Anglo-Boer War. All the officers, however, and a large percentage of the rank and file called out for the commandos in 1914 had had much practical experience of war in Southern Africa.

The Campaign in German South West Africa, 1914-1915

Broadly then, the troops which took the field in German South West Africa in 1914-15 may be classified as follows:—

Active Citizen Force units, which included the pick of the Volunteer Forces serving at the date of Union, 1910; special units in which older soldiers and volunteers of experience—almost entirely English-speaking South Africans—were enrolled; and commandos from the Transvaal and Orange Free State. The units from the first-named province, though preponderantly Afrikaans-speaking, contained many English-speaking men, while the Free Staters represented a more or less equal proportion of the two races.

There was every reason to anticipate that the soldiers of the fighting formations of the Union would prove to be staunch and stubborn fighters, and this anticipation was amply justified on different fronts in the ensuing four years of war.

But the finest efforts of the fighting troops often fail to repair the consequences of incompetent direction, and the best laid plans of a General suffer at the hands of an inexperienced and ill-trained, if zealous, staff.

No military system, therefore, which does not make the best possible provision for the teaching of staff work and the higher regimental duties to its officers, can do full justice to the efforts of the fighting soldier who has a right to expect that those who send him to war shall take every possible step to protect him, as far as may be, from unnecessary risk and use his efforts to the best advantage by ensuring that those who lead and direct him shall be competent for their work.

While the staff work of the three military organisations, which have been described, in the Cape, Natal and Transvaal was based on the system laid down for the British War Office by the Esher Committee, the staffs were so small and the forces so weak, each being not much more than a weak brigade, so far as numbers went, that there was a great want of officers with any experience of general staff duties. The citizen forces provided a source of supply of some administrative staff officers.

As far as the commanders were concerned, General Botha alone of all the senior officers had commanded any force much above 200 or 300 in strength, and was the only soldier in South Africa who had directed any considerable body of troops against a European enemy.

The previous experience of the Commandants, operating rapidly in command of small bodies without any central direction, without any kind of staff system, with no arrangements whatever for the supply of their troops or for the replacement of losses of any kind, even practically without medical arrangements, and, finally, with no lines of communication, enabled them to make great demands upon their men accustomed to suffer hardship in the field.

That these Commandants, suddenly placed in command of as many thousand troops as they had before controlled hundreds, did not realise that the greater numbers needed elaborate staff arrangements cannot be wondered at.

The surprising thing is that here and there an outstanding commander did appreciate the different conditions.

The circumstances last related must all be taken into consideration in any criticism of the conduct of operations in German South West Africa and are specially essential to a proper understanding of the great mobility of the commandos.

German officers, well trained in European methods of staff work, to the end of the operations under-estimated the mobility of the South African troops, even though they early conceived an immense respect for it.

The English-speaking units were all accustomed of course to far more formal arrangements.

We must now turn to the organisation at Defence Headquarters, for it must be realised—as will appear—that it was from PRETORIA alone that the campaign as a whole could be viewed.

Immediately after the Defence Act had become law in 1912 the formation of the Permanent Force (Headquarter, Instructional, and Administrative) was taken in hand.

The forces were divided into two commands. The five regiments of the Permanent Force, the South African Mounted Riflemen, were placed under the command of an Inspector-General (Brigadier-General H. T. Lukin). The first regiment was the Cape Mounted Riflemen already referred to, and the four remaining regiments were formed by transferring personnel of all ranks from the Police Forces of the Union. Though disciplined, these four regiments had no military training when war broke out in 1914. Many of the officers and some of the senior non-commissioned officers had served in the war of 1899-1902.

The Citizen Force, which included the Active Citizen Force and different reserves (liability for service in the defence of

The Campaign in German South West Africa, 1914-1915

the Union continued to the age of sixty) was commanded by Brigadier-General C. F. Beyers, a former assistant Commandant-General of the Republican Forces in the Transvaal.

There was thus no supreme command allowed for, and the Minister of Defence became in effect Commander-in-Chief. There was no military Chief of Staff and this position was virtually filled by the civilian head of the Department, the Secretary for Defence, who was throughout without military status, rank or disciplinary power.

While it may be regarded as a fortunate accident that the first Minister of Defence, in the person of General Smuts, had experience of active service, the obvious unsoundness of such an arrangement, from a military point of view, needs no emphasis.

The Headquarter staff officers were theoretically responsible to the Minister for the duties of their sections, but the latter were water-tight, their heads never met in conference, there was no provision for the co-ordination of staff work, and, in practice, the staff officers dealt solely with the civilian Secretary, who gave them instructions or referred their submissions to the Minister entirely at his own discretion.

When war broke out there were no plans to deal with any military operations.

No arrangements for the expansion of the forces from peace to war strength had been made in any of the several directions in which expansion became necessary, and the Union forces were unprepared.

There is no reason why the system at Defence Headquarters should not have borne a real instead of a purely nominal resemblance to that at the War Office.

From May to November, 1912, fifty officers (twenty-five English-speaking and twenty-five Afrikaans-speaking) had been assembled for some instruction in staff work before taking up appointments in the military districts into which the Union had been divided—all these officers had served in the Anglo-Boer War, fighting against each other, and in the Afrikaans-speaking officers were included several who had rendered distinguished service and brought off many tactical successes against the British forces.

In all the circumstances it was perhaps too much to expect that the latter officers should be profoundly impressed by the methods of an opponent whom they had often bested and,

The Campaign in German South West Africa, 1914-1915

though any instruction was to the good, probably not the least advantage of the course was that it laid the foundations of respect and comradeship between many of those who attended it.

Certain circumstances which contributed to a general unreadiness must in fairness be recorded.

The whole of the system provided for in the Defence Act was only rather more than twelve months old when this strain was thrown upon it. The staff, all too small for its work, though it would have been far better organised and able to perform its work under competent military supervision, was necessarily engaged upon preparatory work, and had not been able to reach a point where, under the most favourable conditions, it could have fully performed its normal functions in relation to the forces smoothly and without interruption.

The industrial troubles of 1913 and early 1914 and the rapid and disturbing events of the Rebellion tended further to confusion.

Four facts in connection with the military forces of the Union must be constantly borne in mind, for they are of the greatest importance to aid a fair judgment of the successes and failures which will be described in the following pages.

1. There was no coherent staff at Defence Headquarters where no provision had been made for the competent military supervision and co-ordination of staff work.

2. The complete omission to prepare in advance any kind of considered defence scheme to deal with probable or possible emergencies was a grave defect.

3. There was a very serious dearth of trained staff officers and particularly of officers for the General Staff.

4. There was an ample supply of fighting soldiers of high value. (The numbers of the latter will be given in detail as the different operations are described.)

The military resources of the enemy must now be considered.

The peace establishment of the German forces in South West Africa in 1914 was 140 officers and 2,000 other ranks organised in mounted companies and field batteries. These were all regular soldiers, picked men specially chosen for colonial service.

There were also 7,000 European males in the Protectorate, most of whom were reservists who had undergone military training, normally engaged for the most part in farming.

A potential increase to the German forces existed in dis-

The Campaign in German South West Africa, 1914-1915

affected South Africans who, however, were from the enemy point of view disappointingly few in number and who, after the first few months, ceased to be a force to be reckoned with.

The forces were organised in mounted companies, of which eight were regular.

The German commander was well supplied with excellent field guns of uniform pattern and throughout the campaign enjoyed a very substantial advantage over his opponent in the matter of artillery. He had also a number of machine guns and a good suply of munitions.

The food resources of the country were placed under strict control and it was unlikely that any shortage of essential supplies would arise for some considerable time.

The German forces were intimately acquainted with the theatre of the operations and had experience of fighting in it.

In addition to other advantages which will be referred to, the enemy forces presented the following:—
1. One undivided command over the whole.
2. A staff, adequate in numbers for its task, of regular officers trained for their duties on uniform lines.
3. A homogeneous force, trained throughout on the same plan and system, of a total strength of some 10,000.

CHAPTER III

Note.—In the following Chapter O.H. denotes Official History and J.C.I. Judicial Commission of Inquiry into the Rebellion.

THE MILITARY SITUATION to be dealt with in consequence of the decision of the Union Government to invade German territory presented the following main features:—

It was clear that the strategy of the enemy would be governed by the consideration that the decision of the war would be sought and arrived at many hundreds of miles from Southern Africa.

It was equally certain that, in the event of failure to detach the Union from the British Empire by means of a wholesale and successful rising within the borders of the former country with such purpose in view, the local German forces could hope for no permanent success in any venture against Union territory.

Until the Rebellion should have proved completely successful, and, equally, in the event of its failure, a strictly defensive policy was imposed upon the enemy Commander-in-Chief.

The actual violation of adjoining territory was first perpetrated by German troops.

On August 19, 1914, a small German detachment occupied a kopje, just within the Union border, which commanded a water-hole at NAKOB in German territory close to the international boundary, strengthening and repairing some old entrenchments on the hill.

Two days later an encounter took place near SCHUIT DRIFT, on the Orange River, when a German sergeant fired upon some Afrikaners—British subjects—who had been residing near the river in German territory and refused to withdraw to the north with their stock when ordered by the German authorities to do so. One of the German detachment was killed by the refugees who retaliated, another mortally wounded and a third captured. The German sergeant was on Union territory in the bed of the Orange River when he fired the shot which started the fight.

Each of these incidents took place so very close to the border that the enemy may be acquitted of any deliberate intention to violate Union soil, and the episodes certainly indicate no intention to invade the Union.

The Campaign in German South West Africa, 1914-1915

Governor Seitz, at his first interview with General Botha in May, 1915, vehemently disclaimed any such thought and sought to throw the onus of aggression on his opponent.

It would seem fair to regard the acts as accidental and due to ignorance of the boundary limit.

The attitude of the German Imperial Government became clear—though of course this information was not available at the outset of hostilities—when a proclamation by Dr. Seitz, dated September 15, 1914, was found at WINDHOEK after the occupation of that town by the forces of General Botha.

It ran:—

"To the Boer People of South Africa.

WHEREAS the British troops have attacked the German police station at RAMANSDRIFT and have come over the German border thus bringing the war to South Africa: I expressly declare hereby that the Germans carry on no war against the Boer people of South Africa. On the other hand I declare that we Germans shall repel the attack of the British troops at all points and by all means and carry to its conclusion the war against the British and against the British only."

It might therefore be assumed that the enemy would conduct his operations so as to delay a decision for as long as possible and to contain as many of his opponent's forces as he could.

It would be necessary to advance against the enemy forces along clearly defined routes determined by the existence of water in sufficient quantity to supply the troops and animals that would be required. Such routes were known to the enemy command and were few in number.

While the advance of the Union forces would entail a continuous prolongation of their lines of communication which along any line of approach would be over very long tracts of country—at first entirely barren and practically waterless—the retirement of the Germans would be effected over country with which they were familiar.

The German commander would be served in his retreat by a railway immediately behind him along any of several possible lines of withdrawal, and would fall back on his supplies.

His adversary would be compelled to bring from the Union everything needed for the equipment and subsistence of his troops.

Reference to the map will show the lines of communication

The Campaign in German South West Africa, 1914-1915

of the contending forces and will suggest the vital importance of adequate transport arrangements by Union Headquarters.

The communications of the Union Expeditionary Force began at PRETORIA and reached to

UPINGTON in the north-west of the Cape Province by rail,

TAUNGS, also by rail, for any force proceeding westward from KURUMAN,

CAPETOWN where the base of the forces moving by sea was established.

From UPINGTON and TAUNGS such roads as were available served any forces operating from either point against German territory.

From CAPETOWN sea routes completed the lines of communication to the ports of PORT NOLLOTH and WALVIS BAY and to LUDERITZBUCHT and SWAKOPMUND in the German Protectorate.

The routes were long drawn-out and involved the use of rail, sea, and mechanical and animal transport, and much handling of stores on their way to their destination.

The map shows too the admirable strategic arrangement of the German railways. They enabled the enemy to concentrate against an invading force far more rapidly than it would be possible for component detachments of the latter, if moving at any considerable distance from each other, to combine for mutual action or support.

There was reason to suppose that when the inland highlands should have been reached some grass veld and slaughter stock might become available, and, if this expectation were fulfilled, the supply situation might be helped to some extent.

This relief, however, could not be confidently relied upon and it was clear that no other supplies would be procurable in the theatre of operations.

Feeding armies in an advance over a desert was not a new problem. It had been dealt with in the expeditions of the Russians against the Turkomans and by the British in the Soudan and the recorded experiences of these campaigns, if studied, should have thrown useful light upon it.

One of the chief difficulties in such a position—and, as it will be seen, it became acute when General Botha decided early in 1915 to move along the SWAKOP River—is that personnel, combatant for the protection of the convoys, or administrative,

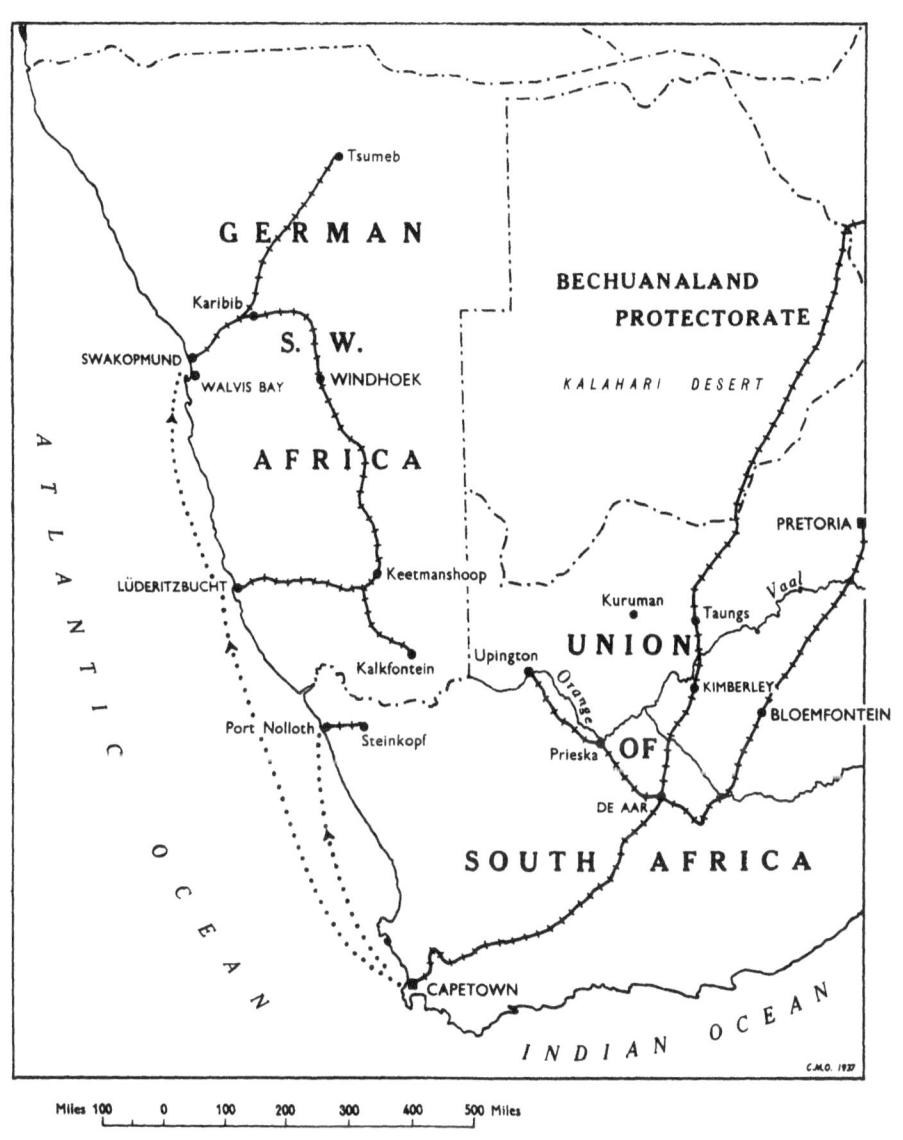

SKETCH MAP SHEWING
LINES OF COMMUNICATION
OF
OPPOSING FORCES

The Campaign in German South West Africa, 1914-1915

must be fed from the wagons en route to the advance depot. The smaller this personnel, the greater the bulk of supplies placed ahead.

The country was abnormally difficult for every kind of transport.

The regulation strength of animal teams had to be increased with a consequent reduction of the number of wagons.

Well up on the final advance in June, 1915, the armoured cars had to be left behind because their chassis were so twisted as to prevent their further forward movement.

While the conditions were worst in the desert belts the going was very difficult for every form of transport throughout the campaign.

The lightest cars would often boil every quarter of an hour or so, and it was necessary to pack the running boards with tins of water for refilling the radiators.

A safe method of advance would have been along the railway lines which would serve to keep the troops, moving slowly ahead, supplied. As a matter of fact this plan did not lack its advocates.

Such a course would, however, have added very greatly to the duration, and consequently the cost, of the operations.

Apart from the delay and heavy additional expenditure which it would entail, such a method of advance would have rendered the great mobility of the South African mounted troops of no value.

It would further have been favourable to the enemy's strategy and thus incidentally have involved the violation of Napoleon's maxim: " It is an approved maxim in war never to do what the enemy wishes you to do for this reason alone that he desires it."

The conveyance of supplies by road (if many of the routes which were employed may be so described) was essential, and the provision of suitable and adequate transport for the purpose a consideration of prime importance.

South West Africa abounds in defensive positions of great natural strength. A numerically inferior force well handled could delay an advance over and over again unless, and until, it was outflanked.

The known superiority of the enemy in artillery was an additional aid to such a defence.

The advance of several forces from the Union would necessarily be on a broad front or arc and the detachments,

The Campaign in German South West Africa, 1914-1915

owing to the paucity of possible routes, must inevitably be widely separated.

To several detachments advancing against him the German Commander-in-Chief could oppose a highly efficient force, capable of rapid concentration in strength superior to any enemy detachment of less than say 5,000 and always with a heavy preponderance of field guns in his own favour.

Such a concentration might at any time achieve success if the selection of a suitable occasion were made.

It followed—and especially in the first stages of the campaign—that, unless grave risks were to be taken, each detachment must at least be equal in strength to any possible concentration against it and that reliable arrangements for the co-operation of detachments and the co-ordination of their movements must be made.

This last condition postulated one direction of the whole operations and the nicest timing of movements.

To sum up:

The main points to be taken into consideration by the military authorities of the Union in framing a plan of operations for an offensive campaign would appear to be the following:—

1. The enemy would be compelled to adopt a defensive attitude with the objects of avoiding total defeat and containing as many of his opponents as possible.

2. An invasion of the Union by the enemy was highly improbable. That such a venture could succeed after the collapse of the Rebellion was impossible.

3. The enemy would have no difficulty in supplying his troops for the probable duration of the campaign.

4. Practically every kind of supply needed for the equipment and maintenance of the Union troops would have to be brought from their own country over long and difficult communications. This condition would be absolute until the desert belts should have been crossed and supply bases fixed on their further edges.

5. An advance by the Union forces confined to a railway route was undesirable as not taking full advantage of the great mobility of the mounted men and because it would be favourable to the enemy's strategy.

6. Consequently the question of mechanical and animal transport became of paramount importance and called for careful investigation and arrangement.

7. The enemy commander was well placed for the defensive

The Campaign in German South West Africa, 1914-1915

action imposed upon him. He was quite aware of the only possible lines of advance against him. He could concentrate forces rapidly and in strength against any opposing detachment if he judged the step to be advisable and potentially productive of good result. He had at his disposal, as well as his railways, a number of unusually strong natural positions along any line of retreat that he might select. His opponent's supply difficulties offered him good chances of delaying an advance by energetic action against the former's long and ever lengthening lines of communication.

8. So long as the enemy held the railways (i.e.—see map facing p. 24—until the line KARIBIB-WINDHOEK should be captured) his power of rapid concentration would remain and must be taken into account by the Union military authorities.

We may now turn to the first plan of operations decided upon at Defence Headquarters PRETORIA (henceforward referred to as " D.H.Q."), where a meeting of senior officers assembled on August 21, 1914.

This meeting was presided over by General J. C. Smuts, Minister of Defence, and attended by Brigadier-Generals C. F. Beyers, Commandant-General Citizen Force, H. T. Lukin, Inspector-General Permanent Force, Sir Duncan McKenzie, formerly Commandant-General in Natal, together with Colonels P. S. Beves, Commandant of Cadets, and P. C. B. Skinner, an officer from the British Army, loaned to the Union Government for instructional duties. Sir William Hoy, General Manager of Railways, was also present.

The decisions reached by this meeting were arrived at " after prolonged discussion " (J.C.I., p. 7), and no doubt, bearing in mind the composition of the gathering, represented a compromise and the reconciliation of divergent views.

The extremely grave position in the Union must have caused the Minister and his political colleagues deep concern and probably precluded the dispatch of any Union forces to a point too far from their own borders.

It was decided (O.H., p. 10) " to occupy LUDERITZ BAY while the wireless station and landing equipment at SWAKOP-MUND were to be destroyed by naval bombardment ", and that " to take pressure from the LUDERITZ BAY expeditionary force " a Union force was to be landed at PORT NOLLOTH to operate against the enemy's southern frontier while another force was concentrated at UPINGTON to threaten his eastern border.

This plan clearly then had as its object the occupation of

LUDERITZBUCHT and any enemy force at that place as the objective of the expeditionary force.

To carry the above intention into effect the following movements were agreed to:—

One force, " A ", under General Lukin, to proceed by sea from CAPETOWN to PORT NOLLOTH; a second force, " B ", to be commanded by Lieut.-Colonel Maritz, District Staff Officer in the north-western Cape, to collect at and operate from UPINGTON; while the seizure of LUDERITZBUCHT was entrusted to Colonel Beves, whose force was to proceed to its destination by sea from CAPETOWN.

The strength of the three forces was as follows:—

" A " Force (LUKIN):
  * 2nd and 4th (Permanent) Batteries.
  8th (Citizen) Battery.
  (Field Artillery each four guns).
  † 1st, 2nd, 3rd, 4th and 5th Regiments South African Mounted Riflemen (Permanent).
  10th Infantry (Citizen).
    (Witwatersrand Rifles.)
  Ammunition Column.
  One Section Engineers.
    Total: 2,420 all ranks.

" B " Force (MARITZ):
  Mounted Rifle Units.
  3 Machine Guns.
  No Artillery.
    Total: 1,000 all ranks.

" C " Force (BEVES):
  7th (Citizen) Battery, six guns.
    (Field Artillery.)
  One Squadron 5th Mounted Rifles.
    (Imperial Light Horse.)
  8th Infantry (Citizen.)
    (Transvaal Scottish.)
  11th Infantry (Citizen).
    (Rand Rifles.)
  One Section Engineers.
    Total: 1,824 all ranks.

---

* One battery was early returned and Lukin took the field with two.
† Each regiment 3 field squadrons.
  Each squadron—100 rifles.

The Campaign in German South West Africa, 1914-1915

The strengths of the forces in terms of field guns and rifles may be put as—
"A" eight guns, 1,800 rifles;
"B" no guns, 1,000 rifles;
"C" six guns, 1,200 rifles;
or 4,000 rifles in all, with a total of fourteen guns.

To meet this strength the enemy could dispose of 7,000 to 8,000 rifles with a heavily superior artillery.

When the three Union forces reached their first destinations they stood on an arc of 500 to 600 miles, without any lateral communication except by mounted dispatch rider, and at a distance as the crow flies (it was, of course, much greater along the lines of communication) of from 500 to 1,000 miles from PRETORIA, whence their co-ordination was to be effected largely by means of hastily arranged telegraph lines and with no one definite chief command.

To these dispositions the enemy central single command opposed a force in close touch throughout its component parts, capable of rapid concentration, almost half as strong again as the total strength of the three Union detachments and at least twice as strong as the two which alone could act in co-operation. It was obvious that the force at LUDERITZBUCHT could do no more than maintain itself there, particularly as apparently "pressure" upon it by the enemy was expected.

In these circumstances, even with proper co-ordination and careful timing, an advance by " A " and " B " forces combined would have been a risky undertaking in a country so suitable for defensive and delaying action by small forces, and presenting the water and road conditions and difficult communications which have been described. The advance of one force without the other would invite disaster.

In point of fact at no time was any kind of pressure exerted by the enemy on " C " Force at LUDERITZBUCHT. Except for patrol action the German commander opposite Beves, and, later McKenzie, remained in his positions until the general retirement northwards.

Had it been otherwise, it is difficult to see how " A " and " B " forces—even in conjunction—could have effectually interfered with any action the enemy might elect to take against LUDERITZBUCHT.

Any advance from the Orange River would be a long business, for the enemy could have detached forces, small but

The Campaign in German South West Africa, 1914-1915

ample for the purpose, to hold back the Union forces from the south quite long enough to cover any offensive action he might contemplate against Beves.

The occupation of LUDERITZBUCHT depended entirely upon the local result of the approach of Beves' force, and it is difficult to understand the supine attitude of the enemy in allowing it to be taken so easily, or, at all events, in leaving it in Beves' hands without any attempt to recapture it.

Possibly the presence of a civil population in the place may have influenced the German commander, and, of course, as will be seen, the point on the coast which was of vital importance did not lie at LUDERITZBUCHT.

So long as the invader remained on the coast there he caused no inconvenience to the Protectorate forces; should he advance, no doubt the latter felt competent to deal with him.

In all the circumstances it would seem that it would have been well to have been content with the achievement of the purpose assigned as that of the first plan, viz.: to occupy LUDERITZ BAY and to have refrained from any forward movement from the south into enemy country until either considerable reinforcements should have been sent to the forces to operate from that direction or arrangements made and put into effect for a diversion elsewhere which would compel the enemy to detach heavily.

Beves reached LUDERITZBUCHT on September 18 and landed his force there without opposition.

The naval bombardment was carried out at SWAKOPMUND.

Other views, however, were held at D.H.Q.

Lukin's ("A" force) first transport ship arrived at PORT NOLLOTH on August 31, and on the following day disembarked the leading personnel of his force. His disembarkation was completed on the night of September 16-17 with the last of his transport.

By September 10 his headquarters and the 1st, 4th and 5th S.A.M.R. regiments were at STEINKOPF. His infantry were disposed along the PORT NOLLOTH-STEINKOPF railway.

On September 11 patrols were sent to the Orange River and on the following day, when authority to enter German territory was received from the Union Government, Lukin sent the 4th and 5th S.A.M.R., under Lieut.-Colonels Dawson and Berrangé, to occupy RAMAN'S DRIFT and HOUM'S DRIFT, respectively,

The Campaign in German South West Africa, 1914-1915

in order to make good the high ground to the north of the Orange River at each place.

By September 15 he held this high ground after some skirmishing and slight casualties, taking a few prisoners.

The enemy in small strength withdrew towards SAND-FONTEIN, about 24 miles from RAMAN'S DRIFT.

On September 19 the water at SANDFONTEIN—the first, except for a scanty and brack supply at GABIS, on the way to WARMBAD—was occupied by 200 rifles from the two forward regiments.

Lukin had decided on the line RAMAN'S DRIFT-WARM-BAD-KALKFONTEIN-SEEHEIM as the best for an advance by his force when such a movement should prove to be practicable. He held the opinion that an advance must be made simultaneously by " A ", " B " and " C " forces " since neither was strong enough by itself to successfully oppose resistance which would be set up against it in the absence of close co-operation between the three forces ".

His transport was enough to maintain his two forward detachments at RAMAN'S DRIFT and HOUM'S DRIFT (45 and 56 miles over very heavy country from his base at STEIN-KOPF respectively). It consisted of " indifferent wagons and donkey teams ". On September 15 he suggested that a light train line should be laid from STEINKOPF to RAMAN'S DRIFT, but the proposal was vetoed by D.II.Q. on the score of expense.

After considering the transport and water position, Lukin came to the conclusion that the greatest strength he could possibly maintain on the river line was that which was already there, viz., 600 rifles, distributed in equal strength at RAMAN'S DRIFT, HOUM'S DRIFT and SANDFONTEIN, with the addition of the 1st S.A.M.R. (another 300 rifles) and one battery of artillery, and these reinforcements left STEINKOPF for RAMAN'S DRIFT.

On September 24 a squadron (Welby) of the 1st S.A.M.R. relieved the two squadrons of the 4th and 5th regiments at SANDFONTEIN, and Lieut.-Colonel R. C. Grant, the commanding officer of the 1st Regiment, with a second squadron and the field battery reached RAMAN'S DRIFT, his third squadron being then between STEINKOPF and the drift, en route for the latter.

The Campaign in German South West Africa, 1914-1915

Lukin with his brigade headquarters arrived at RAMAN'S DRIFT on the morning of September 24.

Lukin was an officer of much experience of active service in South Africa. He had been wounded in 1879 at ULUNDI, served in the Basuto War of 1880-81, and in the Langeberg campaign of 1897, where he had commanded the artillery, and he had gained distinction in charge of the artillery at the siege of WEPENER in the Anglo-Boer War, and as a column commander in the same campaign. He was to conclude a long active military career in command of the South African Infantry Brigade (he commanded it at DELVILLE WOOD) and the 9th Division in France.

He was a highly efficient soldier and quick in action, though he gave long thought to any task he had to undertake before coming to a decision. He was a strict disciplinarian, and, though very tenacious of his opinion once he had formed it, would loyally carry out the order of a superior.

This being his character, he would, as a matter of course, represent all his difficulties and communicate any views he might hold as to the soundness or otherwise of a proposed line of action to D.H.Q.

That he did so on this ocassion is clearly shown on reference to the Official History, for we read on page 14: " Headquarters had to request high pressure to the verge of self-sacrifice on the part of General Lukin to which he most loyally responded."

These are extravagant words to describe orders from superior authority to a soldier accustomed throughout a long professional career to obey such commands.

On September 22 General Lukin telegraphed to D.H.Q. that three weeks must elapse before sufficient supplies could be accumulated on the Orange River to enable an advance of any portion of " A " force to commence from that line.

To this D.H.Q. replied that Ministers hoped that the movement of supplies to SANDFONTEIN (24 miles beyond the " Orange River line ") would be hurried on so that a move to WARMBAD would not be delayed.

In view of this desire for an early advance it is necessary to determine what the chances of effective co-operation by " B " force were. Patently a grave risk would be taken if any advance were initiated before such co-operation had been assured.

" B " Force was commanded by Lieut.-Colonel S. G. Maritz, who by September 20 had assembled 1,000 rifles with three

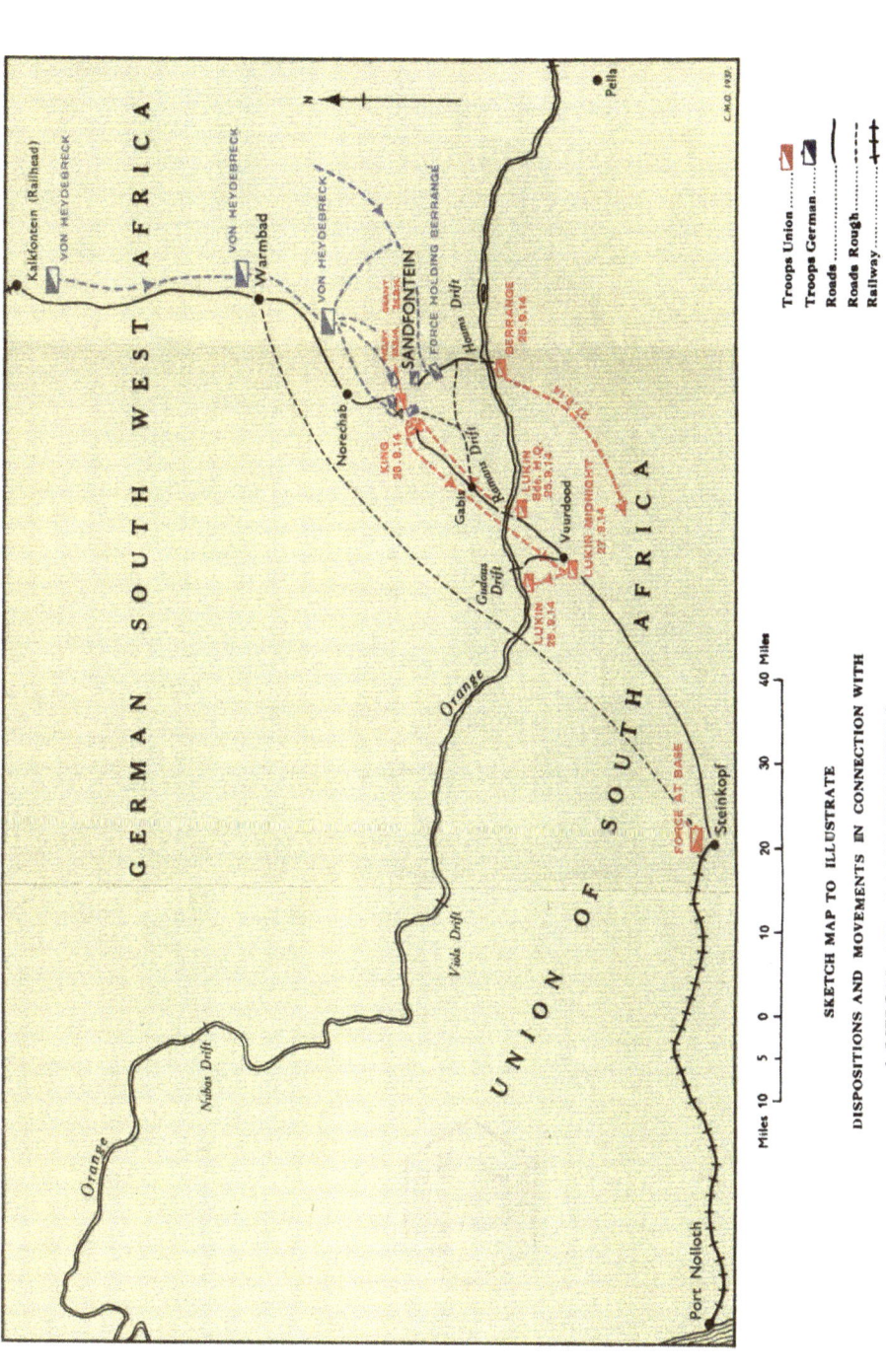

SKETCH MAP TO ILLUSTRATE
DISPOSITIONS AND MOVEMENTS IN CONNECTION WITH
ACTION AT SANDFONTEIN

The Campaign in German South West Africa, 1914-1915

machine guns but without artillery at UPINGTON and KAKAMAS.

Maritz, a former officer in the Transvaal Republican Forces, at the end of the Anglo-Boer War had refused to take the oath of allegiance and trekked into German South West Africa, where he lived for some years, giving the German authorities valuable assistance during the Herero Rebellion. He was very friendly with the Germans.

He returned to the Union, and, after attending the initial course of instruction for staff officers in 1912, was appointed, at the instance of General Beyers, District Staff Officer in the north-west Cape.

He was " a man of violent temper and appears to have been in the habit of frequently expressing bitter anti-British feelings " (J.C.I., p. 15). He was also a fine guerilla fighter possessed of abundant courage and great physical strength and would brook no opposition to any scheme upon which he was bent. His anti-British sentiments were less due to racial feeling, for he could be friendly enough and indeed helpful even to an Englishman if he took a liking to him, than to the loss of his country's independence which, to a man of his temperament, was galling in the extreme and became an obsession.

It was more as the authors of that loss than as men of another race that English-speaking South Africans earned his cordial detestation of which he was honest enough to leave them in no doubt whatever.

He had received his command as " independent of " Lukin (J.C.I., p. 7) and under the most favourable conditions the chances that he would give the latter, with whose regular methods he was wholly unfamiliar and for which he probably had a profound contempt, whole-hearted support were slender indeed.

But he had no intention of giving him any support at all.

The whole details of Maritz's action are given in the Report of the Judicial Inquiry, and for the purpose of a review of the campaign in German South West Africa no more than the following particulars are needed.

The demeanour of Maritz, combined with the grave events in connection with the Rebellion in the Union—notably the accidental shooting of General de la Rey and the resignation of General Beyers—had placed Generals Botha and Smuts and their colleagues " in a very awkward dilemma " (J.C.I., p. 16)

The Campaign in German South West Africa, 1914-1915

and on September 23 a telegram was sent from D.H.Q. to Maritz " to test his loyalty rather than with any hope of practical result " (J.C.I. *ibid*), asking if he could move a strong force to SCHUIT DRIFT from KAKAMAS and advance the UPINGTON force towards the border in the direction of * UKAMAS with a view to possible co-operation with General Lukin in his march towards WARMBAD.

This would of course involve splitting Maritz's force and creating another detachment.

In any case Maritz's reply must surely have put an end to any hope that Lukin could advance otherwise than entirely alone and without any kind of diversion to aid him.

Maritz sent a long telegram to D.H.Q., in which he ridiculed the idea that those members of the Active Citizen Force who were with him were of the least military value and made the significant observation that " it is reported that there are at UKAMAS alone 3,000 Germans well mounted and armed with artillery and I have not a single cannon." He advised the Government to consider well the matter of taking German South West Africa, said he would do his best to support the Government " on this side of the border ", that he could not divide his force (this at all events seemed sound enough) but would move as many as he could in the direction of UKAMAS " for protective purposes ". He added that his " position was very difficult " and that if he was intended to attack German South West Africa he should be glad if " my resignation is accepted " (J.C.I., p. 17).

Maritz eventually went into rebellion with 700 of his men (J.C.I., p. 23) and his actions became a part of the Rebellion and had no more influence on the progress of the campaign against the German forces beyond giving the latter a breathing space of three months. From October to the end of 1914 the whole energies of the Government were bent on crushing the Rebellion and active measures against the enemy across the border temporarily ceased.

---

* UKAMAS in enemy territory roughly equidistant—90 miles—from SANDFONTEIN, UPINGTON and KAKAMAS.

CHAPTER IV

ON SEPTEMBER 25th the disposition of "A" Force was as follows:—

At RAMAN'S DRIFT	Brigade H.Q. (General Lukin) One squadron (100 rifles) 1st S.A.M.R. Three squadrons (300 rifles) 4th S.A.M.R. Transvaal Horse Artillery, four 13-pdrs.
At HOUM'S DRIFT	Lieut.-Colonel Berrangé, three squadrons (300 rifles) 5th S.A.M.R.
At SANDFONTEIN	One squadron (Welby) (100 rifles) 1st S.A.M.R.
en route to RAMAN'S DRIFT	One squadron (100 rifles) 1st S.A.M.R.
At STEINKOPF	Six squadrons (600 rifles) 2nd and 3rd S.A.M.R. One battery four guns.
On the line PORT NOLLOTH STEINKOPF	The Witwatersrand Rifles.

The information forwarded by D.H.Q. as to the enemy dispositions was that the main forces were at WINDHOEK with detachments at KEETMANSHOOP and SWAKOPMUND and a small detachment, possibly at WARMBAD, to watch the Union forces on the border.

This was probably correct for it represents the best possible arrangement by the enemy of his forces.

He protected the heart of his defence at WINDHOEK where were the bulk of all his stores and the large wireless plant (incidentally one of the objectives of the Union forces) and where he controlled the railways by which he assured himself of his power of rapid movement throughout the Protectorate.

The Campaign in German South West Africa, 1914-1915

His detachments would give him ample warning of any movement by his opponents and he could concentrate or employ his forces as he chose.

Lukin, having advised D.H.Q. that the greatest strength he could maintain on the river line and forward at SANDFONTEIN was 800 rifles and the four guns disposed as shown above, took the following precautions.

A telephone line linked up Brigade Headquarters with the detachment at SANDFONTEIN.

The state of the river was wired daily from PRIESKA.

The Officers Commanding at RAMAN'S DRIFT, HOUM'S DRIFT and SANDFONTEIN were ordered to scout their own fronts and exchange information through Brigade Headquarters at RAMAN'S DRIFT.

The intelligence officer and Scouts (local bastards) were at SANDFONTEIN.

It is well known that native scouts have two chief faults. They are unable to give any reliable idea as to numbers or to describe war material and they are at pains often to give the information which their questioner (who often suggests the reply by the form of his inquiry) appears to wish to have.

But, allowing for their inherent defects, it would seem that such a large concentration as moved against the SANDFONTEIN detachment should have been detected by the scouts, if they had carried out their reconnaissance properly.

Lukin who, if he was inclined to be meticulous about the prerogatives of a commander, *never let a subordinate down,* says: " it would be grossly unfair to throw blame on a body of men comprising (sic) the Intelligence Unit which had to overcome great physical obstacles, could obtain information from neither man, bird nor beast (the two last named sources were perhaps not very promising) since the country was denuded of all three ", but, seeing that 10 miles was the shortest radius of the patrol area from SANDFONTEIN, some negligence in the forward reconnaissance may be reasonably assumed.

Lukin's general instructions were to co-operate with Maritz with whom he was to exchange reports and information.

That no information should have come from Maritz is in the circumstances not surprising.

Lukin had wired to Maritz before occupying the Orange River posts asking the latter to co-operate by engaging his share of the enemy forces, but Maritz replied that his force was not

The Campaign in German South West Africa, 1914-1915

sufficiently well organised at the time to enable him to do so.

The only other communications which passed between the two force commanders were a request from Maritz that Lukin would let him know what his intentions were and, in view of rumours prevalent at the time, Lukin's reply in non-committal terms.

Until after the reverse at SANDFONTEIN, which must now be described, *no alteration in the enemy dispositions as originally communicated to Lukin was indicated to the latter by D.H.Q.* and all his information was that which he was able to gather himself locally.

At about 4 p.m. on September 25 the intelligence officer at SANDFONTEIN reported to Brigade Headquarters that a body of the enemy estimated at 150-200 had been at AURUS, 15 to 20 miles north-east of HOUM'S DRIFT on the night of September 24-25 and had been seen on the following day moving towards UMEIS, 8 miles east of HOUM'S DRIFT. Another party of 40 had slept at UMEIS on the night of September 24-25 and it was assumed was the advance guard of the larger body. As a matter of fact, the smaller party was an officer's patrol from Berrangé, and it seems clear, in the light of after events, that the larger body was that which held off an attempt by Berrangé to get to SANDFONTEIN on the 26th and was sent for that specific purpose.

It was also reported that the dust of a southward movement from the direction of WARMBAD towards NORECHAB had been observed, but no indication of its strength was given. The fact of this movement was verified by an officer's patrol.

Lukin formed the opinion that a force " perhaps some 300 strong was intended to attack SANDFONTEIN " and took the following action.

Lieut.-Colonel Grant was ordered to reinforce the squadron at SANDFONTEIN. Welby, at the latter place, was rationed up to the following day, the detachment which Grant took with him (two 13-pounders, a machine-gun section and three troops of the squadron of his regiment at RAMAN'S DRIFT) was rationed only to the evening of the 25th.

The three squadrons of the 4th S.A.M.R., together with the other section of the Field Battery, Lukin kept under his own hand at RAMAN'S DRIFT.

Considering the reinforcement of Welby as urgent, he ordered Grant to leave a troop with his wagons to take up supplies from a donkey convoy expected during the evening and follow him to SANDFONTEIN.

As indicating the scarcity of transport it may be mentioned that all Grant's reserve ammunition was on his supply wagons. In reply to repeated requests for transport for this ammunition he was regretfully informed that it was absolutely unobtainable. Lukin had not enough wagons for this highly important service. Grant's reserve ammunition therefore did not accompany him when he marched at 5.30 p.m., and he never saw it again.

The position at SANDFONTEIN occupied by Lukin's forward detachment was 24 miles from his headquarters at RAMAN'S DRIFT.

The following is a description of it, and the plan facing page 40, though rough, will help to a better understanding of it.

It consisted of an isolated conical kopje between 150 and 200 feet high. The sides of this kopje descended steeply on the east and west, but on the north the slope was more gradual and on the south it threw out a low spur for about 150 yards. The total length of the base of the kopje was about 400 yards. The kopje was completely dominated on the east, south-east and south sides by a higher rocky ridge at ranges varying from 500 to 1,000 yards.

The position was also commanded from the north-east, north and north-west by a semi-circular range of hills at ranges from 1,000 yards upwards.

On the west and south-west the ground was open but rose gradually and commanded the Union position on those sides.

A dry river-bed also ran round the position from the south-west to the east and another from the north-west to the east. These, with outcrops of rock and small dongas, afforded good cover to an attacking force.

West of the kopje at its foot were a well and pump, a stone kraal and three or four detached buildings and sheds.

In the short time available it had been impossible to entrench the position, but Welby, since his arrival on September 24, had constructed schanzes round the kopje. It is not clear, by the way, why this ordinary precaution was not taken by the detachment which he relieved during their five days' occupation.

No suitable gun positions were available, and the guns of the T.H.A. had to be brought into action on open ground at the foot of the kopje on its western side.

Welby, relieving a squadron of the 4th S.A.M.R. under

The Campaign in German South West Africa, 1914-1915

Captain King, had reached SANDFONTEIN at 9 a.m. on September 24, having taken 15 hours to cover 18 miles, and, in the process, followed seven different tracks branching from the main road.

He had been told " there was only one road to SANDFONTEIN ", and the officer in command at RAMAN'S DRIFT had apparently refused his request for a guide, no doubt thinking such aid unnecessary, as he himself was familiar with the route. An example of the difficulty of night work in what was virtually desert country without reliable guiding.

Welby recognised the high ground to the east and south-east as " the key to the whole position " and that if the enemy held it he would make the defender's position " untenable in less than an hour ".

He accordingly occupied this high ground together with a feature to the north-east which commanded the road to WARMBAD. He also placed some of his troops to the west and north-west of his main position, the conical kopje near the water hole and buildings.

Two hours before dawn on September 25 two officers' patrols were sent out from SANDFONTEIN towards WARMBAD, one to the north-west and the other to the north-east.

The second, on return about 4 p.m., reported about 300 mounted men with wagons, and, it was thought, guns, as having been observed from a distance moving in the direction of HOUM'S DRIFT.

On communicating this information to RAMAN'S DRIFT Welby had a telephonic conversation with General Lukin, who had reached the drift the day before.

Replying to his Brigade Commander's questions, Welby said he confirmed the views expressed to himself by Lieut-Colonels Dawson, Berrangé and Eliott, who had previously occupied the position, that it was impossible to hold it unless the surrounding heights were denied to an attacker.

He then called to the telephone the engineer officer who had been sent with him and the latter seems to have given it as his opinion that the position could not be defended against attack and added that the construction of gun pits was impossible.

After pointing out that his rations were 36 hours overdue and urgently needed, Welby asked if his rear was protected and was told it would be looked after by troops from RAMAN'S DRIFT.

General Lukin approved of the steps which had been taken at

The Campaign in German South West Africa, 1914-1915

SANDFONTEIN and advised Welby that Grant would be along in the morning with some more men.

At 4 a.m. on September 26 Welby again sent out two patrols. One of these, under Lieut. Northway, retiring before an enemy body which it had engaged, found a German machine-gun between it and its main body.

Northway endeavoured to capture this party but was shot dead in the attempt and his patrol taken prisoners, a man whom he had sent back earlier with information having also fallen into the enemy's hands.

At 7.30 a.m. Welby had received no reports from his pickets or patrols and at this juncture Lieut.-Colonel Grant arrived with the reinforcement described earlier.

The latter at once recognised the position as " extremely bad, difficult to hold against any superior force, and untenable against artillery ".

Grant too was a soldier of long experience of active service and, had he been given any time to alter the disposition of his force, would very probably have withdrawn to SANDFONTEIN NEK, which will be mentioned later, but he was given no time.

He reached SANDFONTEIN at 7.25 a.m. on September 26. While still talking to Captain Welby and before he had dismounted his men a message was received from the top of the kopje that a column of troops was advancing on the position from the direction of WARMBAD—north-east—and the S.A.M.R. patrols were retiring. At the same time the telephone operator ran up and reported that his line to RAMAN'S DRIFT had been cut.

Grant at once ascended the kopje to view the ground and make his dispositions. He had barely reached the top when two more columns appeared from the east and west moving at a gallop, and occupied the ridges and outcrops on those sides. A few minutes later a fourth column appeared on the south-west, and, to use his own words, " thus, within 20 minutes of my arrival it was evident that my detachment was completely enveloped by a greatly superior force ".

Nothing remained but to make the best of the situation, and to this end Grant distributed his riflemen where they could get the best field of fire, placed his two machine-guns on the southern spur of the kopje which gave them a field of fire to the east, west and south, and took up his own position on the top of the kopje.

The action began about 8 a.m., when Lieut. Adler was

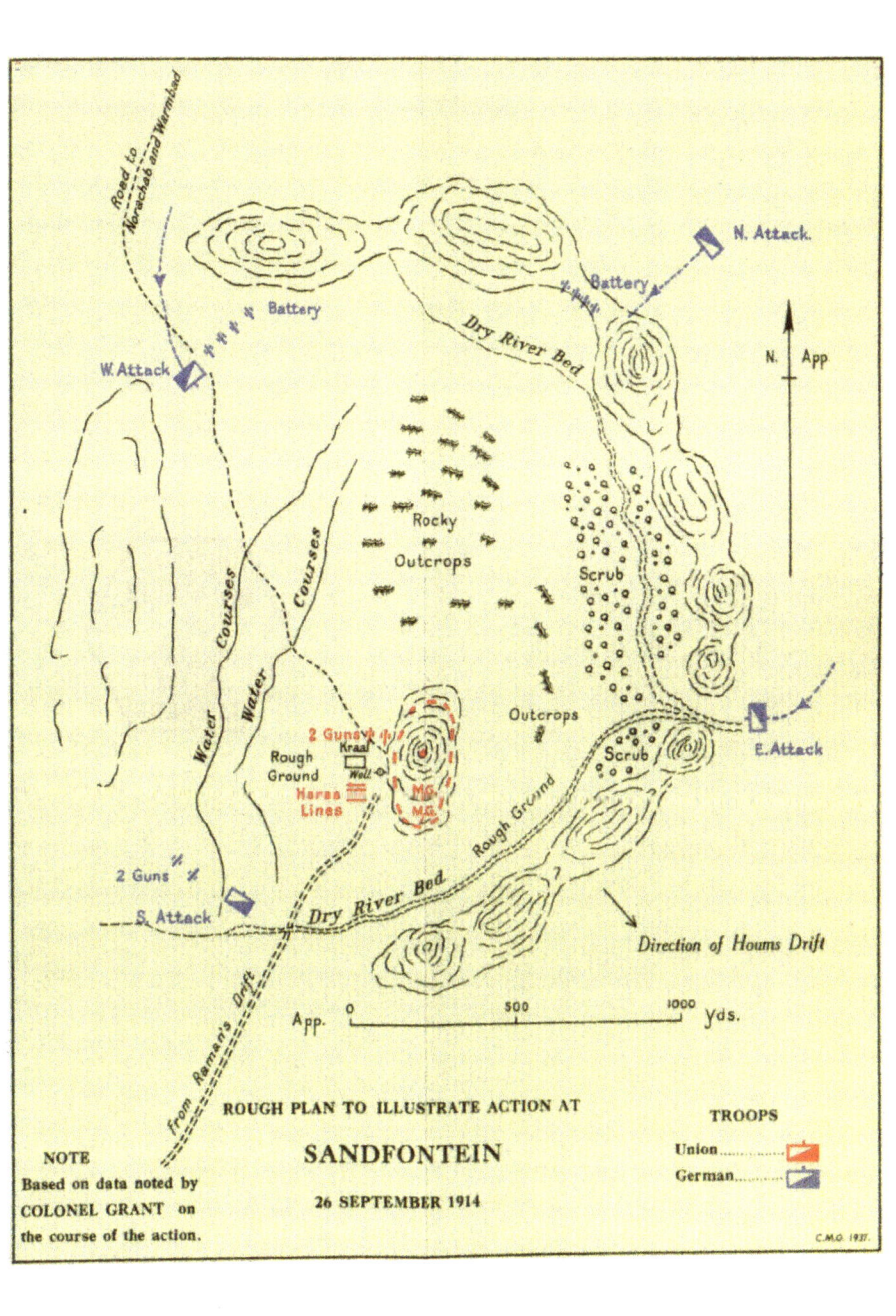

ordered to open on the southern attack with his two 13-pounders, necessarily placed without cover, on the western side of the position.

His fire was at once answered by a battery of four guns on a neck of the ridge to the north-east and shortly afterwards by a second battery of four guns on the west and two more on the south-west.

Meanwhile an infantry attack had developed.

Lines of skirmishers advanced, aided by the dongas and outcrops of rock, and soon formed an encircling ring of riflemen and machine-guns, and the position was soon swept by heavy rifle and machine-gun fire from all sides.

A thin firing line extended round the perimeter of the position maintained a steady and well controlled fire and effectually kept the attack at bay.

The two machine-guns of the defenders maintained a most unequal contest against several enemy maxims and concentrated rifle and artillery fire from three sides. One of the guns was ultimately compelled to cease fire, but the second was never quite silenced.

At 11 a.m. Adler reported that one of his guns was disabled and that he had not enough men left to serve the other and he was told to withdraw his men into the position.

Lieutenant Adler pluckily removed both breech blocks under heavy fire, and Welby's tribute to the young gunners of the Transvaal Horse Artillery should be recorded.

He says: "I must pay these gunners the compliment of expressing my admiration at their behaviour under fire, for it must be remembered that most of them were boys hardly out of their teens, who had never seen an angry shot fired before, and they behaved like veterans."

The enemy now concentrated his gun fire on the horses and mules until the ground where they had been left linked was a shambles. Some broke loose and in a short time only a few were standing and most of these were wounded.

The enemy guns then switched on to the position searching it from end to end with shrapnel in support of the advancing riflemen and rendering all movement within the position impossible.

At about noon Grant was severely wounded and felt compelled to hand over the command to Welby who was at the foot of the kopje on its western side. The order to Welby was

The Campaign in German South West Africa, 1914-1915

shouted by the Adjutant, as owing to the intense fire and the absence of cover it was impossible to convey orders or messages by runner. The same reason made it impracticable for Welby to ascend the kopje and take his post at the top, which was absolutely essential for the exercise of effective command, as it was only from there that the position as a whole and the course of action on all its fronts could be viewed. Grant, therefore, resumed command at a later hour.

In point of fact Welby *did* hear the message and took over the command and continued to act on the assumption that his command was effective until the white flag was hoisted in token of surrender. When this occurred and he asked why the flag had been shown he learnt that Lieut.-Colonel Grant had given the order. The misunderstanding, however, had no effect on the course or outcome of events.

Shortly after the Union guns had been put out of action at 11 a.m., distant machine-gun fire was heard in the direction of HOUM'S DRIFT but died away and was rightly supposed to mark an unsuccessful attempt at advance by Berrangé.

At about 3.30 p.m. a helio light was observed on the top of a high hill towards RAMAN'S DRIFT, but the use of a helio by the beleaguered force was rendered impossible by the close and concentrated fire of the enemy.

At about 3 p.m. the enemy advanced his guns to close range and severely bombarded the position with rapid fire using much percussion shell and firing battery salvoes.

The ring of riflemen worked itself in some places to within 200 yards of the Union schanzes but were thrown back by the steady fire of their occupants.

Grant had from the first regarded his chances of relief as slight for he knew that the forces of the enemy were far superior to any disposable by General Lukin. He was also aware that there were other enemy detachments in the vicinity, that which had held back Berrangé and another which had been seen in the morning on the west moving from NORECHAB towards RAMAN'S DRIFT, evidently to attend to any activity on the part of Lukin.

The reasons which led him to accept the inevitable and surrender are perhaps best given in his own words:

" I had decided to hang on as long as possible in the hope that some unexpected turn of events might bring relief, but, as evening drew on, it became obvious that all hope of succour

The Campaign in German South West Africa, 1914-1915

must be abandoned, and that ultimate surrender was inevitable. Our ammunition was now running very low (it will be remembered that he was without his reserve and only had the 120 rounds in each of his men's bandoliers) more than half my command had been without food since the previous day and were exhausted through want of sleep. The great majority of the wounded were lying where they had fallen, it being impossible to remove them.

Though unaware of their actual extent, I knew that our casualties must be severe. The enemy had now (5.30 p.m.) drawn very close, and, though we had beaten back successive attempts to gain a foothold in the position, it was evident that with a firing line orginally very weak and further attenuated by casualties there would be no hope of repelling an assault delivered under cover of darkness.

The men had displayed great fortitude for 10 hours under most trying conditions, and I felt that to commit them to a hand to hand struggle in the dark against overwhelming numbers would mean their certain annihilation and a useless sacrifice of life *as no military object was to be gained* by further resistance.

I therefore decided to surrender, which was carried out at about 6 p.m."

Against Grant's 190 riflemen and gunners with their two guns a total of about 230 combatants the enemy had concentrated eight times the number of his guns and at least ten times the number of his rifles.

No one will quarrel with his ultimate decision, and that it was deferred so long was due to his own resolution and the gallantry of his men, which called forth the soldierly congratulations of Colonel von Heydebreck.

The Union casualties were 67, or approximately 25 per cent.

If blame may be apportioned for this unfortunate occurrence none of it rests upon Lieut.-Colonel Grant or the soldiers who fought under him.

The unwounded and slightly wounded South African prisoners left on foot for WARMBAD on the evening of the surrender, September 26.

To return to Brigade Headquarters at RAMAN'S DRIFT.

Telephone communication with Welby's detachment was cut early on September 26 (the last message received being " all clear nothing to report ") and soon afterwards guns were heard in action in the direction of SANDFONTEIN. One squadron (King) of the 4th and another (Davidson) of the 5th S.A.M.R. were ordered forward from RAMAN'S DRIFT and HOUM'S DRIFT, respectively, " to reinforce Colonel Grant at or near SANDFONTEIN ".

At about 9 a.m. a wounded rifleman of Grant's wagon escort came back to Brigade Headquarters and reported that the wagons had come up against 90 of the enemy with a machine-gun. King on his way forward came across the wagons burned on the road. This was Lukin's first intimation that the enemy was between him and SANDFONTEIN. He states that at noon the gun fire, " which had not at any time sounded as if more than two guns were in action ", became more and more indistinct and he gathered the impression that Grant had repelled an attack on SANDFONTEIN.

At 5 p.m., however, a message from Berrangé advised him that the enemy was shelling the SANDFONTEIN position with four guns and Lukin then moved out with 130 rifles and the section of artillery reaching SANDFONTEIN NEK about $2\frac{1}{2}$ miles south-west of SANDFONTEIN at 1 a.m., September 27. Here he found King held up, as Davidson was also held up on the HOUM'S DRIFT–SANDFONTEIN road.

At daybreak it became apparent that the Union detachment had surrendered.

Lukin had not been able to reconnoitre the SANDFONTEIN position personally since his arrival on the river on the 24th but it had been reported to him as tenable. As a consequence of distant observation on the morning of the 27th he formed the opinion that " it was untenable if a considerable force of artillery was brought against it ".

The reverse was perhaps not of much importance since no more than a detachment was involved, and it had little influence on the campaign as a whole, but it *was* a reverse and therefore will repay examination.

It is abundantly clear that constant urging to press forward was employed by D.H.Q., which " had to request high pressure to the verge of self-sacrifice " (O.H., p. 14). Any responsibility for the mishap which depends upon insistence on a forward movement must be therefore assumed by D.H.Q., and will be dealt with later.

The local responsibility rested with Lukin, and to arrive at

The Campaign in German South West Africa, 1914-1915

a clear idea as to how he acquitted himself of that responsibility we may answer three questions.

First:
Did the Force Commander place an adequate force on the river line?

The answer to this must be in the negative if a general forward movement was contemplated but in the affirmative if a watching and defensive role were called for.

But in any case it was the limit of strength he could maintain on that line—as has been explained—in view of his shortage of transport, and as it was the utmost he could do he must be held blameless, since the pressure to go forward came from Headquarters.

Second:
Was he right in occupying SANDFONTEIN?

His reasons for doing so he gave as follows:—

" It was an important point on the line of advance contiguous to and therefore commanding the recognised roads from WARMBAD to RAMAN'S DRIFT and HOUM'S DRIFT. It embraced the principal water holes between the above-mentioned points. Its occupation would form a bar to the enemy's reconnaissance patrols and consequently a screen to the concentration of additional troops on the line GUDOUS–RAMAN'S DRIFT–HOUM'S DRIFT. It was in telephonic communication with RAMAN'S DRIFT and at a distance at which it could be quickly reinforced or from which a small force could as quickly retire in the face of greatly superior numbers."

(This last assumption, of course, depended upon timely notice of the advance of the " greatly superior numbers ").

It was therefore decided to occupy SANDFONTEIN " rather with a view to establishing an outpost there than with the object of obtaining a permanent footing, though the latter would be effected in the absence of powerful aggressive action by the enemy ".

In the circumstances the occupation of SANDFONTEIN must be judged permissible if the Force Commander had reason to suppose it to be tenable.

He appears to have been assured that it was by someone in whom he placed confidence.

Against this must be placed Welby's report and a consensus of opinion that the place could not be held, and the opinion of

The Campaign in German South West Africa, 1914-1915

Grant that the position was " extremely bad " was clearly right and whoever reported it as tenable was wrong.

The point should have been determined, for senior officers were on the spot at the two drifts long enough to have cleared the matter up.

Lukin, unable to get forward himself, was guided by the report mentioned, but it is quite clear that SANDFONTEIN NEK and not SANDFONTEIN itself was the place to occupy.

At SANDFONTEIN NEK the water could have been denied to any but a strong force, and this was all that was necessary at the time.

Frequent change of squadrons at the NEK and constant patrolling from the two drifts (HOUM'S and RAMAN'S) would seem, in the light of events, the best course and the decision to attempt to hold SANDFONTEIN itself must be judged to have been a mistake.

The possibility of a strong concentration against a small stationary force was always present.

Had timely information of the strong forces moving on the place been received, the detachment should have been saved.

There must have been some laxity in the forward reconnaisance but there was another serious mistake which will be referred to later, which largely contributed to the fate of the force at SANDFONTEIN.

Third:

Was all that was possible done to try to relieve the force at SANDFONTEIN?

On September 25 there were 400 rifles and four guns at RAMAN'S DRIFT and 300 at HOUM'S DRIFT.

On forming the opinion that a force of some 300 was about to attack SANDFONTEIN, the Force Commander at once sent forward two guns and 100 rifles to that place, keeping 300 rifles and two guns to secure RAMAN'S DRIFT, his Headquarters, and commanding his line of retreat.

On the following day, on hearing gun fire, he dispatched towards SANDFONTEIN 100 rifles from RAMAN'S DRIFT and 100 rifles from HOUM'S DRIFT. On further information he himself took the two remaining guns and 130 rifles and moved in support to SANDFONTEIN, leaving rather less than 200 rifles (the squadron on the way from STEINKOPF had then arrived) at RAMAN'S DRIFT.

It would seem therefore that with due regard for the safety

The Campaign in German South West Africa, 1914-1915

of his forward base at RAMAN'S DRIFT, which was of extreme importance, Lukin did the best he could with the numbers at his disposal.

It is true that 200 rifles remained at HOUM'S DRIFT, but that drift had to be watched, and in any case the hundred or so extra rifles would have been of no avail against the enemy's superior forces.

The question now arises as to whether the forward policy insisted upon by Defence Headquarters was sound or justifiable.

An examination of the facts leads one inevitably to the conclusion that it was neither.

Briefly to recapitulate these facts which have been already noted at length:—

The full strength of the combined forces of Maritz and Lukin was far less than that which the enemy could bring against them.

It was soon apparent that Lukin could look for no assistance from Maritz, whose defection was an episode of an imminent civil war in the Union of which the dimensions could not be determined.

The purpose of the plan in pursuance of which the forces of Maritz and Lukin had been placed on the border had been achieved in the occupation of LÜDERITZBUCHT.

The occupation of WARMBAD, by which so much store was set, as an isolated act would achieve nothing more than did the presence of a Union force on the border but, unless it were carried out in far greater strength than was available on the spot in September, 1914, would be accompanied by grave risk.

Lukin's remarks as follows in a report dated October 4, 1914, are here pertinent:

" The Force under my command (exclusive of those essential for safeguarding as far as possible my lines of communication, i.e. slow-moving infantry) consisted of two 4-gun Q.F. Batteries and approximately 1,200 mounted riflemen ", pointing out that the enemy has shown his ability to concentrate rapidly as far south as SANDFONTEIN a force of at least 10 guns and 1,800 men, he proceeds: " I would draw attention to the extremely dangerous position in which my force would have been placed had the enemy delayed until I had reached WARMBAD with my whole force, with a long and vulnerable line of communication, the cutting of which would have been effected simultaneously with the delivery of an attack on my force."

The transport arrangements for " A " force (Lukin) were,

as has been shown, most indifferent and inadequate for the most ordinary needs of the force.

The determination to advance with one force to WARMBAD in such circumstances was most unsound, the more particularly as, being an isolated act, it could have no military value in the extremely improbable event of success.

Finally, a most regrettable mistake has to be recorded.

Information, from two sources, had reached D.H.Q. at PRETORIA on September 24 that train loads of the enemy had moved south to KALKFONTEIN. This information, of vital importance to "A" force, since it indicated a southward movement of the enemy in strength against it, was embodied in an Intelligence Summary and *posted* to Lukin, whom it reached at GUDOUS on October 7, ten days after the reverse at SAND-FONTEIN.

Had the information of this movement been telegraphed, to use Lukin's words: "A clearer appreciation of the situation would have resulted and the outpost at SANDFONTEIN withdrawn in ample time." Lukin, however, was left in ignorance of the strong enemy concentration against him, and for this blame must rest on D.H.Q.

A staff officer of competence would at once have telegraphed this valuable information "clear line" and obtained an acknowledgment of it.

That this action was not taken must be taken as due to the inefficiency of the staff system at D.H.Q.

The incident at SANDFONTEIN and the circumstances which led up to it emphasised the lack of trained staff officers; the absence of military staff control at D.H.Q., and the lack of appreciation in the same quarter of the enemy's power of concentration.

It was also apparent that the influence that the matter of transport was to exercise on the conduct of operations was not grasped.

On September 27 the situation of "A" Force on the Orange River had to be surveyed. The 2nd and 3rd S.A.M.R. had been ordered up from STEINKOPF and reached RAMAN'S DRIFT at 4 p.m. on September 27.

This step was taken in view of the strength the enemy had exhibited the day before.

Lukin first ordered the retirement of the whole force to STEINKOPF (there was no intermediate position between the

The Campaign in German South West Africa, 1914-1915

latter place and the river), but at VUURDOOD decided to turn to GUDOUS DRIFT where he took his force, less the 5th S.A.M.R. which, in view of the state of their horses, went back to STEINKOPF.

A telegram from D.H.Q. on September 27 ordered "*on account of Maritz's attitude*" the extrication of "A" Force from its position on the river and this (for the reason given earlier) entailed retirement to STEINKOPF. On the following day a second telegram from D.H.Q. expressed the view that "A" Force was strong enough to hold the Orange River position and that a retirement would enable the enemy to pay attention to the smaller forces under Maritz and Beves.

It is difficult to think that these telegrams emanated from the same source, and they seem to indicate considerable confusion of thought at D.H.Q.

In the circumstances Lukin could do nothing to help Beves, who, as it proved, did not need assistance, and Maritz was apparently regarded at Headquarters as at least a potential enemy.

Lukin remained in a defensive position at GUDOUS until October 23, when he was recalled with his force (less the Witwatersrand Rifles) to the Union for the Rebellion which occupied the energies of the Government for the ensuing three months.

CHAPTER V

IN THE LAST chapter the view was expressed that the dispositions of the German Commander-in-Chief protected " The heart of his defence at WINDHOEK ".

To realise the significance of this statement we must be clear as to what the loss of this place would mean to the enemy.

It was not that it was the capital.

Capitals have often been the objective of strategy.

In the American Civil War of 1861-65 Lee and Jackson constantly compelled the Northern generals to abandon the advance by threatening WASHINGTON.

In the Anglo-Boer War Lord Roberts made Bloemfontein and PRETORIA his objectives clearly influenced by the action of the American generals.

The value of WINDHOEK, *qua* capital, was merely sentimental, and the enemy would have no difficulty in removing—as he did—everything he wished to take away in the shape of war material and stores.

But, as commanding the railway to the south and to KARIBIB, the junction with the narrow-gauge railway to TSUMEB in the north, the possession of WINDHOEK was of vital importance to the defensive arrangements of the German Commander-in-Chief.

With its loss would go his power of rapid concentration throughout the length of the Protectorate, of which the value and effect had been so signally emphasised at SANDFONTEIN.

Deprived of this power his mounted troops would have to rely upon their own mobility unaided.

The enemy commander was well aware of the mobility of the mounted troops which were about to move against him, the war in South Africa of twelve years earlier teemed with instances of its value, he knew he would be greatly outnumbered and no doubt recognised that the South African mounted riflemen were more mobile than his own, though to the last he never fully appreciated the extent of their superiority in this respect.

With KARIBIB and WINDHOEK in his opponent's hands, the best he could hope for would be that he should extricate his forces in full strength and continue the struggle north of the

The Campaign in German South West Africa, 1914-1915

KARIBIB—OKAHANDJA line with the whole of his troops concentrated.

It is generally allowed that success at the decisive point will ensure ultimate success, and that difficulties elsewhere, and even temporary reverses, are removed and compensated for by such success.

Exactly where the decisive point is is sometimes a disputed point and it is the work of the sound strategist or tactician to detect it.

In this case the decisive point was, for the reasons given, obvious, and the capture of WINDHOEK would compel the retirement of any enemy detachments south of that point to the north. Should they elect to remain in the south, their capture would be a simple matter and quickly effected, while any movement further south without supplies or any line of communication along which supplies could be sent to them would render their capture easier still.

Any effort to enter the Union would therefore invite the early destruction of any enemy force which might attempt it.

In such circumstances Union territory would be amply secured by the establishment of suitably placed entrenched posts with good lateral communication and arrangements for the concentration of forces behind them in support in the very improbable event of such assistance becoming necessary.

The concentration of all necessary strength *and the provision of the means of keeping the mounted troops mobile* for an advance against WINDHOEK by the most direct and shortest route was clearly the right course to adopt.

We have seen how Lukin was reduced to immobility and compelled to allow half of his force to remain idle at STEINKOPF as a consequence of inadequate transport arrangements, and his predicament should have made it quite clear that, in such a country as South West Africa, the provision of the full transport *necessary to keep the mounted troops on the move* was a condition indispensable to their employment to the best advantage.

Once the movement of these troops against the enemy was arrested, their chance of effecting surprise—the immense advantage conferred on them by their mobility—would disappear.

While the importance of an advance such as that last mentioned—viz. on WINDHOEK by the shortest route—was

The Campaign in German South West Africa, 1914-1915

recognised by D.H.Q., the need for concentration of all energy for the purpose was not.

The dissipation of effort which had been a feature of the earlier movements persisted and arrangements were made for a strong advance from the south against what might be estimated, and what actually proved to be, small detachments.

The number of Union troops available being what it was, the employment of so many in the south made little difference except to the extent of the expense caused by their maintenance, but the diversion of the transport needed for them was—as will be seen—a serious matter.

At the end of the year, 1914, the internal situation in the Union became settled enough to allow operations in South West Africa to be resumed.

WALVIS BAY and SWAKOPMUND were plainly points from which a movement against WINDHOEK should start, and on December 25 a force, composed as under, from CAPETOWN landed at WALVIS BAY under the command of Colonel P. C. B. Skinner.

        Seven guns Field Artillery.
        Two Infantry Brigades (each 3 battalions).
        One regiment Mounted Riflemen.

Reconnoitring towards SWAKOPMUND on January 3, 1915, Skinner found the place abandoned and occupied it.

General Botha sailed from CAPETOWN on February 6 on the auxiliary cruiser " Armadale Castle ", placed at his disposal by the Naval Commander-in-Chief at SIMONSTOWN, and on the 8th reached LUDERITZBUCHT, where he landed and met General Sir Duncan McKenzie who had taken over command of " C " Force—now the Central Force and reinforced—from Colonel Beves.

McKenzie's advanced force was at TSCHAUKAIB with detachments along the railway line back to LUDERITZBUCHT.

The enemy held AUS opposite McKenzie eastward along the railway line.

AUS was a remarkably strong position and considerable emphasis was from time to time laid by the Intelligence Department at D.H.Q. on a reported intention of the enemy to resist any attempt to capture it and on the formidable nature of such an undertaking by the Union forces.

General Botha had arranged before leaving the Union that he should exercise a general control over McKenzie's movements

The Campaign in German South West Africa, 1914-1915

in order that any possible measure of co-operation in connection with the advance on WINDHOEK should be assured.

He accordingly now discussed with McKenzie the manner of the latter's next forward movement from TSCHAUKAIB.

McKenzie stated his views which were, briefly, that he should occupy some place short of GARUB—between TSCHAUKAIB and AUS—and thence combine the occupation of GARUB with an attack on AUS.

He proposed to advance to a place on the desert six miles or so short of GARUB whence an infantry advance was to end in the occupation of GARUB. His mounted troops, having started the evening before, were to advance on AUS and come in on the position from its southern flank.

The advantages of this plan were held to be that the chance of surprising the enemy would be greater than if any other method were adopted, and that the occupation of GARUB as a step preliminary to the attack on AUS would give warning of the intention and lead to the abandonment of the position and damage to the water and railway which a surprise might prevent.

General Botha's views were that a certain line of action would be looked for by the enemy, and that whether the advance were carried out from GARUB or six miles short of it, the chance of surprising the enemy was the same.

He also considered that the following advantages would accrue from the occupation of GARUB before attacking AUS.

First: GARUB afforded a good base naturally capable of strong defence with a good water supply.

Second: The denial of these advantages to the enemy who, occupying GARUB six miles away, as contemplated by McKenzie's scheme, would see all movements against him and be able with ease to offer resistance to an infantry advance over the open plain.

Third: A railway up to GARUB to which retirement would be easier, if it became necessary, than it would be to a point on the open plain across six miles of desert.

He saw the following disadvantages in McKenzie's plan:

An extra six miles for the infantry advance on AUS; the facility afforded to the enemy for an attack on either of the separate advancing forces; increased separation in consequence of the longer marches of the two forces; and difficulty of inter-communication if the infantry should fail to seize GARUB.

General Botha thought that the enemy with his intimate

The Campaign in German South West Africa, 1914-1915

knowledge of the ground, which was new to the Union troops, would quickly divine the purpose of the movement. He also expressed the opinion that the enemy would do the same amount of destruction in any case as the position at AUS would allow of more or less leisurely evacuation.

He finally laid stress on the moral effect of the occupation of GARUB with its natural facilities as a tangible advantage which would encourage troops, which had necessarily been long inactive, far more than an advance to yet another open position on the desert.

The distances were as follows:—
LUDERITZBUCHT to TSCHAUKAIB ...... 30 miles.
TSCHAUKAIB to GARUB .... 34 miles.
TSCHAUKAIB to AUS .... 40 miles.

In the end Aus was evacuated by the enemy without fighting as a consequence of General Botha's own movements in the north and its occupation called for no operations. The above particulars, however, are given as they may help to show the nature of the problems to be undertaken.

General Botha left LUDERITZBUCHT in the evening and reached WALVIS BAY at noon on February 9, landing on the morning of the following day. Here he was informed that probably some 500 of the enemy were before SWAKOPMUND, from which no extended movement had been made by the Union garrison there.

On the following morning General Botha arrived at SWAKOPMUND where he took over the command of the Northern Force from Colonel Skinner who assumed the command of an Infantry Brigade.

The position of the forces is shown in the map facing page 56.

The new dispositions were as follows:—

Northern Force (General Botha) at SWAKOPMUND: To be brought up to—
Two (4-gun) batteries Field Artillery.
(One battery was allotted to each of the Mounted Brigades.)
1st Mounted Brigade (Colonel C. J. Brits), approximately 2,200 rifles.
2nd Mounted Brigade (Colonel J. J. Alberts), approximately 2,500 rifles.
These were "commando" brigades, and constituted the

The Campaign in German South West Africa, 1914-1915

Field Force with which General Botha made his first advance to RIET.

The following were employed on protective duty covering the railway construction, as a garrison for SWAKOPMUND, and on the lines of communication back to WALVIS BAY:—

One infantry brigade (Colonel P. C. B. Skinner).
One infantry brigade (Colonel J. S. Wylie) (each of three battalions).
Two unbrigaded infantry battalions.
One mounted regiment.
One battery and one section (six guns in all) Heavy Artillery.

(*Note.*—All the forces had the usual allowance of administrative, medical and engineer units.)

Central Force (Brigadier-General Sir Duncan McKenzie), LUDERITZBUCHT to TSCHAUKAIB:—

Two (6-gun) batteries Field Artillery.
Two mounted brigades (each of two regiments).

The above, with an additional mounted brigade sent in March, 1915, composed McKenzie's Field Force with which he moved on GIBEON, and contained approximately 1,800 rifles.

The following were employed as garrison at LUDERITBUCHT and along the lines of communication.

Seven infantry battalions (in two brigades) and two (4-gun) batteries Heavy Artillery.

Eastern Force (Colonel C. A. L. Berrangé):—

One Section (12-pdr.) Heavy Artillery.
Four regiments Mounted Riflemen; 1,200 rifles.

Southern Force [Colonel (later Lieut.-General Sir) J. L. van Deventer *]:—

One battery (4-gun) Field Artillery, 5,000 rifles, representing twenty-nine commandos.

This force operated in five, and later four, columns, the principal commanders being Colonels Celliers, Bouwer and D. van Deventer.

---

* General van Deventer later commanded the British East African Expeditionary Force.

The Campaign in German South West Africa, 1914-1915

Roughly stated the proposed lines of advance of these four " Forces " were:—

Northern: SWAKOPMUND on WINDHOEK.
Central: LUDERITZBUCHT on AUS and eastward.
Eastern: KURUMAN on KEETMANSHOOP.
Southern: UPINGTON (via SANDFONTEIN, WARM-BAD) on KEETMANSHOOP.

For these movements D.H.Q. disposed of some 13,000 mounted rifles and 26 guns, and of these 8,000 and 18 respectively were to be employed in the south, some 5,000 and 8 being directed against the decisive point at WINDHOEK.

The Central, Southern and Eastern Forces were widely separated once more.

The enemy before the SANDFONTEIN affair had kept the bulk of his troops north when no threat of any kind was offered in that direction, and it might be reasonably assumed that he would at least not reduce his strength about WINDHOEK when a serious threat materialised with the occupation of WALVIS BAY and SWAKOPMUND by strong Union forces including some 5,000 mounted men.

We have already seen that the transport allotted to Lukin, less than half the size of van Deventer's force, was far below that which was needed, and when it is realised that Berrangé's advance was to be over 200 miles of arid desert, involving (O.H., p. 36) " a special motor transport and water supply service ", it would seem that, only if the forces moving on the decisive point in the north were fully equipped with everything needed for as rapid an advance as possible, should such expenditure of effort, and incidentally money, have been made in the south.

It will have been noticed that the mounted troops of General Botha, and to a large extent those of van Deventer, were commandos.

The Active Citizen Force was represented, in the latter instance especially, in the 10th Mounted Brigade under Colonel Bouwer which contained Hartigan's Horse (Hartigan), 17th (W.P.) Mounted Rifles and 14th Dismounted (mounted for the campaign) Rifles under van der Westhuizen and Steyn respectively.

A Commando Brigade was organised as follows:—

It was commanded by a colonel (later a brigadier-general)

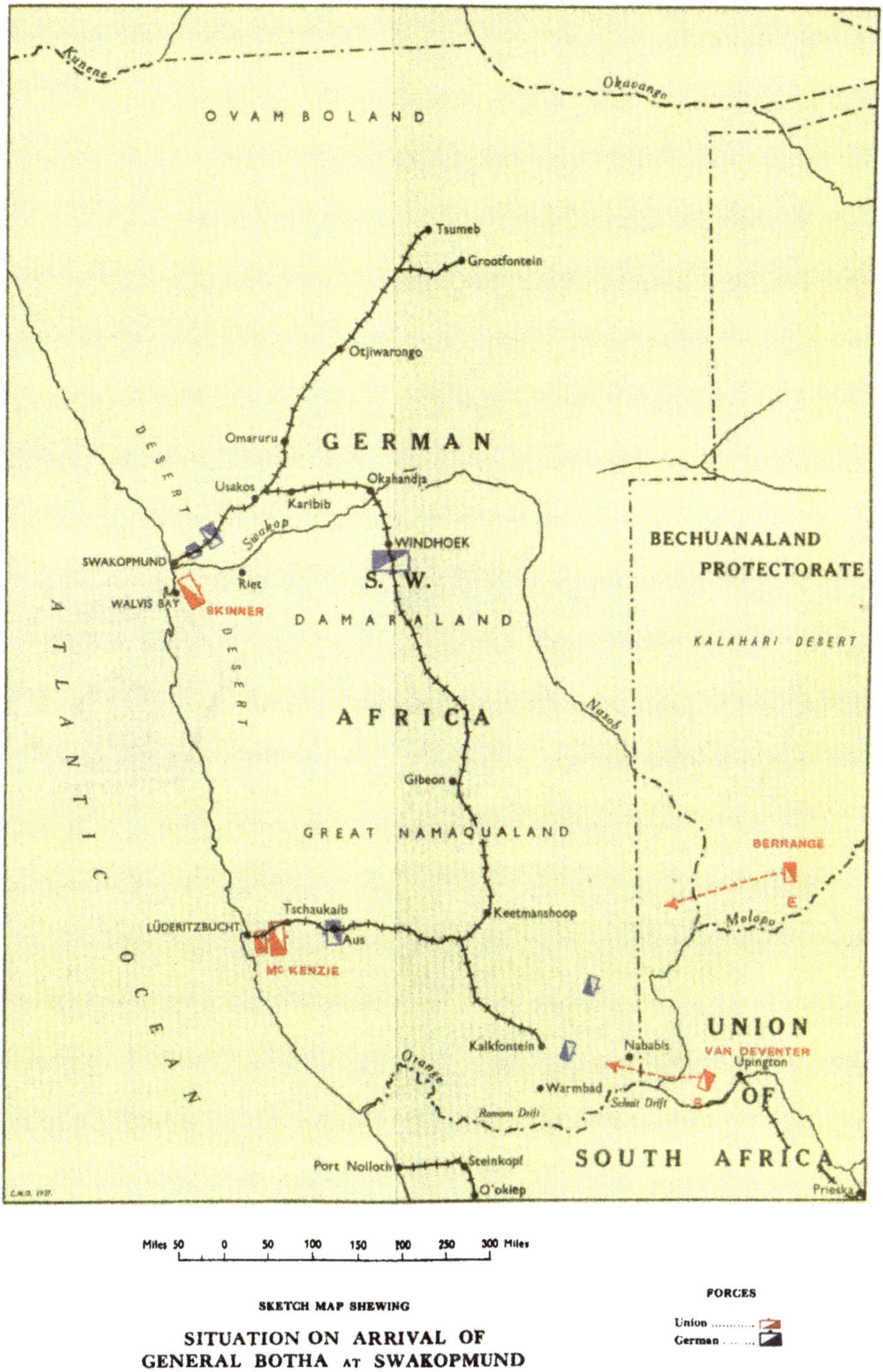

SKETCH MAP SHEWING

SITUATION ON ARRIVAL OF
GENERAL BOTHA AT SWAKOPMUND

FEBRUARY, 1915.

FORCES

Union ....
German ....

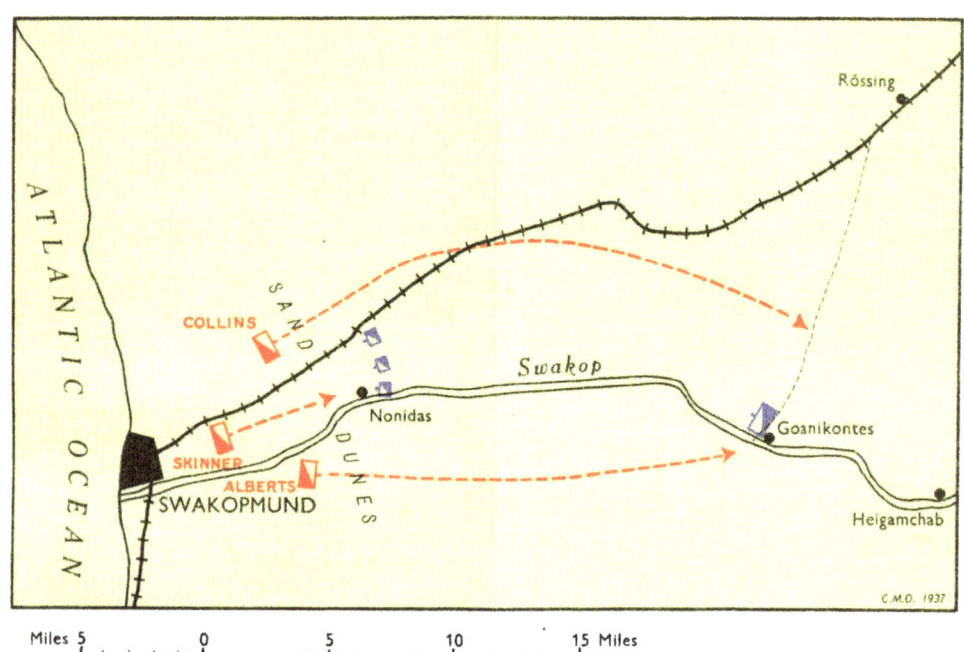

SKETCH MAP OF MOVEMENT OF
GENERAL BOTHA'S FORCE
FROM SWAKOPMUND

23 FEBRUARY 1915

The Campaign in German South West Africa, 1914-1915

whose staff comprised a brigade-major, staff captain and aide-de-camp, or " galloper ", and administrative staff officers.

The brigade consisted of two wings, each commanded by a colonel commandant who had a wing adjutant and a secretary as his staff officers.

Wings were self-contained and could be detached without any special arrangements.

The units (commandos) were recruited on a territorial basis and each was under a commandant, a lieut.-colonel or major as the size of the commando or sometimes the personality and record of the commandant suggested.

There was no fixed establishment for the strength of a commando, but the plan of sub-division under field cornets and assistant field cornets was common to all.

General Botha's first movement from SWAKOPMUND was undertaken to clear the enemy from his position of observation outside the town and to gain power of movement and reconnaissance.

Information as to the strength of the enemy opposed to the Northern Force was mainly based on intercepted wireless messages—the total strength of the enemy was of course more or less accurately known—and, as the country was new to the Commander of the Union force, it was not until February 23 that a movement was made from the town.

The plan was an attack on the ground held by the enemy due east of SWAKOPMUND combined with another attack on GOANIKONTES, an oasis and small settlement in the SWAKOP River bed 20 miles inland, apparently headquarters of the force in observation of the town. See map opposite.

For this purpose the forces were divided into three detachments with a general reserve.

An infantry brigade (Skinner) with artillery was to attack the enemy position east of SWAKOPMUND.

Colonel Alberts with the right wing of his (2nd) mounted brigade and two machine-gun sections was to deal with GOANIKONTES, moving on the right of Skinner.

Colonel-Commandant Collins with his own (left) wing of Alberts' brigade would move on Skinner's left to the rear of the enemy position and place himself astride the track from GOANIKONTES to ROSSING.

Skinner occupied his objective, the rising ground above NONIDAS, without incident in the early morning, but the

The Campaign in German South West Africa, 1914-1915

mounted troops were all delayed in consequence of the guides losing their way. One force, marching in a circle all night, found itself at dawn close to its starting point.

The enemy slipped away, but, judging from the condition of his camps, with some degree of hurry, and owing to the delay some tactical success was perhaps lost.

Collins in a skirmish with an enemy rear guard took some prisoners.

The rising ground beyond the town and NONIDAS was occupied, as were GOANIKONTES, 20, and HEIGAMCHAB, 25 miles up the river, respectively.

Reconnaissance was now maintained to ROSSING which was occupied when the railway reached it rather more than a month later.

It is probable that the enemy received news of activity in the Union lines. Thousands of natives were employed on the railway, at the coast, and in the transport. To prevent odd ones coming in and slipping out was a matter of extreme difficulty.

General Botha now turned to the consideration of his next move.

There were two lines of advance in the direction of WINDHOEK open to him.

Along the railway line to USAKOS or along the SWAKOP River to RIET.

USAKOS and RIET were distant from SWAKOPMUND across the desert belt 80 and 60 miles respectively.

Report said that, once the intervening desolate belt should have been crossed, grass veld would be found.

Grass meant forage and mobility to the commandos and if report spoke truly, the passage of the desert would bring relief in the problem of supply.

The merits of the two lines had been weighed, and, as has been mentioned, the railway had supporters. One officer—an influential member of Parliament—had come to Capetown from LUDERITZBUCHT to emphasize to General Botha that an advance along the railway line was the only possible method.

It was stated that D.H.Q. had allotted the transport of the Northern Force on the understanding that the view last mentioned was to be adopted.

If this was the case the evil of working on a preconceived notion was well illustrated. It might explain the inadequacy of the provision in this all important respect.

The Campaign in German South West Africa, 1914-1915

The enemy had removed all the 2-ft. gauge track between the coast and ROSSING and stacked it at USAKOS 80 miles inland, but from ROSSING eastwards long stretches were left intact.

It was decided to relay the line to USAKOS with 3 ft. 6in. gauge brought from the Union and this was done as far as EBONY station, about 10 miles short of USAKOS. By the time EBONY had been reached construction work had to give way to urgent strategic need, and the original 2-ft. gauge was used to the north from USAKOS which became the junction for the TSUMEB railway.

It was estimated that it would take until the end of May to connect USAKOS by rail with the coast. As a matter of fact, the first train entered USAKOS on May 15, on which date WINDHOEK had been in possession of the Union forces for three days.

General Botha could either advance slowly ahead of the railway, feeding and watering his troops by its aid and holding, as a matter of necessity, the line of approach to SWAKOPMUND on his right flank from SALEM and RIET along the SWAKOP, or move along the river leaving a protective force covering the railway construction.

The seizure of KARIBIB would enable a switch of the lines of communication to be made to the railway as soon as the latter should have reached USAKOS, but, until then, a heavy sand track which would require a large quantity of transport material and animals was the only route by which the advancing force could be supplied.

If he had tied himself to the railway, General Botha would have entirely sacrificed the mobility of the commandos. It would also take all his personal influence to keep the burghers, anxious to get home, sitting on a railway line.

He accordingly selected the river route, with its obvious defects and risks, as strategically the sounder and quicker of the two.

The decision was, however, bold, and argued a robust confidence in the hardihood and grit of the commandos.

As if in good omen, when the choice had been made, the SWAKOP River came down in one of its heavy rare floods and intercepted wireless messages gave information of general heavy rain inland and as far south as KEETMANSHOOP and AUS.

CHAPTER VI

THE WELCOME INDICATION of rain inland had made it clear that, if the mounted troops of the Union could reach the grass, which was understood to begin at RIET, their mobility would be increased to an extent which would allow of wide movement, and General Botha accordingly advised D.H.Q. of his intention to direct 5,000 mounted men from SWAKOPMUND towards WINDHOEK as soon as possible.

When a careful review of the situation had been made and a clear idea had been formed as to what the proposed advance would entail in the way of preparations and supplies of all kinds, it became apparent that there was a grave shortage of transport.

It must be observed that the original Northern Force had been largely added to and that until General Botha had examined the situation on the spot and formed his plan a proper estimate of his requirements could not be arrived at.

But from the point at which he made up his mind he urged unceasingly the need for far greater transport facilities, soon pointing out that everything depended upon a rapid and decisive thrust in the north, and that, to attain this end, the forces in the south might be very much reduced and that the transport thus released should be sent where it was so badly needed.

The only units which arrived at the scene of operations with their full transport were the 1st and 2nd Mounted Brigades, each of which had first line transport, and a brigade train. The latter could carry one—capable of being stretched to two—day's supply.

The Infantry Brigades, the Medical and Veterinary units and the Machine-gun Brigade were all short of the transport allowed by their establishments.

There was nothing whatever beyond this in the way of transport and the mobility of the mounted troops was most seriously affected.

Only with the railway close behind the troops could the subsistence of the latter be guaranteed with such an exiguous allowance of transport.

What there was was further diminished, as in the heavy ground 12 mules was the least number with which a wagon

The Campaign in German South West Africa, 1914-1915

could be worked. The addition of two mules to each team of ten—the regulation allowance—meant sacrificing a certain number of wagons.

The first step was to obtain an immediate increase in the daily lift of supplies from WALVIS BAY.

Two alternatives confronted those responsible:—

Either all railway construction must be stopped until, by using all native labour to load and unload supplies and filling rolling stock with food instead of railway material, enough supplies ahead of daily demands should have been brought up to form a reserve.

Or the advance along the SWAKOP must be abandoned to push the railway on.

Railway construction after a long series of discouraging checks had just begun to make smooth and regular progress, but General Botha regarded the need for bringing the enemy to an early engagement as paramount and, accordingly, railway construction ceased from February 23 till March 2.

Meanwhile HUSAB, 30 miles from SWAKOPMUND along the SWAKOP River, had been occupied by the 2nd Mounted Brigade and was selected as the advance supply base, and the work of conveying supplies from railhead near NONIDAS to this base was begun. RIET was 30 miles from HUSAB.

Infantry garrisons were placed at GOANIKONTES, HEIGAMCHAB and HUSAB and all mounted troops—except the Imperial Light Horse sent to Skinner now covering railway construction with his brigade—were withdrawn to SWAKOPMUND where they could be fed.

Enough food and fodder must be placed at the water-holes to enable the advancing force to be subsisted in its passage of the desert without drawing upon the reserve required after the advance from HUSAB.

The protection of the convoys moving in full view of the craggy hills bordering the SWAKOP was of importance.

The smaller the escort, the greater the bulk of supply which reached the other end.

Escorts were gradually reduced to vanishing point as the enemy showed no intention of interfering with the convoys.

This indulgence on the part of the German Commander was much appreciated, and General Botha gained some light on his opponent's attitude.

Colonel von Heydebreck had recently lost his life by an

The Campaign in German South West Africa, 1914-1915

experimental bomb explosion, and throughout the campaign there was no repetition of such initiative as the late Commander had shown.

Reconnaissance showed that motor lorries could be used for some distance on the hard Namib desert soil and this was of some help.

On March 16, after stripping every unit of its transport and using every means of conveyance to hand, 5½ days' supplies had been collected at HUSAB for the mounted force which was to make the attempt to reach WINDHOEK.

The heavy pulling and incessant 16 days' work in the deep sand had taken heavy toll of draught animals which were handed back to the units in poor and tired condition.

To be independent of the country—which until the capture of WINDHOEK produced little but water in scanty quantity—not less than 400 wagons were required. At this time the Northern Force had little more than one tenth of that number.

Relying, however, on the mobility of his burghers, and, always with his mind on the grass which might be found at RIET, General Botha determined on the venture.

He had hoped that McKenzie would move forward on AUS coincidently with his own advance.

The latter had occupied GARUB and reported AUS to be held by the enemy. His last arrived Mounted Brigade (his third) had recently disembarked and its horses had not recovered from the effects of their voyage and the water at GARUB was not fully developed.

In these circumstances General Botha decided to advance alone.

The mobile force was composed of the 1st and 2nd Mounted Brigades.

The 3rd Mounted Brigade, recently assembled after disembarkation, was to remain at SWAKOPMUND, but ready to move forward if it were urgently required.

The task of protecting the railway—of which the head was 15 miles from SWAKOPMUND on March 20—was assigned to Colonel Skinner with his (3rd Infantry) Brigade.

The 4th Infantry Brigade under Colonel Wylie (less the Rand Rifles at GOANIKONTES, HEIGAMCHAB and HUSAB) was to take up the forward position at NONIDAS.

Little or no information had been gained as to the strength of the enemy which would have to be reckoned with. A fairly comprehensive distribution of the enemy forces had been pieced together from such information as had been received and from deductions which had been made from time to time. Intercepted wireless messages had given useful information, and the practice of mixing " clear " with " code " in the messages had simplified this source of information considerably.

Contact with the enemy and access to the natives were, however, of much importance in order to arrive at some degree of certainty.

Accordingly ample forces were left for the protection of the base and lines of communication.

A thorough knowledge of the country, uniformity of staff and regimental system, a well-trained and homogeneous force, power of rapid concentration, ample war material, and, for the time being at all events, supplies, together with the favourable nature of the terrain presented a combination of decided advantages possessed by the German Commander which, if skilfully and resolutely turned to account, with a greatly superior artillery at his disposal, might go far to counterbalance any actual disparity of numbers.

The composition of the two mounted Brigades to move forward was as follows:—

1st Mounted Brigade.

Right Wing (Colonel-Commandant Piet de la Rey):
KRUGERSDORP, POTCHEFSTROOM " A " and POTCHEFSTROOM " B " Commandos ...... 1,089 rifles.

Left Wing (Colonel-Commandant Lemmer):
MARICO, LICHTENBURG, BLOEMHOF and WOLMARANSSTAD Commandos ...... 1,200 rifles.

Total strength ...... 2,289 rifles.

Transvaal Horse Artillery Battery ...... 4 guns.

2nd Mounted Brigade.

Right Wing (Colonel-Commandant Badenhorst):
HEIDELBERG " A ", HEIDELBERG " B ", STANDERTON " A ", STANDERTON " B " and ERMELO " A " Commandos ...... 1,311 rifles.

The Campaign in German South West Africa, 1914-1915

Left Wing (Colonel-Commandant Collins):
BETHAL, CAROLINA, ERMELO " B ",
MIDDELBURG " A ", MIDDEL-
BURG " B " Commandos .... 1,253 rifles.
Total strength .... 2,564 rifles.
4th Permanent Field Artillery Battery 4 guns.

The Commander of the 1st Mounted Brigade was Colonel C. J. Brits. He later became a Brigadier-General and served after the campaign in German South West Africa in East Africa as a Major-General in command of a Division under General Smuts.

Coen Brits was a well-known personality.

As a young man in the Anglo-Boer War he had been a successful Commandant under General Botha, and had been noted for boldness and capacity though, of course, had not held any independent command nor had he controlled any considerable body of troops. He had been associated with General Botha in the charge at BAKENLAAGTE, which overwhelmed Benson's rearguard, and other bold tactical successes.

He spoke no English (at any rate never used it), had a genuine contempt for anything like the formal methods of a regular army which he expressed in telling terms, and was a law unto himself, except that he had for General Botha a great affection and offered him an unvarying and unlimited personal loyalty. He paid little attention to anyone else.

It is said—the story has often been repeated—that at the beginning of the war in 1914 Brits, ordered to mobilise his commandos, did so and telegraphed to General Botha: " My burghers are ready, whom do we fight, the English or the Germans? " He was ready to move against either " enemy " as General Botha might direct.

He was of forceful character and—like so many of his countrymen—of splendid physique and a stout fighter, but lacked some of the essential qualities of generalship.

Extended responsibility and the intrusion of doubt as to the best of several possible courses to pursue have often affected the resolution of a soldier ready to act with boldness in a clear-cut situation.

Colonel Alberts—also an ex-Commandant—had been less prominent in the Anglo-Boer War but was a man of influence— a member of Parliament—and much easier to work with than his fellow Brigadier.

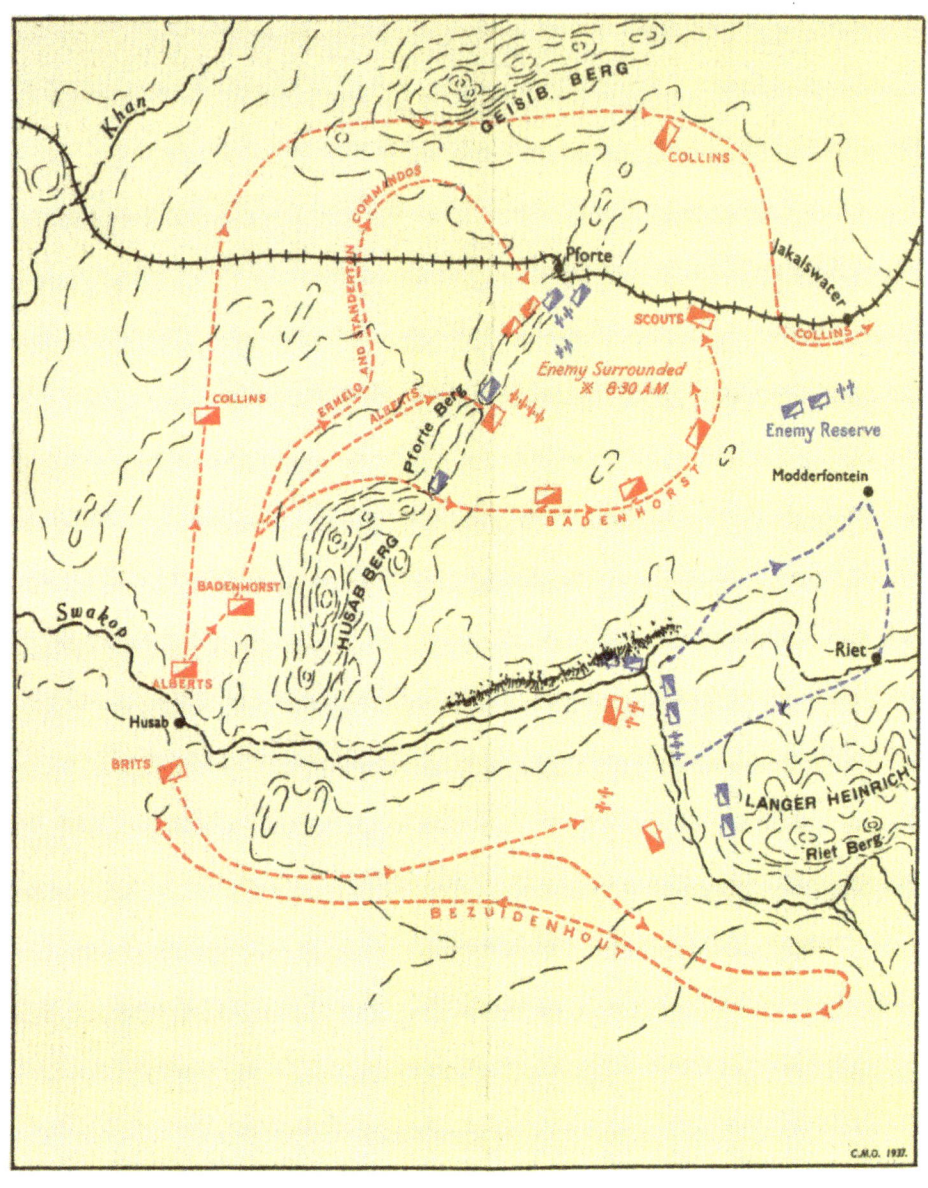

SKETCH MAP TO ILLUSTRATE ENGAGEMENTS AT
RIET, PFORTE AND JAKALSWATER
20 MARCH 1915.

The Campaign in German South West Africa, 1914-1915

All the commandants and officers were veterans of the Anglo-Boer War and represented the pick of those, their qualities and characters were well known to their commander-in-chief, and the whole of the personnel had served through the Rebellion.

Employed on the lines to which they were accustomed and led by a commander who was a master of their tactics, they were a formidable force.

On March 18 the 1st Mounted Brigade left its camp at NONIDAS and the 2nd Mounted Brigade moved from GOANI-KONTES, both on HUSAB.

At HUSAB a patrol reported the enemy in position at PFORTE just south of the KHAN-JAKALSWATER railway line. RIET was known to be held.

On moving from HUSAB on the evening of March 19 (the 1st Brigade at 8 p.m., following the 2nd which left at 6 p.m.) the two brigades separated.

The 1st was ordered to move against RIET and attack the enemy there at daybreak. The forked roads west of LANGER-HEINRICH were to be reached under cover of darkness.

From this point the BLOEMHOF Commando (Commandant Bezuidenhout), approximately 300 rifles, was to continue its march by way of KLEIN TINKAS–MITTEL TINKAS–SCHWARZ KUPPE against RIET, approaching it from the south-east, while the remainder of the Brigade (1,800 rifles) was to advance against the enemy position, by the road north of LANGER HEINRICH, from the west. See map opposite.

General Botha accompanied Brits, and, moving behind his brigade, bivouacked for the night March 19-20 at WITPOORT.

Alberts received instructions in the following sense.

His right wing (Badenhorst) of 1,200 rifles, accompanied by himself to move against PFORTEBERG and south of it.

His left wing (Collins) to move north of the PFORTEBERG and, after dropping a commando to connect with Badenhorst, to divide, half the wing moving against JAKALSWATER and the remainder against SALEM, crossing the railway line north of JAKALSWATER.

The railway line referred to is the old KHAN railway line running from KARIBIB via HABIS, ABABIS KUBAS and JAKALSWATER past the KHAN to SWAKOPMUND.

A glance at the map will show clearly the intention of General Botha's plan of envelopment. It gave the enemy a

The Campaign in German South West Africa, 1914-1915

foretaste of their opponent's mobility which was to be turned to advantage later over a greatly extended area.

The Commander-in-Chief left his bivouac at HUSAB at dusk on March 19 in the wake of his commandos rapidly slipping past him with the silent level motion peculiar to them on trek and accentuated by the smoothness of the sandy track.

Dawn on March 20, which found General Botha well on his way to RIET, was marked by frequent gun fire at that place and from the direction of PFORTE.

Arrived opposite RIET, after halting further back for reports, he found Brits engaged with the enemy who was in an exceptionally strong position astride the main road to, and covering, the RIET water-hole.

The German right was on the river (SWAKOP) and its left rested on the foothills of LANGER HEINRICH, a high mountain also known as RIETBERG.

This position was roughly bisected by the main road which ran east and west. Six German guns were in battery just off, and to the north of, the road in a very rocky position where, though covered from view, they were subjected to heavy fire all day from the four guns of the Transvaal Horse Artillery, of which two came into action—virtually in the open, for low sand dunes alone broke the dead level of the desert—on the right and two on the left of Brits' centre.

On each side the artillery remained stationary all day.

The Union guns at a range of 2,800 yards held those of the enemy immobile, and inflicted severe damage upon them both as regards personnel and material, while the ranging of the Germans was most indifferent and their fire consistently ineffective.

The position confronting the 1st Brigade commanded an open field of fire down from the centre of Brits' position to the bed of a dry spruit whence the ground rose covered by heavy outcrops of rock to the site of the German guns.

The space opposite the enemy between the mountain, LANGER HEINRICH, and the broken ground bordering the SWAKOP River was totally bare and sandy and strewn with small pebbles, and, though quite devoid of cover from fire, afforded by its contours concealment here and there.

Brits' centre was on the slope of the rise nearest to the enemy position.

On his left, south of the road, the German commander had

The Campaign in German South West Africa, 1914-1915

posted dismounted riflemen, who covered with their fire the ground over which an attack from the side of LANGER HEINRICH would develop, and which, though occasional ridges of rock gave cover, presented many open patches.

The enemy right on the river was exceptionally strong. The river banks, especially on the side held by the enemy, were fringed with natural positions. Huge castellated rocks in profusion afforded impregnable cover, while machine-guns, in the use of which the German forces, here as in East Africa, were adept, skilfully posted, enfiladed the open approach across the river bed.

After deciding that his presence was necessary, General Botha quickly reached the centre of Brits' position where he met the Brigade Commander with a small knot of personal attendants but without his Brigade Major and with no troops.

The action had begun at about half past six in the morning and very early in the day practically the whole force was in action; the major portion on the left of the road. The four Transvaal Horse Artillery guns had taken up a position in the open a short distance to the right and in rear of the position occupied by the mounted men.

As no troops were held in reserve, the 100 rifles of the Commander-in-Chief's bodyguard were brought up to protect the guns.

Brits had sent a force of 300 rifles up to the heights of LANGER HEINRICH with the object of testing the left flank of the enemy, but when it became clear later in the day that Bezuidenhout's Commando had not reached its objective, the LANGER HEINRICH or right flank was reinforced by another commando 300 strong with the object of turning the enemy's left flank. Owing to the rugged nature of the mountain progress was slow, with the result that the force on the right flank took very little part in the day's fighting.

Three hundred rifles had, of course, been sent by General Botha's order on an encircling movement and thus Brits' available force was reduced to 1,200 rifles.

The action had begun when the enemy had fired upon Brits scouts when the latter approached the dry spruit already mentioned. Sustaining one or two casualties the scouts made for cover on their left and were reinforced by a commando.

The situation having become stationary, Brits sent his

The Campaign in German South West Africa, 1914-1915

Brigade-Major, Major Brink, to investigate it, again reinforcing the left of his attack by another commando.

Brink found the enemy in strong positions up to the bank of the SWAKOP River; he tried to initiate a movement across the river but owing to the precipitous cliffs on the river bank a crossing by mounted troops could not be effected, which made the turning of the enemy's position impossible, and the attack on this side remained stationary as before.

The movement from the river side would seem to have come about in consequence of the swerving of the scouts in the direction where good cover lay. It is not easy to understand otherwise why a serious effort should have been made from the river in view of the obvious advantage of position which lay with the enemy in that locality.

Brits was far too experienced a judge of a good position for an attack by his riflemen to have failed to recognise the much greater suitability of the foothills for such a purpose. Posted in the rocks on the left of the enemy position the men of the commandos would be placed where their method of fighting was best served and on equal terms so far as the ground went with their opponents.

There was no reason to suppose that Bezuidenhout would not reach the rear of the enemy in the course of the day and there was no point in delivering anything more than a holding attack until his movement should become effective.

In these circumstances a small force directed against the enemy right would have been ample.

Further, if a serious attack were contemplated with a view to dislodging the enemy it should have been delivered on the left of the latter to drive him towards, and not away from, Alberts.

It would seem then that so early to detach troops to his own left and leave himself without any reserve was an error of judgmen on the part of the Union brigade commander.

With a reserve, his attack by his right might have been reinforced far earlier than was possible and been of substantial aid in the general plan of envelopment.

Late in the afternoon enough troops had been reclaimed to strengthen the right attack, but by this time the enemy was in full retreat evidently apprised of the turn of events at PFORTE.

The most important factor, however, at RIET was the failure

The Campaign in German South West Africa, 1914-1915

of Bezuidenhout to find the opening in the mountain range by which he was to place himself on the enemy line of retreat.

Apparently it only existed in the imagination of the cartographer who had shown it on one of the very indifferent maps with which the forces had been provided. It was only with the greatest trouble that any attention whatever to the important matter of maps could be obtained at D.H.Q.

"The Riet Mountain was connected by very formidable hill features, which did not even present a bridle path, so that this detachment had to return." (O.H., p. 41.)

Unfortunately the Commandant *omitted to report his failure to find any path or his intention to return*. Early notice of this would quite likely have suggested the speeding up of efforts at RIET.

Having elected to retire Bezuidenhout did it thoroughly, and passing RIET, whence the guns must have been audible, went back to the starting point at HUSAB.

Meanwhile more success had been attained at PFORTE.

From the advanced base at HUSAB the 2nd Mounted Brigade's reconnaissance patrols obtained early contact and definite information as to the disposition of the enemy forces which was found to be located on the PFORTE RANGE.

It will be observed that the enemy had skilfully selected a defensive position of great strength. See map facing page 65.

The natural features of the PFORTE RANGE extending at right angles from the VALSCHER HEINRICH or HUSAB BERG astride the KHAN–JAKALSWATER railway line to the GESIB BERG afforded the Germans an important commanding position capable of strong defence.

The only line of approach in the attack was over flat open desert country devoid of any vegetation and without any possibility of concealment for man or beast. The high ground moreover provided the enemy with excellent facilities for observation as well as a clear and unrestricted field of fire.

Alberts, who was entrusted with the task of moving against the enemy forces at PFORTE, completed the concentration of his right wing, Badenhorst, at HUSAB on March 19 and to avoid observations during the advance made a night march, arriving on the 20th in an attacking position close to the PFORTE RANGE before dawn.

It was decided to launch an immediate and simultaneous attack at two points, viz.: the ERMELO and STANDERTON

The Campaign in German South West Africa, 1914-1915

" B " Commandos were instructed to attack the Ridge and secure a footing at the Railway Gap while SWART'S Scouts were detailed to seize the Nek at the foot of the HUSAB BERG.

The advance of the two Commandos was checked by heavy artillery fire, but meanwhile SWART'S Scouts surprised the enemy and after slight opposition secured the key position of the HUSAB NEK.

This important and early tactical success was instantly exploited by pushing forward two additional Commandos to consolidate the position and to assist the enveloping movement. During the advance the two Commandos were subjected to heavy machine-gun fire, but owing to the uncertain light and thick dust due to the charging horsemen, no casualties were sustained.

The encircling movement was carried out at great speed and continued up to and including the occupation of the railway line, thereby effectively cutting the enemy's communications and his line of retreat to JAKALSWATER.

The immediate effect of these developments was to compel the enemy to resort to fresh dispositions to meet the threat in his rear. The artillery which had earlier checked the attempt to secure the railway gap was now forced to withdraw from its forward position and to take up a fresh position on the eastern slopes of the range.

In the meantime the ERMELO and STANDERTON Commandos, taking advantage of the momentary cessation of artillery fire, resumed the advance and promptly seized a portion of the PFORTE RANGE in the vicinity of the Railway Gap.

The Reserve Commando and Artillery were meanwhile ordered to advance and occupy the first gap in the PFORTE RANGE and to assist in the attack.

The 4th Permanent Field Artillery had been brought into action and took up its position in the open just east of the Gap.

Within one hour after launching the attack the foremost troops were in action on the railway line eight miles away. The success attained at the start and the enterprise displayed in the subsequent manoeuvre were mainly due to the swiftness of the Commandos, which still characterised the spirit of the Boer forces as manifested in the South African Campaign of 1900-1902 and constituted a typical example of the rapidity of Commando movement.

However, in consequence of the heavy dust raised by the

The Campaign in German South West Africa, 1914-1915

rapidly moving troops and prevailing mirage, only a confused idea of the situation below could be formed by the two commandos which had occupied the heights.

Artillery was just below them, at some 300 yards distance and firing eastward, i.e. in the original direction of the enemy and away from the two Commandos, and in order to clear his mind the Commandant of the Standerton Commando, Piet Botha, descended its eastern slopes and was close to the guns before he recognised them as German and engaged with Badenhorst.

Finding himself suddenly amongst the enemy and unable, without grave personal risk, to beat a hasty retreat to his Commando, he at once demanded an interview with the German Commander whom he called upon to surrender. Upon being refused he quickly ascended the ridge and rejoined his troops, luckily avoiding temporary capture.

The resistance of the enemy was soon overcome, as the force had now been surrounded and subjected to heavy gun and rifle fire. At 8.30, and just two hours after the first shot had been fired, the action at PFORTE culminated in the surrender to Colonel Alberts of 9 officers, 200 other ranks and two guns.

A small party held out manfully at the Railway Gap till 3 o'clock in the afternoon but after being subjected to artillery fire they too gave in.

The spent condition of Alberts' horses and the absence of any water in this area enforced a halt upon him and he had to be content with the success he had achieved.

It will be remembered that the third movement in General Botha's plan of envelopment had been entrusted to Colonel-Commandant Collins with his own wing of the 2nd Mounted Brigade.

The mission of this force, which entailed a night march of 40 miles at least, was to block the enemy line of retreat, divert his general reserve and intercept any reinforcements which might appear from the direction of KARIBIB. Incidentally, one troop train of the latter was captured but had to be abandoned in the subsequent retirement.

Generally, the diversion caused by this advance was relied upon to keep the RIET and PFORTE positions unsupported by reinforcements.

At about 5 a.m., March 20, Collins had reached the PFORTE railway about $5\frac{1}{4}$ miles from PFORTE station towards KARIBIB.

The Campaign in German South West Africa, 1914-1915

This being too near PFORTE, a portion of the force was sent to cut and hold the railway east of JAKALSWATER while another detachment was directed on JAKALSWATER to seize and occupy that station.

At 6.30 a.m. Collins, who was without artillery, was attacked by the general reserve of the enemy, and, caught in three detachments, was compelled to retire with the loss of 43 men who were captured after their horses had been killed by gun fire.

The task involved a very long march at night in unknown country.

JAKALSWATER was actually occupied, but its evacuation was enforced by gun fire from MODDERFONTEIN.

Collins directed his retirement on HUSAB, and, in consequence of his omission to advise Alberts of the fact was very nearly dealt with by the latter as another enemy body.

The general reserve was content to cover the German retreat and took no steps to intervene at RIET or PFORTE and Collins' movement, though producing no material result, did undoubtedly serve the valuable purpose of keeping the general reserve at MODDERFONTEIN occupied.

The general characteristics of the commando soldier and their causes have been dealt with in an early chapter, but, before offering any comment on the operations which have just been described, it may be advisable to examine more closely the effect which their special features had upon the tactical action of the commandos.

The burger in the ranks of the commandos of 1899-1902 and 1914-15 was a good shot, a fine horseman accustomed to ride for long distances, a man of frugal habit of life, and a bold and self-reliant scout who ranged with confidence far ahead of his main body. This latter fact enabled the commandos behind their scouts to move over long distances with great rapidity, implicitly relying on their scouts to clear up the country miles ahead.

Every mounted brigade in German South West Africa had its " scouts ", from 25 to 50 strong, under a selected commander whose name they usually bore, thus " de la Rey's Scouts ", " Lemmer's Scouts ", " Swarts' Scouts ", and so on.

Special scouts were a feature too of the Republican Armies in 1899-1902. They contained some of the more adventurous spirits and, especially in the case of Theron's Scouts, led by Danie Theron, performed numberless feats of audacity. Danie

The Campaign in German South West Africa, 1914-1915

Theron was eventually killed on the Gatsrand in September, 1900.

The Scouts therefore were a feature of the commando organisation.

The burgher in the commando possessing confidence that, if he did not commit himself too deeply, he could always extricate himself from a tactical situation which threatened to become difficult or unpleasant, readily adopted an initial aggressive role in action.

The same individualism which made the burgher self-reliant tended to render him indifferent to orders which did not square with his own idea of the best method of fighting, and, in consequence, it was rarely that an attack was pushed beyond its first tangibly successful phase, while counter attack to retrieve a situation was seldom resorted to.

The tactical action of the commando was instinctive and based on views and habits common to all members of it, and, thus, while each individual acted on his own judgment, the fact that all the members of the unit were imbued with the same ideas resulted in uniform, though spontaneous, action to meet any sudden change in a tactical situation.

The immediate turning away of the Ermelo and Standerton Commandos when coming under artillery fire at PFORTE and their subsequent occupation of a good fire position is a case in point.

This individualism also had its effect on the commandants, who consequently went far afield and were apt to forget that they were part of a whole, and not virtually independent as they had so often been in the Anglo-Boer War.

It was often with the greatest difficulty that information could be gathered during movements by the central command.

This failure to recognise the need for co-operation and interchange of information is well illustrated by the action of the Bloemhof Commando which, having failed early in the mission assigned to it, returned to the base at HUSAB without any notification of its non-success or subsequent action to its Brigadier whose guns were in action and must have been plainly audible. Even Collins, a leader much above the average in many respects, omitted to keep Alberts posted as to his movements, though difficulty of communication may have had something to do with this.

In the closing stages of the Anglo-Boer War, and it was then

The Campaign in German South West Africa, 1914-1915

that most of the commandants who were in responsible positions in German South West Africa came to the fore, *no extensive tactical combinations ever occurred.*

Success was obtained by local leaders at the head of small bands of devoted followers who were the finest soldiers (the " Bitter-enders ") of the Republican armies, tested in many fights and bound by a camaraderie and mutual trust born in the common dangers and exploits all had shared.

That in such circumstances the close control and staff work that is necessary in the handling of larger units and the conduct of far more comprehensive operations should have been often absent is not surprising, and these circumstances must be kept in mind in offering criticism. The criticism is made with the object of recording mistakes which may be avoided in future and in no sense as implying blame.

In a body such as the commando the personality of the leader counts for much.

In the Rebellion, where a determined and influential leader was opposed to the Government forces, his commando was one to be reckoned with.

In German South West Africa General Botha, and in German East Africa General Smuts, were either with, or immediately behind, and in the closest touch with, the fighting troops throughout their advances. The presence of their Commander was looked for by the commandos whose soldiers would have entirely misconstrued the action of a commander who conducted their operations remote from them.

Brits sent his Brigade-Major (the title of whose office conveyed nothing whatever to him) to his left flank because of the staff officer's personality and because of his own confidence in the judgment and capacity of the individual.

At RIET and PFORTE alike it was the intial action of the scouts which settled the form and trend of the attack and it must be allowed that in this respect Brits had the worst luck, for the turn of his scouts was inevitably to the nearest cover, i.e. the SWAKOP River, where they found themselves up against a virtually impregnable position.

Brits decided to reinforce them with a commando, wisely enough, but this was all that seemed necessary, for the position on his side of the river was also extremely strong. It could have been held against any force the enemy was likely to employ against it, and holding the enemy was all that was needed here.

The Campaign in German South West Africa, 1914-1915

The German commander's decisive flank was his left which threatened his guns and his line of retreat and was vulnerable and without any of the abnormal defensive features of the river. It was highly improbable that he would take any risk on his left to attack by his right.

By sending a second commando to the river on his left, Brits left himself in the early morning without any reserve whatever. His dispositions on his right had further depleted his resources.

Had he waited long enough to judge more deliberately of the situation and developed a strong attack early in the day—for which he had, to begin with, ample strength—it is difficult to see how the German commander could possibly have saved his guns and it is probable that any withdrawal on his part would have been attended with heavy loss.

The loss of the services of his Chief of Staff—though in point of fact the latter no doubt did good work forward—tended to weaken Brits' power of control.

In consequence of the early dissipation of the Union forces no enterprise could be undertaken against the weaker enemy left until an hour in the afternoon when the German Commander had secured his retirement.

The action emphasises the truth of Napoleon's dictum that " Victory is to him who has the last reserves ", and the need for a gradual introduction of troops into the fight until the situation to be dealt with shall become clear enough to enable the commander to employ those which he has kept under his hand decisively.

The action at RIET became a stalemate early in the morning and remained so until late afternoon when the enemy withdrew.

The fight at PFORTE was as rapid as that at RIET was drawn out, and here again the action of the scouts had most to do with the course of the operations.

The terrain although of a formidable nature lent itself here, once a footing had been seized on the PFORTE RANGE, to rapid and enveloping movements in keeping with commando tactics.

The rapid advance of the scouts to a fire position between PFORTE BERG and HUSAB BERG and their initiative in pushing on when through the gap, together with the quick recognition of the opportunity afforded to the main body of the 2nd Brigade by the weakening of the southern PFORTE BERG gap to reinforce the opening through which the scouts had

The Campaign in German South West Africa, 1914-1915

passed, are reminiscent of many characteristic and effective rapid movements of the Anglo-Boer War and are typical of the Republican tactics at that time. The fact that everything went right does not detract from the value of the leadership and support accorded to it which went to the success.

Commandant Piet Botha's estimate of the importance of the height commanding the PFORTE railway gap too is in keeping with the tactical sense and judgment of ground which was so general throughout the commandos.

The actual fight at PFORTE was over so quickly that staff arrangements came little into calculation and its favourable result must be ascribed to a highly intelligent use by all concerned of what used to be called "Boer tactics" in a situation specially adapted for their employment.

The casualties of the forces were as under:—

Union Forces:
  Killed: 2 officers, 11 other ranks.
  Wounded: 5 officers, 36 other ranks.
  Prisoners: 43 other ranks.

German Forces:
  Left on the field killed: 4 officers, 12 other ranks.
  Wounded: 1 officer, 20 other ranks.
  Prisoners: 9 officers, 275 other ranks.
    with 2 guns.

CHAPTER VII

THE RIET-PFORTE operations had taken place in the most trying heat and the scantiness of water had caused general exhaustion of men and animals.

On the day following the fight, Major Brink, the Brigade Major of the 1st Mounted Brigade, with some of the least tired men and horses of the commandos, was sent to reconnoitre in the direction of MODDERFONTEIN.

Arrived at this place he found a standing camp abandoned by the enemy with a considerable quantity of supplies. He sent for wagons, and this welcome temporary aid to the resources of the Union commissariat was made good use of.

The position at MODDERFONTEIN, combined with the discovery of documents which no General Staff would have left behind except under dire necessity, and, if compelled to do so, would have burnt, established for once and all the presence of the bulk of the enemy forces opposite General Botha and confirmed beyond any doubt that detachments, for the purpose of observation only, were in the south.

The information was at once conveyed to D.H.Q. with a repetition of the request for much increased transport.

Brink also intercepted a train coming from the direction of KARIBIB. It was a hospital train and, after reference to General Botha, was allowed to return to the enemy lines.

It was clear that the enemy retirement had been precipitate and one effect of the action of March 20 was that the Germans never stood again until the last and greatest enveloping movements of their adversary compelled them to do so and surrender. Hereafter the German Commander yielded long tracts of the most difficult country without any attempt to defend them.

On the night of March 20-21 the Union troops occupied the positions vacated by the enemy which were however without water which, since leaving HUSAB, had been obtained by digging in the river bed.

The detection of a wire at one of the holes saved a commando from heavy casualties for the place had been mined.

All spots where troops were likely to congregate or to pass in the advance, were heavily mined and the sites of the mines were chosen with much skill, but, as a rule, the luck experienced by the commando on this occasion held.

The troops, too, soon developed an acute sense of the kind of places to avoid.

The German officer who was responsible for laying all the mines, and, after the surrender, went all over the country with the engineers removing them, expressed a becoming relief that so little result had followed his widespread efforts to do damage!

RIET water-hole was occupied early on the morning of March 21 where a well in the river-bed furnished an ample supply of good water for any force likely to need it.

The 2nd Mounted Brigade was sent back to IDA MINE for water, there being none at PFORTE.

General Headquarters and the 1st Mounted Brigade remained at RIET and patrols secured JAKALSWATER, and SALEM and DORSTRIVIERMUND were found to be clear.

A vigorous pursuit might have had far-reaching results, but circumstances were to prevent this.

General Botha remained at RIET until March 24 and made arrangements for some forward reconnaissances up the SWAKOP. By the 24th, however, his supplies had entirely disappeared, as had the hope that it might be possible to bring enough from SWAKOPMUND to maintain a forward movement. The condition of the best horses would only allow of one more day's work.

While the water supply at RIET was equal to any demand likely to be put upon it, the veld which had been hoped for was practically non-existent. The most slender evidence of the border of the grass country alone was apparent.

General Botha was therefore forced to order his mounted troops back to SWAKOPMUND where they could be fed from the ships.

This step was all the more distasteful because the troops had responded to all the calls made upon them, and, after a tangible success, were anxious to press on and bring the campaign to a speedy conclusion.

To the burgher and the infantryman alike, desirous of returning to their homes and, in many cases, undertaking further service elsewhere, another long wait was a dreary and depressing prospect.

There was, however, no alternative and, by March 26, the Commander-in-Chief was back at the coast, and the slow process

The Campaign in German South West Africa, 1914-1915

of building up a stock of supplies at RIET, this time 60, instead of 30, miles away was resumed.

A garrison of 600 infantry under Colonel Wylie was placed at RIET, with a commando for reconnaissance work, and the remainder of the field force retraced their steps.

Nearly five weeks were to elapse before another move could be made against the enemy.

Before leaving RIET on his return to SWAKOPMUND General Botha had arranged for a reconnaissance of the narrow-gauge railway from ROSSING to JAKALSWATER to decide if it were possible to repair and make use of it.

Expert advice was against the step as extremely difficult and undesirable, but the enemy had extended the railway from JAKALSWATER to RIET and it was realised that without some means of supplementing the meagre transport there was small chance of making any headway. The Commander-in-Chief decided the point by personal observation.

The project seemed to him to be feasible and it was put in train at once and almost completed by April 24.

From the documents at RIET the sites of the mines round the KHAN were ascertained and the mines rendered inoperative.

Other information from the same source indicated an intention of the enemy to infect water with bacteriological matter. In point of fact, though remonstrances were addressed to the German Commander about the poisoning of water supplies, no harm occurred to the advancing troops.

On March 27 General Botha left for LUDERITZBUCHT by sea and met McKenzie on March 29.

It was plain, in view of the position of the Northern Force in relation to WINDHOEK, that the enemy would have to concentrate quickly and that the former could be employed against the capital or the USAKOS–KARIBIB–OKAHANDJA railway with equal facility.

The Central Force was therefore ordered to move at once against AUS from GARUB, where McKenzie reported his forces assembled and ready to advance. Beyond suggesting the employment of mounted troops on *both* flanks of the enemy position, the plan was left to McKenzie to devise.

The AUS wireless had been silent for two nights and it was desirable to verify the presence of the enemy or his abandonment of the position.

After his return to his own Headquarters the Commander-

The Campaign in German South West Africa, 1914-1915

in-Chief was informed on March 31 that AUS had been evacuated.

The probability of this event had been communicated to D.H.Q., as had the information that from native and prisoners' statements, corroborated by intelligence derived from captured documents, strong enemy parties had left the south for the north.

Intimation was now received that the Southern (Van Deventer), Eastern (Berrangé) and Central (McKenzie) Forces were to be combined in two divisions as the " Southern Army " under the command of General Smuts.

The Southern and Eastern Forces under Van Deventer were one (the 2nd) and McKenzie's Force the other division (the 1st).

It is now time to record events in the south.

It will be remembered that Van Deventer with several columns was to advance on KEETMANSHOOP from RAMAN'S DRIFT via WARMBAD while Berrangé moved on the same objective from KURUMAN across the KALAHARI.

The Southern Force was faced by Major Ritter with a battery of artillery and four mounted companies based on KEETMANSHOOP; there were also early in 1915 in its vicinity some 800 rebels under Maritz, to whom had been sent by the Germans one mounted company, four field guns, and a pom-pom.

This force attacked Van Deventer on January 24 at UPINGTON but were heavily defeated and melted away, the German portion and a few of the hardier rebels retiring on Ritter's force. This was the last appearance of any rebel contingent, and from the end of January the German troops only were opposed to Van Deventer.

On February 4 Ritter attacked a Union force at KAKAMAS with 400 rifles and four guns but was repulsed about 11 a.m., leaving behind 12 killed and 12 prisoners.

On March 8 Major Smith, of the Southern Force, attacked NABAS, 10 miles north of UKAMAS, in the course of the advance on KEETMANSHOOP. Surprising the enemy he compelled his retirement with a loss of 1 killed and 3 wounded, together with all his transport and supplies which fell into the hands of the Union Commander.

Later in the advance on March 27 Colonel Dirk van Deventer —brother of the Force Commander—attacked some 200 rifles of the enemy at PLATBEEN and compelled his retirement with a loss of 14 prisoners and 6 wounded and, again, all transport and supplies.

The Campaign in German South West Africa, 1914-1915

On April 20 Dirk van Deventer again attacked 300 rifles of the enemy with two guns at KABUS with about 1,400 rifles of his brigade. Here he established contact with the Eastern Force (Berrangé), 300 rifles of the latter co-operating with him. The German force retired with the loss of 2 killed and 16 wounded.

Colonel Bouwer advanced with his brigade from RAMAN'S DRIFT, and, moving by way of WARMBAD and KALKFONTEIN received the surrender of KEETMANSHOOP.

The Eastern Force in its westward march had several similar encounters.

On March 19 Captain van Vuuren with 100 rifles attacked 200 enemy rifles at RIETFONTEIN. The enemy retired, once more with the loss of his transport and supplies, and left 4 killed, 20 wounded and 2 prisoners on the field. Van Vuuren lost 1 killed and 2 wounded. This was a highly creditable performance by the Union troops, but the retirement of twice their number from an important water-hole leaving their supplies ana transport behind is eloquent of the desire of the enemy at all costs to get away and offer slight resistance.

On April 20 Berrangé's men joined with Dirk van Deventer attacked the enemy at KOES, capturing several hundred head of cattle.

On the 16th of the same month Berrangé attacked 300 of the enemy with two guns at KIRIES WEST forcing his retirement with the loss of 4 killed, 1 wounded and 8 prisoners.

On April 20 Berrangés men joined with Dirk van Deventer at KABUS as has been seen.

This last date, April 20, brings us some weeks ahead of the record of General Botha's operations, but KABUS was the last engagement in the south except McKenzie's affair at GIBEON, which will be described later, and the disbandment of the Southern Army was ordered on May 5.

Though the fights had been on a small scale, the marching of the Southern Force and the endurance of its soldiers were no less remarkable than the performance of the Union troops in other parts of the scene of operations.

If the numbers of the enemy detachments given as facing the Southern and Eastern forces from time to time are compared with those of Von Kleist's force in his retirement, it will be realised that the latter represented the concentration of all the German forces in the south.

The Campaign in German South West Africa, 1914-1915

Von Kleist's strength at GIBEON when attacked by McKenzie was 700 rifles and 2 field guns.

The guns are obviously those at KIRIES WEST and KABUS and the rifles the aggregate of all the detachments of which the strongest which came into action against Berrangé or van Deventer was 300.

Extrication of their troops was all that concerned men who left all their transport and supplies behind even in the hands of a force half their strength.

To deal with these 700 rifles and two guns the Union Defence Headquarters deployed 14,312 mounted men (see O.H. p. 60).

The lines of advance of the Southern and Eastern Forces are shown in the map facing page 56.

RIET was now reinforced. It was within easy striking distance of greatly superior forces, and it seemed reasonable to assume that the enemy would make some attempt to adjust the balance after his defeat, and the post at RIET appeared to offer him the best chance of doing so. Its value to the Union Commander too was obvious.

In the event, the curious lack of enterprise and want of grip which characterised the enemy command were again apparent and RIET was left unmolested.

The garrison of the Rand Rifles was strengthened by the addition of the 1st Durban Light Infantry while the river posts were taken over by the South African Irish. Wylie's (4th) Infantry Brigade was thus distributed from RIET to GOANI-KONTES.

Wylie's mounted men at RIET (200) were furnished from the 2nd Mounted Brigade and 400 of the 1st Mounted Brigade were placed at HUSAB.

On April 1 the work on the KHAN railway was begun and the advanced troops were placed on the line ARANDIS–KHAN–JAKALSWATER–RIET where they protected the SWAKOP River line and would screen the early stages of the next forward movement.

On the same day Cornelius van Wyk, chief of the REHOBOTH bastards, reached the Union lines at WALVIS BAY and came to interview General Botha at SWAKOPMUND.

Van Wyk, who came unaccompanied, was an intelligent old man of Bastard race who, since the outbreak of war, had remained in his own territory at REHOBOTH, south-west of WINDHOEK.

The Campaign in German South West Africa, 1914-1915

The interview was mainly important for the emphatic instructions which General Botha gave to the old chief strictly to refrain from participating in hostilities. It was made plain that while the Union Government would see that no harm was done to the natives it would insist that the latter should abstain from any unfriendly action to the Germans with whom it was well able to deal.

As General Botha put it: " My quarrel is with the Germans. Your people must be outside the fighting line. I want you to act wisely. Do not involve yourselves in this war."

It was gathered from the Chief that the OTJIMBINGWE country between RIET and WINDHOEK was " good, plenty of grass and good water ".

At this time the enemy was found to be patrolling ONANIS, south-west of RIET and DIEPDAL, and two companies of infantry with a small mounted detachment were placed at SALEM where there was an excellent water supply. Its denial to the enemy and conservation for the advance outweighed the further undesirable strain on the supply situation.

About this time Skinner at ARANDIS was visited by an aeroplane but on no occasion did its efforts from the air produce result. It soon ceased to function, and, from later information, the intrepid German who risked his life on this ricketty engine of war was very fortunate in getting off with a prolonged stay in hospital as his personal experience of its final crash.

General Botha now considered the plan of his next forward movement.

On April 11 McKenzie was instructed to reconnoitre towards BETHANIEN and endeavour to get into touch with the natives whom he was to reassure and advise of the intention of the Union authorities to leave them undisturbed.

By this time intelligence—in consequence of patrol action and contact with natives—was far more definite, and it was possible to gauge the situation with some degree of certainty.

The enemy forces concentrated, or concentrating, in the north were known to be disposed mainly in the area contained between KARIBIB–USAKOS–KUBAS–GOAS and in occupation of WINDHOEK.

Though information was fairly regular as regards the forces in the area defined above, nothing could be learnt about, nor had any native come through from, the country between WINDHOEK–OKAHANDJA–OTJIMBINGWE–GREAT BARMEN.

The enemy had received a physical, and even more effectual moral, set-back at RIET and PFORTE. This was borne out by his reluctance to take any chance at RIET where he could engage the garrison on terms advantageous to himself.

The most important consequence of the action of March 21 had been his abandonment of the south and consequent northward movement.

It was therefore assumed that there were few enemy forces south of WINDHOEK and that even these would accelerate their movement from the south at the first sign of renewed activity by the Northern Force.

General Botha decided upon the defeat of the enemy in front of him and the simultaneous isolation of WINDHOEK as the main objects of his next operations.

He planned to attack the German forces where they were known to be concentrated with as strong a force as possible, and at the same time to destroy the telegraph and railway lines at a suitable spot between KARIBIB and OKAHANDJA. WILHELMSTAL was decided upon as the point of this destruction, as it was near enough to enable the force concerned to maintain touch with G.H.Q. and far enough from KARIBIB and JOHANN-ALBRECHT'S HOHE to make the surprise of the enemy possible.

Reference to the map facing page 104 will show that unless a force could be sent by way of USAKOS to north of the WINDHOEK-USAKOS railway line, the interception of the enemy was most improbable as a result of the operations.

This course was out of the question.

As will be seen, the transport position and its influence upon the supply question made the provision of wagons for a force strong enough to hold the retiring enemy impossible. If he could not be held and his further movement north arrested, there was nothing to be gained by sending any force to USAKOS.

The obviously sound plan of getting round the enemy flank by USAKOS was therefore ruled out perforce, and it was hoped that the great mobility of the mounted troops might to some extent compensate for the omission.

Once more lack of transport prevented the possibility of the settlement of the campaign at this stage.

The newly-formed Southern Army was committed to its advance and no release of transport from the south could be expected.

Though the interception of the entire enemy force seemed impracticable, and it appeared that its escape to north of the KARIBIB–OKAHANDJA line would be effected, the occupation of WINDHOEK and seizure of the railway line from the capital to KARIBIB would have far-reaching effect.

This success would also, incidentally, attain the objectives of the expedition indicated by the British Government as " a great and urgent Imperial Service ", viz.: " to seize such part of German South West Africa as will give them (Ministers) the command of SWAKOPMUND and LUDERITZBUCHT and the wireless stations there or in the interior ".

Preparations were therefore pushed on.

All units were once more stripped of their transport and the filling up of RIET with supplies was begun.

On April 16 advice was received from D.H.Q. that the Central Force had been handed over to General Smuts and removed from the control of General Botha.

As any Union forces in the south had been disregarded as probable factors, this decision was not regarded as of much local importance.

On April 18 it was ascertained that the rate of progress which had been hoped for in the restoration of the KHAN–JAKALSWATER railway could not be maintained, and it became necessary to take stock of the position with a view to dependence upon animal transport if the advance was to be set in motion on the date which had been fixed.

The maximum rate of railway construction was 1,200 yards a day. Nothing could be done to alter this, for it was governed by the weight (400 yards of railway material) which the light engines could hold back going down the gorge to KHAN and the number of trains (3) which could be run daily.

Four-and-a-half days' rations had been collected at RIET on this date for the force which was to undertake the advance.

By using all the transport of the force, *without intermission,* this reserve could just be maintained but could not be increased.

The situation which had faced the Commander-in-Chief at HUSAB a month earlier once more confronted him at RIET.

Some additional transport had come from the Union, but the force to be fed was nearly three times as large as that which took part in the RIET–PFORTE operations.

One hundred and thirteen wagons were at this time employed on the work of conveying supplies to the forward base.

The Campaign in German South West Africa, 1914-1915

The return of the transport to the units would, if reliance could be placed on the timely arrival of considerable transport from the Union, leave 85 mule wagons and 30 donkey wagons —the latter in the end had to be put to work straight off the ship—to feed the force of approximately 13,000 troops and 15,000 animals which was to move inland.

With 400 wagons it might have been possible to maintain two or three days' supply with the troops.

Another urgent request message was addressed to the Union putting the situation clearly and urging that in order to deal with the enemy in front of the Northern Force decisively every wagon and mule which could be scraped together should be sent up.

General Botha was the Prime Minister of the Union as well as its Commander-in-Chief and he now pointed out to his colleagues in the Cabinet the need for every effort to terminate the campaign and save as much expenditure as possible.

Parliament had not been unanimously enthusiastic about the expedition, and severe criticism of any mistakes or excessive expenditure in regard to its conduct might be looked for as inevitable.

It was also asked that a reduction of the forces in the south might be considered as it was felt that a sustained effort in the north might quite likely end the campaign.

D.H.Q. now stated that 300 wagons could be sent if some Heavy Artillery Units were held up.

At this time the Northern Force had been compelled to eat the transport oxen of such Heavy Artillery as it had, rendering it immobile, and needed no Heavy Artillery.

It is difficult to understand why, in view of the repeated reports as to shortage of transport and consequent difficulty in keeping the troops fed, the forwarding of personnel which meant further strain on the precarious supply situation should have been contemplated and the urgent need for the 300 wagons failed to be grasped at D.H.Q.

The wagons were at once asked for, and the move of the 6th S.A.M.R. to the Northern Force cancelled for the time.

General Botha decided again to advance on April 26 though the supply position was little more satisfactory than it had been on the occasion of his movement to RIET.

It was anticipated that the light railway would be working to JAKALSWATER, and the appearance of 300 wagons " from

The Campaign in German South West Africa, 1914-1915

the blue " led to a more sanguine view as to the probability of keeping on the move.

Patrol engagements were becoming more frequent and Wylie's patrols reached SPHINX and TSAOBIS and constant reconnaissance, especially towards OTJIMBINGWE, was carried out on the routes of the coming advance.

No. 1 Division of the Royal Naval Armoured cars reached SWAKOPMUND and became available for the operations.

CHAPTER VIII

IN ORDER TO preserve the continuity of the record of General Botha's ensuing operations, it will be well first to deal with the final operations of the Union forces in the south.

Those of van Deventer and Berrangé have been described up to the point where their contact with the enemy ceased, and, with their subsequent occupation of KEETMANSHOOP, this portion of the Southern Army took no further part in the campaign.

It will be remembered that on April 11, shortly before General McKenzie's force was removed from General Botha's control, the Commander-in-Chief ordered the Commander of the Central Force " to reconnoitre towards BETHANIEN ".

In compliance with this instruction, McKenzie moved from AUS with the following force:—

* 7th Mounted Brigade.
* 8th Mounted Brigade.
* 9th Mounted Brigade.
  12th (Citizen) Battery Field Artillery.

Approximately 1,500 rifles with 6 guns.

Moving rapidly, McKenzie reached BEERSEBA at dawn on April 22 with his 8th and 9th Brigades and two guns capturing 20 prisoners with cattle, sheep and goats and some wagons.

The natives here, as elsewhere throughout McKenzie's march, hailed the Union troops " with great joy " and at once provided McKenzie " with men to gain information of movements of the enemy in the vicinity ".

Learning that " an enemy battery " was moving from the south and that it would probably pass through BEERSEBA, McKenzie halted for the 22nd to allow his 7th Brigade and the rest of his guns (4) to come up.

Aroused on the following morning before daylight by shots from the outposts the Natal force found that a body of the enemy was passing along the north-east side of BEERSEBA in the direction of KOKERBOOMNAUTE.

---

* From Natal; each brigade of two regiments.

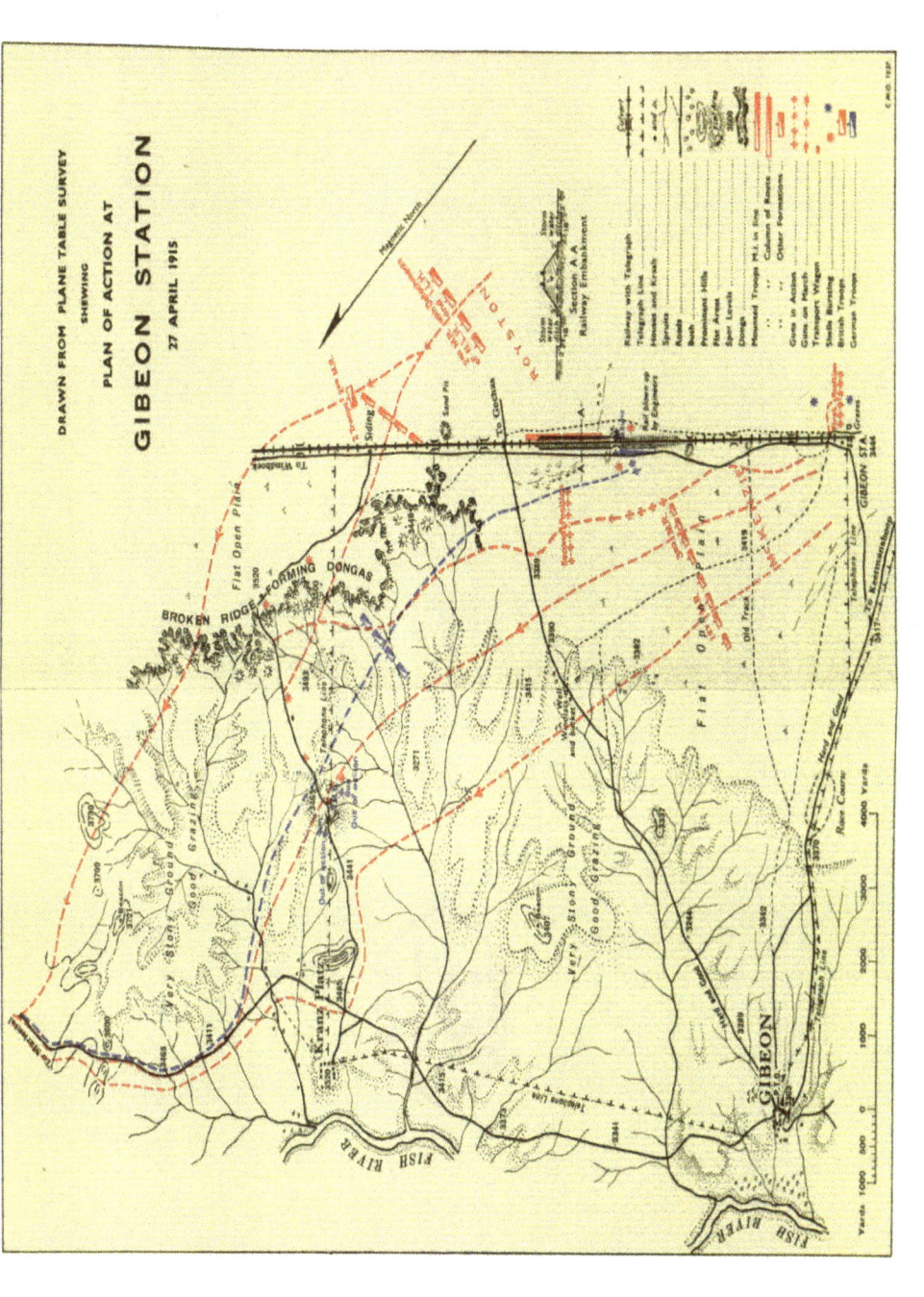

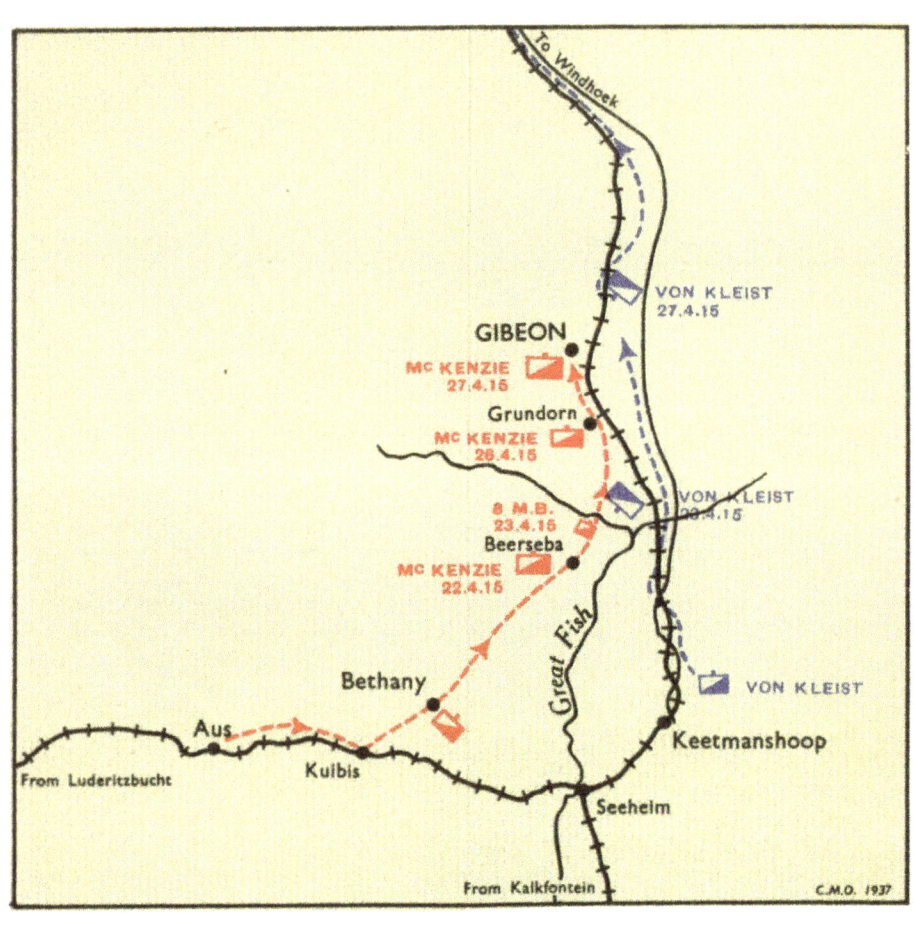

SKETCH MAP ILLUSTRATING
McKENZIE'S MARCH TO GIBEON

The Campaign in German South West Africa, 1914-1915

The 8th Mounted Brigade with a squadron of the Natal Light Horse at once followed the enemy for 13 miles to the FISH River.

The ground was rough, stony, and difficult, and an extended advance was much impeded, and the enemy, moving along the road, fought rear guard actions at all suitable spots.

The Union troops, losing one man severely wounded and another captured and killing one and wounding three of the enemy and taking some prisoners, were compelled to abandon the chase.

The detachment now halted to await the arrival of the main body which moved at 9.30 p.m. on April 23.

Capturing some German signallers who were endeavouring to catch up their own troops ahead, the force reached KOKERBOOMNAUTE where information of the enemy still retiring along the railway was obtained.

On the evening of April 24 McKenzie with his whole force again started in pursuit.

Reaching GRUNDORNS on April 26, he tapped the telegraph line and learned that the enemy force then at GIBEON were under orders to resume the retirement that night.

McKenzie's advanced troops also informed him that late in the afternoon a train could be seen at GIBEON station, while the dust of three columns moving rapidly north towards the station was also visible.

When this information reached McKenzie he was with his force midway between GRUNDORNS and GIBEON stations and he at once moved on.

On the march at 8 p.m. a demolition party with some scouts was dispatched to destroy the railway line north of GIBEON station and prevent the escape of the train, and at 8.45 p.m. the 9th Mounted Brigade together with a regiment from the 8th, the whole under Lieut.-Colonel Royston, was sent forward with instructions to move widely round and to the east of the enemy camp at GIBEON station.

Royston was to place himself astride the German line of retreat and to co-operate with his Force Commander in an attack which the latter would deliver at dawn from the south. Royston was also advised of the dispatch of the demolition party.

At 10 p.m. McKenzie with the remainder of his force arrived at a point about two miles south of GIBEON, where he halted until 5 a.m., April 27.

The Campaign in German South West Africa, 1914-1915

At 11 p.m. the demolition party blew up sixteen rails two miles north of GIBEON station and, eluding several enemy patrols sent out to intercept them, rejoined the main body.

Royston reached a point on the railway, 2½ miles north of the station, at 1 a.m. on the 27th. The ground here was flat and bare of any kind of cover. The railway ran on an embankment and there was no cover from enfilade fire in the trench alongside.

It was bright moonlight, but Royston's men failed to notice a culvert on the line and some 80 yards south of the position which they took up. This culvert, combined with a water-course embankment on either side of the line, afforded good cover for the machine-guns and riflemen of the enemy who later turned this advantage to good account.

Royston aligned three squadrons of the Natal Light Horse on the railway embankment facing west with a fourth squadron in reserve a short distance in rear of the line.

Two squadrons of the Imperial Light Horse were extended in support of the N.L.H. and on the right of the latter.

The Umvoti Mounted Rifles were dismounted to the left rear of the I.L.H.

At 2 a.m., while the above dispositions were in process of arrangement, enemy scouts appeared along the line from the left of Royston's position and detecting the presence of the Union troops, whose fire they drew, retired on their own force.

The fire of Royston's men at once drew that of the enemy machine-guns and riflemen posted at the culvert and on the water-course embankment already mentioned as having escaped notice. From this quarter the Union troops were heavily and accurately enfiladed.

The I.L.H. were then extended facing south in the direction from which the enemy fire was coming.

By 3 a.m. Lieut-Colonel Davies, commanding the I.L.H., in view of the large number of casualties which were being sustained, ordered the N.L.H. and I.L.H.—Royston was away from the scene having gone to order up the Umvoti Mounted Rifles—to go back to their horses, and later Royston on his return ordered a general retirement. In consequence of a gap in the line this last order did not reach 72 men, who were left behind on the railway bank and compelled to surrender at daylight when they found themselves surrounded.

The Campaign in German South West Africa, 1914-1915

Royston also lost 3 officers and 21 other ranks killed and 49 wounded.

He withdrew for 3 miles and awaited daylight, when he moved back towards the railway to co-operate with McKenzie in agreement with his instructions.

The latter, finding Royston some distance away, left his bivouac at 5 a.m. and attacked the enemy in front of him.

Moving towards GIBEON station he sighted the enemy immediately west of the railway and 2½ miles north of the station and the latter opened with his guns on the advancing Union forces.

The 1st M.R. moved on the west, the 3rd M.R. in the centre, while the 2nd M.R. were directed to move against the enemy left to the east of the railway and road. They were joined by a squadron from each of the N.L.H. and I.L.H., the only co-operation Royston was able to afford.

The German guns were quickly answered by those of the 12th Battery which soon picked up the range, and the fire of these guns, together with the rapid advance of the mounted men round the flanks of the enemy, caused the latter to retire and take up a position on high ground just south of the KRANZ-PLAATZ road.

The quick advance of the mounted men and the accurate shooting of McKenzie's guns compelled the German Commander again to retire after a short but stubborn defence under cover of a strong rear guard.

In this retirement the enemy was forced to abandon his two field-guns together with two machine-guns.

His retreat by the KRANTZPLAATZ road being barred by the 1st M.R., von Kleist (the German Commander) withdrew in a northerly direction across country to the GIBEON–MARIEN-THAL road.

A running fight, in the course of which the men taken from Royston earlier were recovered, now ensued to a point at which McKenzie found further pursuit impossible and he collected his force at GIBEON village.

The total losses of McKenzie's force were 3 officers and 21 other ranks killed and 10 officers and 56 other ranks wounded.

The enemy left 11 killed, 30 wounded and 188 prisoners on the field, and McKenzie also took a train, two field-guns, four machine-guns, a quantity of ammunition and wagons and stock.

The Campaign in German South West Africa, 1914-1915

Major von Kleist had with him some 800 men in all, distributed between five companies, some detachments, the garrisons of KEETMANSHOOP and GIBEON, with two field-guns and six machine-guns.

He now made a wide detour to the east of WINDHOEK and made good his escape to the north.

An idea of the march of the Natal men (the 2nd Imperial Light Horse under Lieut.-Colonel Davies were the only unit which did not come from Natal) may be obtained from the map facing page 89.

They had covered 200 miles in the 12 days, which terminated with the successful action, through rough and badly watered country devoid of supplies in anything like the quantity required for their subsistence.

Night operations are notoriously difficult and especially so when there has been no opportunity for previous reconnaissance as in this instance. Taking up a position at night in such circumstances involved very considerable risk, and the omission to notice such a danger spot as the culvert already mentioned can hardly be regarded as more than bad luck. Had it been possible, no doubt a review of the situation, which should always be made at daylight, would have shown the mistake.

The enemy who held the ground was quick enough to realise the possibilities of the situation and took full advantage of them.

The temporary effect of the reverse sustained by Royston was nullified by McKenzie's prompt action and efficient handling of his mounted men, and the operations so well planned by him and so resolutely carried out by his troops suffer in no way by comparison with the finest marches in this campaign of rapid movement.

The Natal troops finished their long and trying task in the desert by a highly creditable success which must have gone far to compensate them for their dreary sojourn at LUDERITZ-BUCHT and TSCHAUKAIB.

They had, however, shot their bolt, and von Kleist moved on to the north.

He was rapidly on his way there in any case, and, fine though McKenzie's work was, it exercised no effect whatsoever on the course of the campaign, for von Kleist would have pursued precisely the same course if there had been no Union troops nearer to him than their own border.

The Campaign in German South West Africa, 1914-1915

It was pressure in the north that brought him back there.

McKenzie's mounted men took no further part in the campaign but, moving slowly north by very easy stages, were returned to the Union from WINDHOEK.

While these events were happening in the south, the monotony of the watch of the infantry on the railway in the northern desert was broken.

Railhead on the broad gauge reconstruction had reached TREKKOPPIES, roughly midway between SWAKOPMUND and USAKOS.

Skinner, who was in command, was a keen soldier of considerable nervous energy and was well versed in his profession. He left the Union service at the end of the German South West African campaign, and went back to his own, and commanded a brigade, and afterwards a division, on the western front in Europe with distinction.

At 3.30 a.m. on April 26 a telephone message was received at G.H.Q. SWAKOPMUND from Colonel Rodger, in command at TREKKOPPIES in the absence of Skinner.

The latter on the night of April 25-26 was some 18 miles along the line towards EBONY on reconnaissance with three squadrons of the 1st Imperial Light Horse and a detachment of the 2nd Transvaal Scottish when about 1 a.m. on the 26th he observed a strong mounted force with guns marching in the direction of his camp. Thick dust prevented an accurate estimate of its strength and, dropping two troops, one to observe the enemy and the other to cover the withdrawal of the infantry which had been placed as a connecting link, Skinner returned unnoticed by the enemy to his camp and positions at TREKKOPPIES.

Such was the gist of Rodger's message.

It happened that the garrison was without artillery, for two 12-pounders had been withdrawn for field operations and were en route across the desert for NONIDAS. Two 4-inch guns were standing at SWAKOPMUND railway station about to go forward and the train carrying them was at once dispatched.

Meanwhile Skinner called in the Rhodesian Regiment from ARANDIS on the railway behind him.

At 5.45 a.m. the enemy blew up the railway line, but to the north instead of the south of Skinner's camp, and the effort was therefore wasted.

At 7.40 a.m. the enemy artillery—two batteries—came into

action from a range of hills extending parallel to the railway line to the north-west at a distance of about 5,000 yards.

Concurrently the German commander developed a dismounted rifle attack from the north and west where the terrain afforded good cover.

The attack was pushed with resolution but broke away before the combined fire of the infantry and Royal Naval armoured cars which rendered valuable support. They had reached TREKKOPPIES two days earlier.

At 10.30 a.m. the attack died down, and, upon evidence of an intention by the enemy to retire, Skinner at once set a counter-attack in motion.

The enemy, however, increased his artillery fire and Skinner, without guns, could not make much impression on the retiring force.

The South African casualties here were 3 officers and 6 other ranks killed and 2 officers and 30 other ranks wounded. The Germans left on the field 2 officers and 5 other ranks killed, 2 officers and 12 other ranks wounded and 1 officer and 12 other ranks as prisoners.

Thus at two widely separated points simultaneously a dreary experience of desert garrison work was relieved by the actions at TREKKOPPIES and GIBEON.

McKenzie's men from Natal and Skinner's Cape, Transvaal and Rhodesian infantrymen showed that, whatever effect their irksome task had had upon them, deterioration of discipline or spirit was not a feature of it.

A prisoner captured in a patrol action on the RIET front the same day stated that a larger force was advancing to attack RIET and SALEM.

The enemy did attack the latter post, but withdrew after a trifling engagement.

Shortly before this General Botha had fixed April 26 as the date of the beginning of his next movement, and whether the enemy, doubtless aware of this intention, attacked to cause some delay or on the wrong information which he received that the TREKKOPIES garrison had been considerably reduced is not known.

It is now time to resume the thread of the record of General Botha's operations which was interrupted to relate the GIBEON and TREKKOPPIES affairs.

The Campaign in German South West Africa, 1914-1915

On April 24 information, which was correct, was obtained of an enemy force at BARMEN (GROOT and KLEIN). This was the first information which had come to hand from that quarter, and it tended to confirm the view that the enemy concentrations were about KARIBIB–UBIB–GOAS–KUBAS and OKAHANDJA–BARMEN so disposed as to watch for an advance against KARIBIB or OTJIMBINGWE. (See map facing page 97.)

On April 25 five days' supplies had been placed at RIET and the orders to begin the advance on the 26th were issued.

The forces were divided into two commands, that of Brits comprising the 1st and 2nd Mounted Brigades which had taken part in the RIET–PFORTE operations, while the second was given to Brigadier-General M. W. Myburgh and contained the 3rd and 5th Mounted Brigades. Brits was also now a Brigadier-General.

The two new brigades were also commando brigades, the 3rd being from the Transvaal and the 5th from the Orange Free State.

The units of the latter were organised as regiments and, while all the Transvaal Brigades were preponderantly Afrikaans-speaking, the two races were more or less equally represented in the Free State Contingent.

Myburgh now joined the Field Force for the first time.

He was an able soldier and a staunch supporter of General Botha under whom, like all the other senior officers in the Transvaal Commandos, he had served in the Anglo-Boer War. He was well fitted to command a detached force.

Broadminded and tactful he numbered many of his English-speaking comrades among his friends. He was withal determined and a good disciplinarian, and enjoyed the well-deserved confidence of his chief. He was an admirable subordinate who never made difficulties and might be relied upon to carry out his instructions and to use good judgment if called upon to make an independent decision.

He was tall, even among tall men, powerfully built and the picture of robust manhood, and his unexpected death a few years later was a loss to the country in general and its military forces in particular.

He represented a Transvaal constituency in the Union Parliament.

The two commands were composed as follows:—
BRIGADIER-GENERAL BRITS.
1st and 2nd Mounted Brigades.

1st Mounted Brigade.
Colonel Lemmer.

Right Wing.	Left Wing.
Col.-Cdt. P. de la Rey.	Col.-Cdt. A. P. Visser.
KRUGERSDORP,	LICHTENBURG,
POTCHEFSTROOM " A ",	MARICO,
POTCHEFSTROOM " B "	WOLMARANSSTAD,
Commandos.	BLOEMHOF
1,026 rifles.	Commandos.
	1,124 rifles.

1st Mounted Brigade.
2,150 rifles.

Transvaal Horse Artillery.
4 guns.
One Section Machine-guns.

2nd Mounted Brigade.
Colonel Alberts.

Right Wing.	Left Wing.
Col.-Cdt. Badenhorst.	Col.-Cdt. Collins.
HEIDELBERG " A ",	ERMELO " B ",
HEIDELBERG " B ",	CAROLINA,
STANDERTON " A ",	MIDDELBURG " A ",
STANDERTON " B ",	MIDDELBURG " B "
ERMELO " A "	Commandos.
Commandos.	1,019 rifles.
1,104 rifles.	

2nd Mounted Brigade.
2,123 rifles.

One section 12-pdrs.   Machine-gun section.
One section howitzers.
Total force = 4,273 rifles, 8 guns.

The Campaign in German South West Africa, 1914-1915

On April 24 information, which was correct, was obtained of an enemy force at BARMEN (GROOT and KLEIN). This was the first information which had come to hand from that quarter, and it tended to confirm the view that the enemy concentrations were about KARIBIB–UBIB–GOAS–KUBAS and OKAHANDJA–BARMEN so disposed as to watch for an advance against KARIBIB or OTJIMBINGWE. (See map facing page 97.)

On April 25 five days' supplies had been placed at RIET and the orders to begin the advance on the 26th were issued.

The forces were divided into two commands, that of Brits comprising the 1st and 2nd Mounted Brigades which had taken part in the RIET–PFORTE operations, while the second was given to Brigadier-General M. W. Myburgh and contained the 3rd and 5th Mounted Brigades. Brits was also now a Brigadier-General.

The two new brigades were also commando brigades, the 3rd being from the Transvaal and the 5th from the Orange Free State.

The units of the latter were organised as regiments and, while all the Transvaal Brigades were preponderantly Afrikaans-speaking, the two races were more or less equally represented in the Free State Contingent.

Myburgh now joined the Field Force for the first time.

He was an able soldier and a staunch supporter of General Botha under whom, like all the other senior officers in the Transvaal Commandos, he had served in the Anglo-Boer War. He was well fitted to command a detached force.

Broadminded and tactful he numbered many of his English-speaking comrades among his friends. He was withal determined and a good disciplinarian, and enjoyed the well-deserved confidence of his chief. He was an admirable subordinate who never made difficulties and might be relied upon to carry out his instructions and to use good judgment if called upon to make an independent decision.

He was tall, even among tall men, powerfully built and the picture of robust manhood, and his unexpected death a few years later was a loss to the country in general and its military forces in particular.

He represented a Transvaal constituency in the Union Parliament.

The two commands were composed as follows:—
BRIGADIER-GENERAL BRITS.
1st and 2nd Mounted Brigades.

1st Mounted Brigade.
Colonel Lemmer.

Right Wing.	Left Wing.
Col.-Cdt. P. de la Rey.	Col.-Cdt. A. P. Visser.
KRUGERSDORP,	LICHTENBURG,
POTCHEFSTROOM " A ",	MARICO,
POTCHEFSTROOM " B "	WOLMARANSSTAD,
Commandos.	BLOEMHOF
1,026 rifles.	Commandos.
	1,124 rifles.

1st Mounted Brigade.
2,150 rifles.

Transvaal Horse Artillery.
4 guns.
One Section Machine-guns.

2nd Mounted Brigade.
Colonel Alberts.

Right Wing.	Left Wing.
Col.-Cdt. Badenhorst.	Col.-Cdt. Collins.
HEIDELBERG " A ",	ERMELO " B ",
HEIDELBERG " B ",	CAROLINA,
STANDERTON " A ",	MIDDELBURG " A ",
STANDERTON " B ",	MIDDELBURG " B "
ERMELO " A "	Commandos.
Commandos.	1,019 rifles.
1,104 rifles.	

2nd Mounted Brigade.
2,123 rifles.

One section 12-pdrs.   Machine-gun section.
One section howitzers.
Total force = 4,273 rifles, 8 guns.

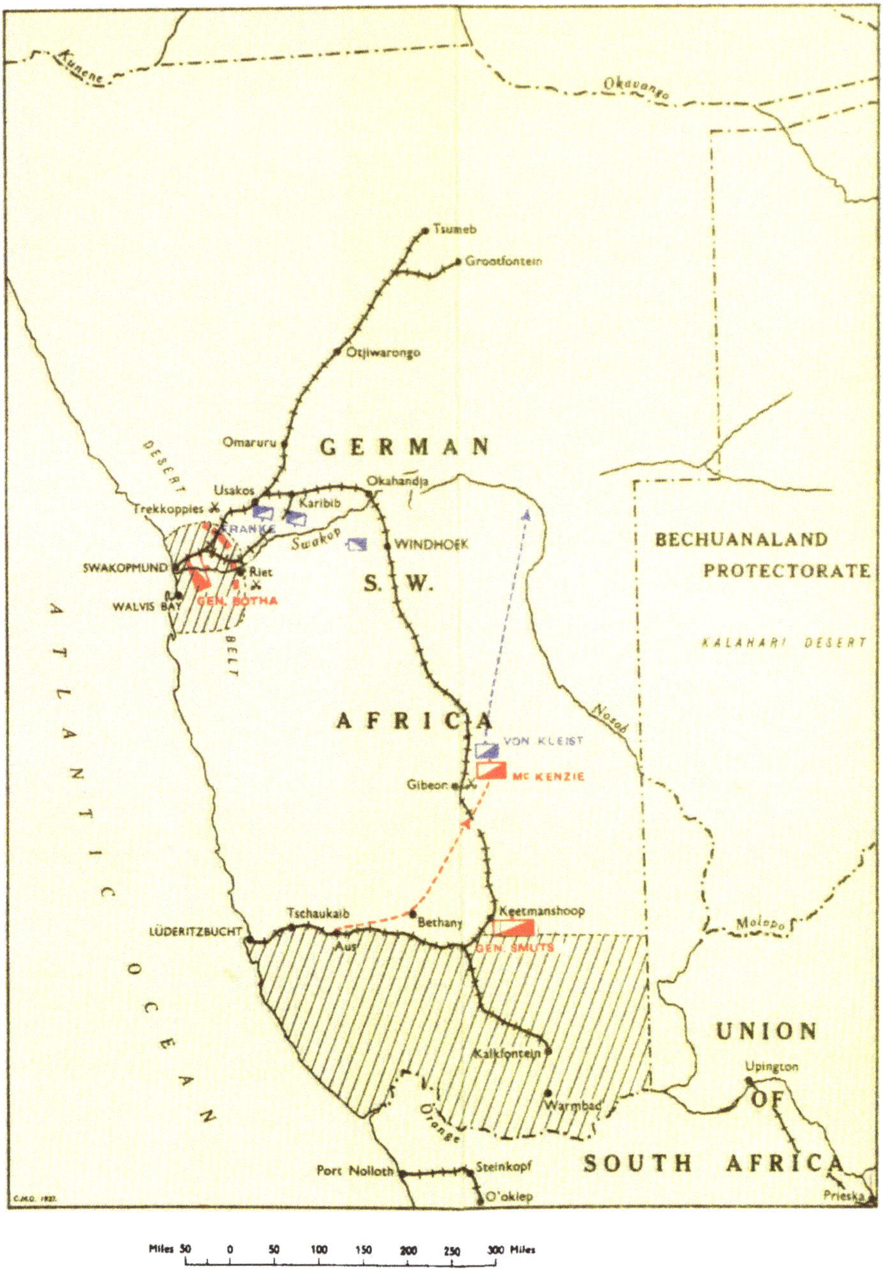

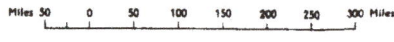

SKETCH MAP SHEWING

GENERAL SITUATION ON
GENERAL BOTHA'S SECOND ADVANCE

26 APRIL 1915

BRIGADIER-GENERAL MYBURGH.
3rd and 5th Mounted Brigades.

3rd Mounted Brigade.
Colonel Mentz.

Right Wing.	Left Wing.
Col.-Cdt. Jordaan.	Col.-Cdt. van Tonder.
WAKKERSTROOM, UTRECHT, VRYHEID, PAULPIETERSBURG, and PIET RETIEF Commandos. Botha's Natal Horse.	LYDENBURG, PIETERSBURG, WATERBERG, RUSTENBURG, PRETORIA Commandos.
1,267 rifles.	1,354 rifles.

3rd Mounted Brigade.
2,621 rifles.

4th Permanent Battery.
4 guns.
Machine-gun section.

5th Mounted Brigade.
Colonel H. W. N. Botha.

Right Wing.	Left Wing.
Col.-Cdt. Nussey.	Col.-Cdt. Fouché.
1st, 2nd and 3rd regiments.	4th, 5th and 6th regiments.
917 rifles.	1,057 rifles.

5th Mounted Brigade.
1,974 rifles.

2nd Permanent Battery.
4 guns.
Machine-gun section.
Total force = 4,595 rifles, 8 guns.

TOTAL FORCE UNDER GENERAL BOTHA: 8,868 rifles and 16 guns.

The Campaign in German South West Africa, 1914-1915

In addition to his mounted troops, General Botha made Wylie's (4th) Infantry Brigade available for field operations and the force was almost three times the strength of that which had left SWAKOPMUND five weeks earlier in March.

The lines of communication had now assumed an added importance and the following organisation was arranged:—

The O.C. Troops WALVIS.
Section: WALVIS–RAND RIFLES SIDING (EXCLUSIVE).
Troops: A detachment.

The O.C. Troops SWAKOPMUND.
Section: SWAKOPMUND–RAND RIFLES SIDING (INCLUSIVE).
SWAKOPMUND–HUSAB.
SWAKOPMUND–Kilo 13 on railway.
Troops: 2 squadrons Southern Rifles.
D.E.O. Rifles.

The O.C. Troops Northern Line.
Section: Kilo 13–RAILHEAD.
Troops: 1st Imperial Light Horse.
3rd Infantry Brigade.
R.N. Armoured Cars.
Two 12-pdr. guns.
Two 4-in. guns.

The O.C. Troops RIET.
Section: RIET and RIET–KHAN railway.
Troops: 2nd Durban Light Infantry.

As soon as the situation at TREKKOPPIES had cleared up, the Commander-in-Chief left SWAKOPMUND for RIET, having set his troops in motion.

CHAPTER IX

THE STRATEGIC SITUATION at this time is clear from the map facing page 97.

The main German body, disposed before WINDHOEK, OKAHANDJA, KARIBIB, awaiting the next move by General Botha who, holding the line TREKKOPPIES–JAKALSWATER–RIET, is about to advance.

In the south the advance of the Southern Army has ended, its objective, von Kleist's force, 200 miles ahead of it, having disengaged itself with loss from McKenzie whose mounted troops are also incapable of further effort.

Von Kleist, moving rapidly north, is available to be called to the main body or to continue his retirement. The rapidity and comprehensive effect of the next operations of the Union Commander-in-Chief over the following week compel von Kleist to adopt the second course, moving widely to the east of WINDHOEK to avoid interception by the rapidly moving commandos.

General Botha has now the whole concentrated German Force before him.

By the evening of April 28 the four mounted brigades, with their artillery and other units, had concentrated at RIET where the Commander-in-Chief had arrived the evening before.

Wylie's infantry were collected at JAKALSWATER.

On the morning of April 28 General Botha met his principal officers in consultation and explained his plans for the ensuing operations, which were as follows:—

General Myburgh (3rd and 5th Mounted Brigades) to march in the evening, 4 p.m. of the 28th—the 3rd Brigade leaving RIET at the hour named followed two hours later by the 5th—via SALEM, WILSONFONTEIN and FRANKE on TSAOBIS; two commandos to be detached from the 5th Brigade to move up the SWAKOP River to HOREBIS and thence to TSAOBIS direct.

General Brits (1st and 2nd Mounted Brigades) to leave RIET 24 hours behind Myburgh, the two brigades moving at the same hours as those of Myburgh on the 29th. The 2nd to preceed the 1st Brigade.

Brits, taking the 1st Brigade, was to move in two detachments against KUBAS by way of DORSTRIVIER and GAMIKAUB

The Campaign in German South West Africa, 1914-1915

River. The 2nd, under Alberts, was directed on POTMINE, where one wing was to be left in reserve, and the other to be detached, as the whole movement developed, to OTJIMBINGWE, whence it would reconnoitre towards GREAT BARMEN.

Colonel Wylie was to be ready to advance on KUBAS, by way of SPHINX and DORSTRIVIER, on receipt of orders.

G.H.Q. was placed at POTMINE.

These movements were all preparatory to an attack on the enemy south of KARIBIB and a wide turning sweep by Myburgh between KARIBIB and OKAHANDJA.

A letter was now received from Cornelius van Wyk, the old REHOBOTH chief, who reported a collision between his people and German troops who, he alleged, had attacked him after his refusal to allow his men to serve under arms as guards over the South Africans who were prisoners of war. Such a service would of course release German troops for the field.

General Botha in reply expressed his "surprise and disappointment" at the events reported, seeing that "his express wish was that the coloured people should keep themselves outside the war" and added that he desired "with the greatest earnestness again to say that he (van Wyk) must not go on with this war, rather trek back some way with his cattle and people". Provided he did this, van Wyk was assured of protection and advised immediately to get into touch with the commandos trekking towards GIBEON and place himself and his stock behind the Union lines.

Some considerable stress was laid by the German Governor, Dr. Seitz, on several occasions during a conference which was to take place three weeks later, upon the "arming of natives" by the Union authorities, and it seems important that the attitude of General Botha, which was the reflex of that of his political colleagues, should be recorded. It is curious to note that it did not occur to the Imperial Governor who was such a stickler for preserving the dignity of the white races—His Excellency made much of this at GIFTKUPPE—that to employ natives to take charge of white prisoners of war would at least be inconsistent with his expressed views.

Skinner at railhead was instructed to do anything he could to demonstrate towards AUKAS within a few days on a date to be communicated to him.

General Botha left RIET at 8 p.m. on April 28, but being

unable to pass the mounted troops and their transport in the river bed, which was here very narrow and rough, slept for the night by the roadside and moved on to SALEM the following morning.

Throughout the campaign he rode with his commandos and travelled, as they did, without a tent.

All through the night of April 28-29 and the following day from dawn to midnight the march on TSAOBIS was maintained by Myburgh's forces, close upon which General Botha followed, reaching KALTENHAUSEN at 11.30 p.m. on the 29th. The temperature—it was bitterly cold—gave evidence of the aptness of the name of the place.

The contrast to the severe heat of the day, during the march of 40 miles, of which 35 were without water, was striking.

The whole distance from RIET had been covered in less than 18 hours.

The route—alternately of deep sand and hard granite-like rock—lay through narrow defiles which had to be made good before the entry of the columns and which had been freely mined.

The South African soldiers had by this time acquired a useful knack of detecting mines and knowing where to expect them and the casualties from this source were far fewer than they would have been earlier.

Some explosions occurred in the river-bed—3 men were killed and others severely wounded—but this comparatively slight loss may be attributed to the watchfulness of the troops and their avoidance of the narrower parts of the track (where horsemen would tend to bunch) by riding round them.

The need for careful work by the scouts added to the merit of the rapid march.

Arrived at KALTENHAUSEN—TSAOBIS water supply was drunk out by the troops which arrived first almost at once— General Botha consulted with Myburgh and Manie Botha (the 5th Brigade commander and his nephew) and half an hour later, at midnight, the 3rd Mounted Brigade (Mentz) left on another 25-mile march to OTJIMBINGWE, in the direction of which an enemy patrol had withdrawn, with the object of surprising the place at dawn. An hour later—1 a.m., April 30— the Free Staters rode out in the tracks of their Transvaal comrades.

Four hundred men, some incapacitated by sickness, but for

The Campaign in German South West Africa, 1914-1915

the most part whose horses had succumbed to the trying march, were left by Myburgh at KALTENHAUSEN.

A few hours later at daybreak the brigades were in action beyond OTJIMBINGWE where they captured an officer and 23 of the enemy.

The main body escaped by galloping through a gap left in the surrounding troops just before the omission was noticed and could be made good. Want of knowledge of the locality robbed the commandos of the full result of their march.

The two brigades had passed over 70 odd miles of extraordinarily difficult country and appalling roads in 36 hours.

Good water, which was here very near the surface of the SWAKOP, and some grazing and stock were found at OTJIMBINGWE.

General Botha reached the latter place at daybreak on May 1.

Though slight damage had been done to the enemy, who had avoided any chance of becoming committed to an engagement and had given up long stretches of country ideal for stubborn delaying action, the first phase of the operations had been rapidly and successfully concluded.

General Botha now made his final dispositions.

Myburgh was instructed to push on with his advance, and to move on the evening of May 2 with his whole force to UITDRAAI on the northern OTJIMBINGWE-WINDHOEK road, where he was to halt for the night of May 2-3. Proceeding on the 3rd as far as the cross-roads at QUAIPUTZ he would halt in daylight and give the appearance of settling down for the night.

Resuming the march, however, immediately after nightfall the whole force was to move—one brigade in advance and the other in support—rapidly to WILHELMSTAL, where the destruction of the railway and telegraph lines was to be effected.

From WILHELMSTAL Myburgh was expected to move westward on KARIBIB, reconnoitring north of the railway and doing his best to interpose as strong a detachment as possible across the OTAVI railway and road north of KARIBIB.

This last step would involve very heavy demands on the mounted men and their horses, but even this outside chance was good enough to take to head off or damage the retreating enemy.

The dimensions of the task may be calculated from the map, and, for the time being, the brigades will be left to it.

The country to be traversed was very broken and rugged and

The Campaign in German South West Africa, 1914-1915

still eminently favourable to the defence, waterless, and devoid of any supplies except for some grass here and there.

The comparative uselessness of the wireless equipment with Myburgh—a feature of all such plant with the Northern Force—and the distance at which the movement remained from G.H.Q. throughout its execution, made communication far more difficult than had been expected.

General Botha, before leaving SWAKOPMUND, had asked General Smuts to come north and confer with him, and on reaching POTMINE on May 2 found the latter awaiting him.

Here was received intelligence of the occupation of KUBAS by an advanced detachment of Brits which had sustained 7 casualties by mines. The place had been abandoned, and, away on the left, Skinner reported STINGBANK, on the railway, clear.

This indicated some withdrawal by the enemy and Alberts was immediately ordered to OTJIMBINGWE with his whole brigade.

Until the exact direction of the enemy should be known he was placed—at OTJIMBINGWE—where he could move without delay towards KARIBIB or GREAT BARMEN.

The force which had retired before McKenzie had still to be taken into account, **and its exact movement after leaving** GIBEON was not yet clear. In the event of course it gave WINDHOEK a wide berth, passing it well to the east.

This early withdrawal was eloquent of the sensitiveness of the enemy about his flanks which became henceforward apparent.

On May 3 Mentz sent in reliable information of the retirement of the enemy northwards by road and rail from KARIBIB.

All information now tended to confirm Mentz's report, and Myburgh was again apprised of General Botha's **view of the** importance of getting a brigade on the OTAVI line.

Once more the German Commander was retiring hastily, surprised by the rapidity of the advance and the turning movements which were a feature of it.

After Generals Botha and Smuts had conferred, the latter, after waiting to acquaint himself with the situation, left on his return south on May 4.

On this day Wylie reached KUBAS with his infantry and Skinner was ordered to set in train the movement on AUKAS for which he was holding himself prepared.

The direct advance on KARIBIB was now begun, and

between 1 and 2 a.m. on May 5 the 1st Mounted Brigade, with which was General Brits, left its bivouacs. General Botha, moving from POTMINE, joined the left wing at UKUIB.

The left wing moved by KEINAS and WILDENRACH; Brits with the right by KUBIS, ABBABIS and HABIS from GAMIKAUB MUND.

A signalling post with a wide range of observation was established on OTJIPATERA BERG with the hope of picking up some of the columns to the east.

A halt was called at KEINAS, found unoccupied, at 7 a.m., and WILDENRACH was reached by the left wing at midday. Here a halt was again made and communication established with Alberts by heliograph.

A message from Myburgh gave details of mines laid on the railway for 10 kilometers ahead of Skinner.

From WILDENRACH 300 rifles of the BLOEMHOF Commando were sent on to reconnoitre KARIBIB, which was hurriedly evacuated by patrols after an exchange of shots with the commando.

At 5 p.m. General Botha with the left wing of the 1st Mounted Brigade entered the town, and was followed two hours later by Brits with the right wing.

The forces bivouacked round the town.

The march had again been without water. Such supplies as there had been had been destroyed by the enemy who, in fear of envelopment, had, as before, foregone the opportunities of holding up the columns in their advance and compelling them to return to the SWAKOP for water.

The 35-mile march had taken about 12 hours.

The first town containing any German population in the north thus fell into General Botha's hands.

64 European males, 100 females and 129 children remained in the town together with 300 natives.

Broad and narrow-gauge rolling stock and engines were secured, and the railway works and water arrangements were found to be in good order.

Myburgh had in the meantime occupied WILHELSTAL and JOHANN ALBRECHTS HOHE.

The Freestaters, under Manie Botha, captured 3 large engines with a smaller one and 30 trucks at WILHELMSTAL.

Myburgh reported that he had been able to find water and subsist his forces on stock which he had captured and said that

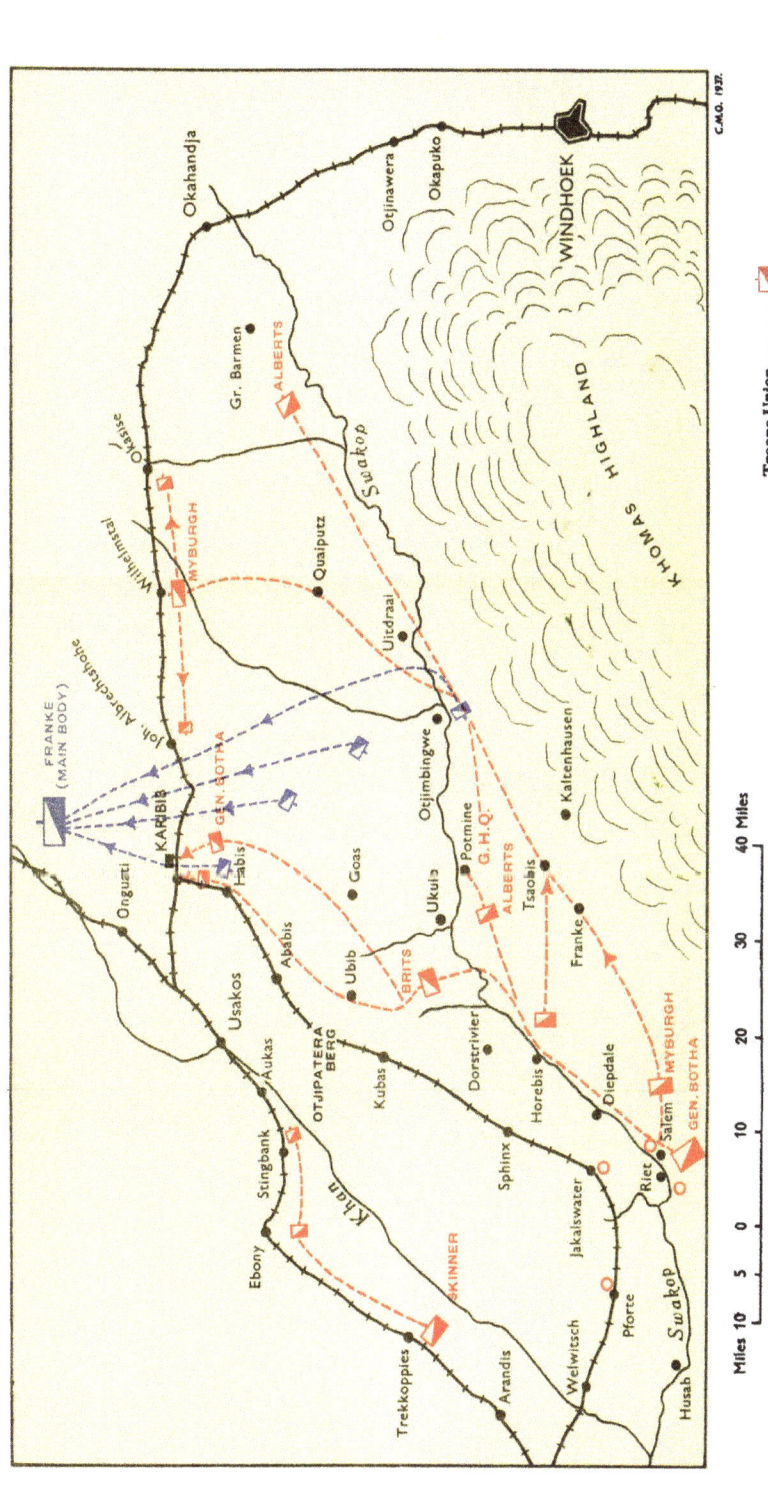

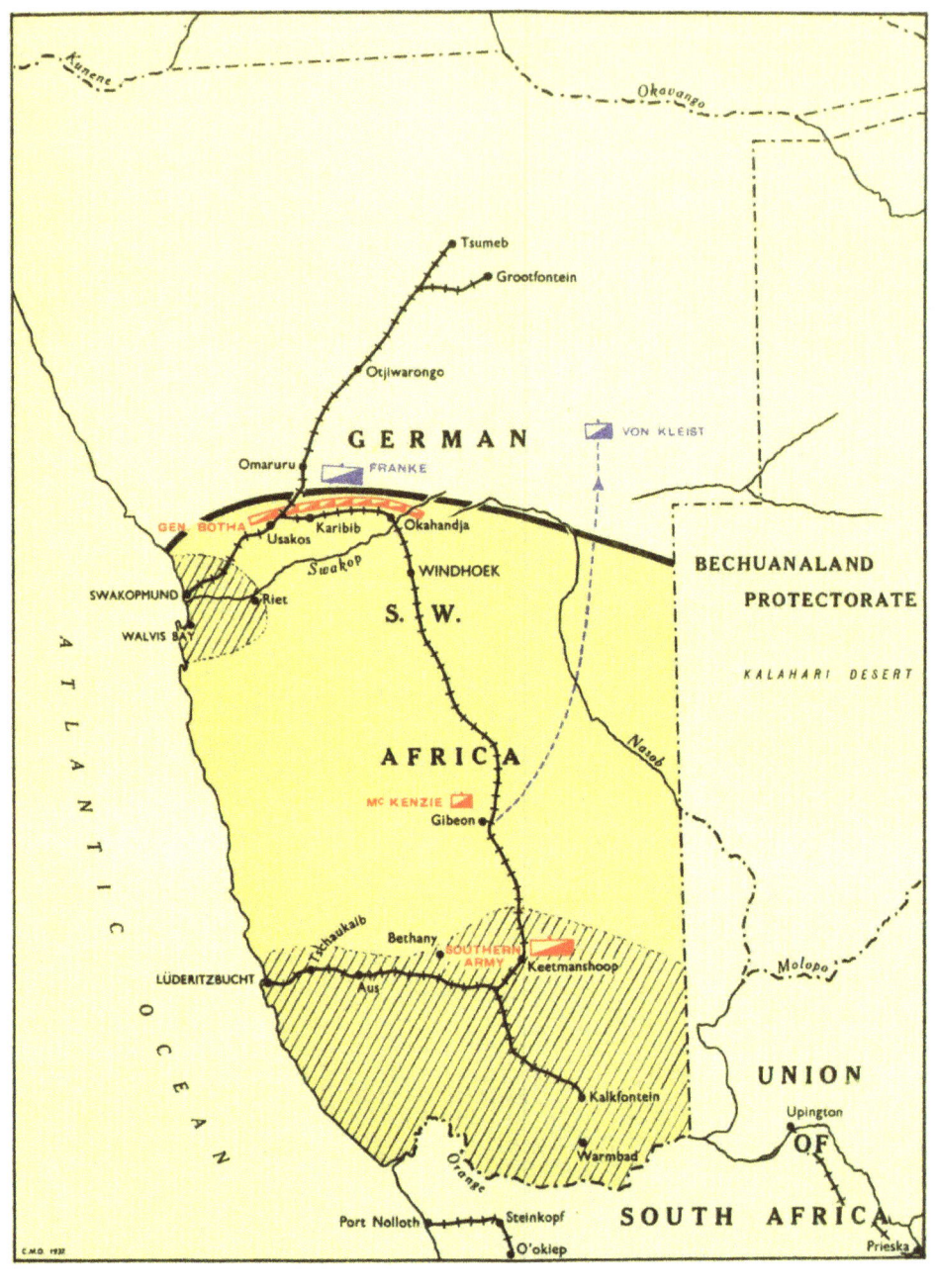

SKETCH MAP SHEWING
STRATEGIC RESULT OF GENERAL BOTHA'S
FIVE DAYS OPERATIONS
28 APRIL TO 3 MAY, 1915.

The Campaign in German South West Africa, 1914-1915

grazing was good as was the condition of his horses despite the heavy strain of continuous marching.

He had sustained no casualties since leaving OTJIM-BINGWE, and had taken a dozen prisoners.

He was sending the 5th Brigade towards KARIBIB, retaining with him the 3rd at WILHELMSTAL, whence he was arranging the occupation of OKAHANDJA.

The interception of the enemy had proved impossible but, as the map opposite shows, great strategic results had been gained in the short space of a week.

On April 28 the German Commander held by far the greater part of the Protectorate and held and covered the capital, WINDHOEK, and the railway which gave him power to concentrate and take the initiative.

His opponents controlled merely that small portion of the country that lay behind their outposts.

A week later General Botha's movements had deprived the enemy of the capital, of his power of concentration for attack, of the initiative and of two-thirds of the settled portion of the Protectorate.

The German Commander north of the KARIBIB–OKAHANDJA line was placed strictly on the defensive.

A striking example of the value of action against a decisive point.

At KARIBIB the Northern Force came into contact with the German civil population for the first time.

On the morning of May 6 General Botha rode into KARIBIB from his bivouac just outside.

Here the German broad-gauge railway from OKAHANDJA and WINDHOEK ended and the narrow-gauge system to USAKOS and OTAVI began.

The village, an important railway centre, was dry and uninviting, much like some places which are to be found in the north-west of the Cape Province, destitute of trees or gardens and consisting of two streets running parallel to the railway line. A contrast to USAKOS, its neighbour, which, well watered, planted with pepper trees and picturesquely situated, was far more pleasing to the eye.

The allowance of hotels to the population was on the generous scale which was to be noticed in all the towns entered by the Northern Force, and two of these, both empty of guests and one entirely deserted, were used for G.H.Q.

General Botha was met by a deputation headed by Justice Kühnest and consisting of the Burgomaster, doctor, and one leading citizen.

At the ensuing conference the town was formally handed over by the deputation who asked that the people might remain in their homes and not be deported—a step which had proved necessary at LUDERITZBUCHT.

They stated they had provisions for two months—they were the only people who for the next few weeks or so would have enough to eat at KARIBIB—and sought permission to take milk from a neighbouring farm for the 129 children, " among whom were many babies ".

The main military points in the discussion were:—

The people in the town, if they remained quiet and refrained from all communication with anyone outside the lines, would be allowed to stay and their supplies—which incidentally would have been of great value to the new-comers—would be left to them.

General Botha again emphasised that the natives were to be kept " out of this struggle between whites ".

The deputation, though unwilling to make a definite assertion, gave it as their opinion that WINDHOEK would not be defended as there were " a lot of women and children there ", a condition which also obtained at OKAHANDJA.

It was thus clear that the enemy's retirement was complete, and that he had transferred the care of his families to his opponent.

The South African soldiers were now to experience some weeks of very short commons and the following incident is a tribute to their self respect and restrained bearing.

While the conference was in progress, a Union soldier, finding a bag of meal in what seemed to be an empty house, took it to supplement the small ration of meat which was all that he and his comrades had had for some days.

The owner of the house, who was, with most of the population, looking on at the conference, took prompt advantage of the encouraging attitude of the invaders and lodged a complaint with the Provost Marshal.

General Botha at once summoned the commandants whom he made personally responsible for keeping their own burghers out of the town, with the result that next morning the commandants—all physically powerful men—cleared the town by

The Campaign in German South West Africa, 1914-1915

the aid of their strong right arms and put an end for good to any looting, if the very natural action of the hungry soldier deserves such a description.

The single bag of meal was the only article of food taken from the civil population without their own consent and without paying a very handsome price.

Some idea of the supply position after the capture of KARIBIB at this time may be gained from the following remarks by Lieut.-Commander Whittall—commanding the R.N. Armoured Cars—in an account of the campaign. The experience he relates befell him *some weeks* after the first occupation.

"Next day I essayed the journey with more success and arrived in KARIBIB a couple of hours after starting (from USAKOS). Things there did not presage an early advance. To say that a state of virtual famine existed does not exceed the truth. Everyone was on the shortest of short rations. Even the hospitals were living from hand to mouth.

The nursing sisters had been living for days on ration biscuit and a little sugarless tea and with hardly any prospect of better conditions in the immediate future.

At G.H.Q. things were just as bad, and it was put pretty bluntly that new arrivals were not at all welcome under the existing conditions. I had known how matters stood and had therefore brought along in the car a few supplies that made all the difference in the way I was regarded by the Headquarters' mess, and made me quite popular for the time being."

The stoical grit of the soldiers of the fighting formations and of the units which served them in South West and East Africa will always be remembered by anyone who witnessed their hardships with unstinted sympathy and admiration.

In a lengthy leader two days before the occupation of KARIBIB the German paper *Süd West* made a well-deserved acknowledgment of the conduct of the South African soldiers, whom it referred to as " troops of a Teutonic nation ". They had, where they had taken possession of South West African places, conducted themselves " in such a way as becomes civilised soldiers " behaving " properly and courteously ". Cash had been paid for cattle and anything needed and *" they did not object in the least to the prices asked by the farmers "*. The London politicians would certainly not await " the stormy entry of the pressing Germans " and German South West would remain German on the map when the European war was ended.

On May 6 the forces which had taken part in the advance were distributed as follows:—

Brits ...... {1st Mounted Brigade KARIBIB.
2nd Mounted Brigade OTJIMBINGWE (ordered to move on GREAT BARMEN).

Myburgh {3rd Mounted Brigade WILHELMSTAL one wing ordered to OKAHANDJA.
5th Mounted Brigade JOHANN ALBRECHTS HOHE.

Wylie ...... 4th Infantry Brigade KUBAS.

AUKAS was occupied by the Imperial Light Horse from Skinner.

Mentz, with the left wing of his brigade, established himself at OKAHANDJA and had instructions to reconnoitre well to the east and to be ready to deal with von Kleist should he get contact with the latter in his movement to the north.

Alberts from BARMEN connected with MENTZ by throwing out a detachment of 500 rifles in his direction.

The forces were thus disposed preparatory to the occupation of WINDHOEK.

Touch was obtained with Skinner on May 7 by the junction at USAKOS of a patrol of the Imperial Light Horse with 200 men of the Bloemhof Commando (from Brits) and the Union forces stood linked up on a front of 200 miles from SWAKOPMUND to OKAHANDJA as a consequence of General Botha's last movements.

At this time supplies with the troops, except for cattle and some grazing, were totally exhausted.

The meat enabled the commandos to live for some time. The burgher of the country units was able to live without discomfort on a diet of meat, with little else, for a time considerably beyond the point where his comrades of the infantry and other town-recruited formations became ill as a consequence of such monotonous fare. This ability to exist on such a diet was one of several important factors which contributed to the mobility of the commandos.

The reasons for this shortage were as follows:—

The lines of communication running from the base at SWAKOPMUND by way of the SWAKOP River and thence by

The Campaign in German South West Africa, 1914-1915

the route followed in the advance on KARIBIB were not less than 150 miles in length.

The mules of the wagons—far short of what were needed— were worn out by the constant strain of pulling over the heavy tracks of deep sand and rock over the whole route.

For three weeks only driblets of supplies came into KARIBIB at rare and uncertain intervals. A welcome first instalment was two truckloads from JAKALSWATER which two officers had brought in on their own initiative aided by a debilitated engine and occasional manhandling.

The light KHAN-JAKALSWATER railway had reached the last-named place on April 29 but 60 miles of rough, waterless and forbidding country intervened between JAKALSWATER and KARIBIB.

It was clear that with so many troops ahead, the heavy, exhausting and irregular lines along the SWAKOP, though the river had been an indispensable aid to the rapid advance, had become a hindrance and that communications must be switched with all possible dispatch to the SWAKOPMUND-USAKOS railway line.

It was at this juncture that it was decided to terminate the broad gauge at EBONY and to rely from that point to KARIBIB (where the German 3·6 in. gauge to WINDHOEK and the south began) and to the north to OTAVI upon the excellent German 2-ft. gauge.

On May 15 the forward base of the Field Force was moved from HUSAB on the river to USAKOS on the railway, and for the rest of the campaign transfer of all forward supplies was effected at EBONY from broad to narrow-gauge rolling stock.

At this date the new lines were working through to KARIBIB and a great improvement in the supply position had resulted, though the mobility of the troops had not been restored.

The ten days, from May 5 to May 14, during which small stray quantities of supplies were sent up by both routes under extraordinary difficulties, were a prolonged nightmare to General Botha and his staff and a most trying time for the troops.

The relief afforded to the troops in what, considering the circumstances, must be regarded as a short time, is to be attributed to the energy and capacity of Lieut.-Colonel Collins and Major Beaton and their associates of all ranks of the South African Railways. Later, Colonel Hoy (the General Manager) came to KARIBIB and remained there until the railway position was practically safe.

The combination of obstacles which arose to hinder progress and upset work was sometimes calculated to depress the most sanguine optimist.

General Smuts was now on his way to confer a second time with General Botha, as it was obvious that the forces must be reorganised for a further campaign in the north.

The following General Staff Memorandum prepared for General Botha in his conference with General Smuts gives an idea of the situation.

" 1. *Purposes to be Served by Forces.*

On the occupation of WINDHOEK and the retirement of the enemy north it is possible to gauge the situation and estimate its requirements with a degree of certainty which has been out of the question hitherto.

Three main purposes to be served by the forces seem to be indicated as follows:—

(a) The defeat of the enemy in the field.

(b) The protection of lines of communication which are in touch with the Field Force and may be within striking distance of the enemy.

(c) The occupation and pacification of such territory as is so remote from that in possession of the enemy as to render attack by the latter improbable.

The whole of the forces in German South West Africa will, it is assumed, be under the command of the G.O.C.-in-Chief.

2. *Division of Territory for the Allotment of Forces.*

(a) Field Force Territory in which operations will be carried by the Field Force.

Approximately all territory north of the OTAVI * line to KARIBIB; the railway line from KARIBIB to WINDHOEK; and an imaginary line from WINDHOEK to, say, GOBABIS. It seems highly improbable that territory east of GROOTFONTEIN–WATERBERG–WINDHOEK will be the scene of any hostilities and it may quite likely prove that much of it may be taken over by the force of occupation below.

---

* The German narrow-gauge railway from SWAKOPMUND to KARIBIB and thence to OTAVI was known as the OTAVI Railway.

The Campaign in German South West Africa, 1914-1915

(b) Lines of Communication. Under this heading are WALVIS and the railway thence to SWAKOPMUND; thence the railway line via ROSSING–ARANDIS–EBONY—USAKOS–ONGUATI–KARIBIB–JOHANN ALBRECHTS HOHE–OKAHANDJA up to but excluding WINDHOEK.

Such lines of communication as at present exist, e.g. the KHAN railway and SWAKOP River, falling as they do, behind the lines mentioned above, will come under the G.O.C. Force of occupation.

The Lines of Communication should, it is recommended, be divided into three sections until they are extended further north, viz.: No. 1 Section WALVIS to USAKOS inclusive; No. 2 Section from USAKOS exclusive to KARIBIB inclusive; No. 3 Section from KARIBIB exclusive to WINDHOEK exclusive.

Experience * has shown so far that the absence of an Inspecting Officer of L. of C. is a most serious defect, and it is accordingly recommended that there should be an Officer Commanding L. of C. who will exercise general supervision. His headquarters would probably be the best placed at USAKOS.

(c) Force of Occupation. The remainder of the territory should, it is suggested, be taken over by a Force of Occupation. This portion of the territory being either remote, or protected, from the enemy, can now be administered and pacified, and, as far as may be, the civilian population may resume its ordinary avocations. The area to be thus controlled is the whole of German South West Africa bounded by the SWAKOPMUND–WINDHOEK, WINDHOEK – KEETMANSHOOP, KEETMANSHOOP–LUDERITZBUCHT railways and to a certain extent the territory south of the imaginary line WINDHOEK to GOBABIS mentioned in (a).

3. *Troops Required.*

(a) Field Force. It is suggested that a force of 8,000 mounted men should be retained for the Field Force and should be obtained from troops now in the field on such lines as may be determined. It is recommended that the force should be organised in four brigades but that the organisation of the wings should be altered somewhat in detail so as to enable these formations to be detached as completely self-contained units. Experience has shown that the staff work for a formation of

---

* This allusion was in respect of the Rebellion and the Lines back from CAPETOWN to PRETORIA in the G.S.W.A. campaign.

more than 1,000 men is more than some of the staff officers can cope with. The defect is mainly apparent when wings are detached under conditions which render it necessary that ambulances, signallers and such details should accompany them. The latter are sometimes overlooked and the wings should be self-contained to avoid the chance of such mistakes. This will be possible to arrange with the great reduction in the combatant troops.

(b) *Lines of Communication.* For these it would seem necessary to have the following troops:—

No. 1 Section: H.Q. SWAKOPMUND.
One Infantry Brigade.
No. 2 Section: H.Q. KARIBIB.
One Infantry Brigade.
No. 3 Section: H.Q. OKAHANDJA.
One Infantry Brigade.

The two last-mentioned Brigades will, on the advance of the Field Force, extend, behind it, up the OTAVI (northern) line.

(c) Force of Occupation it is recommended should be the 6th (Permanent S.A.M.R.) Mounted Brigade.

(d) *Artillery.* It is recommended that the five 13-Pounder Q.F. Batteries (20 guns) should be allotted to the Field Force, as should the 6-in. Howitzers, any guns required for the L. of C. being found from the Heavy Artillery Brigade.

(e) *Signalling.* There should be at least five sets of field wireless, one for each brigade and one for the G.O.C.-in-C. Signallers should be allotted on a wing basis and not to brigades, as at present. This will mean an additional allowance of signallers, but, as in several other details, there is less likelihood of units being sent away without proper means of communication if the wing staff officers have their own allowance of such services.

(f) *Medical.* Medical organisation on an active service basis will be necessary for the Field Force and L. of C., but may be undertaken on a peace basis for the Force of Occupation.

4. *Field Headquarters and Bases.*

General (Field) Headquarters should be established at KARIBIB and it is proposed to move the balance of G.H.Q., now at SWAKOPMUND, to this place.

The Campaign in German South West Africa, 1914-1915

5. *Transport.*

Brigade trains should be doubled at least. They are far too small to be of practical use and they should be so organised as to be able to detach half the wagons for any wing without arrangement or notice.

The A.Q.M.G. should be instructed to state fully, after being told the details of the reorganisation, his requirements for the equivalent of Divisional Supply Parks, *additional to Brigade Trains.* This most important matter has so far been entirely neglected.

Every unit should have its full transport before any movement takes place.

6. *General.*

It would appear that, if the above suggestions are adopted, reduction on a large scale can at once be effected in expenditure on the campaign, for after four mounted and three infantry brigades have been provided, the rest of the military work in German South West Africa can be performed by the S.A.M.R. This will include the protective supervision of all railways other than those on the L. of C. (as above defined).

Judging from appearances a very great proportion of staff officers of the (temporary) administrative staff could at once be dispensed with.* There seem to be numbers of these officers in different capacities.

The forces in the south can also all be done away with as separate forces, though they may be drawn upon to make up the personnel necessary for the continuance of the campaign. All the staffs of these forces can be released, and it would seem advisable to employ all permanent staff officers thus available with the reorganised forces using officers with staff experience and releasing here to some extent temporary staff officers ".

The memorandum is quoted as, apart from giving an idea of what arrangements were necessary, it indicates some weak spots which had come to light.

To the new situation Generals Botha and Smuts now gave their attention.

On May 8 the latter, having, with characteristic energy, out-

---

* Numbers of officers—many with high rank—were sent up from PRETORIA on different " missions " without being asked for and sometimes without any notification of their purpose or dispatch.

stripped the whole of his staff, of which respresentatives, if report might be believed, were to be found shed at intervals along the sand and sea routes as far back as AUS, left SWAKOPMUND for KARIBIB accompanied by Colonel Hoy. He even outpaced the latter and, having braved the unknown difficulties of the road from USAKOS to KARIBIB, was found by a patrol unconcernedly walking towards his destination.

The patrol having furnished the General with a horse proceeded to escort him with some measure of ceremony to G.H.Q.

He at once discussed the situation with the Commander-in-Chief.

Asked how long it would be before reorganisation could be effected and the next move begin, the General Staff gave six weeks as the earliest date possible, provided all General Botha's requirements were met without undue delay.

It was a matter of simple calculation. General Botha had no intention of moving until the supply situation should have been satisfactorily settled, and by this time it was easy to estimate how long it would take for all that was required to come up. By a coincidence, the estimate of six weeks proved correct to the day.

General Botha's next operations would entail far more extended flank marches, and if, as was intended, the enemy was to be surrounded, the flanking forces must be followed by supplies to enable them to move continuously for three or four weeks. These forces would soon lose touch with G.H.Q. and would not regain it until the encirclement of the German forces should have been completed.

No enforced check in the operations, if they were to be a success, could be contemplated and the mobility of the mounted troops must be sustained till the end.

On the third and final advance General Botha's sole objective was the enemy force now concentrated.

On his first and second advances there were other objectives, e.g. the railway, the capital, and the wireless installations, and the escape of the enemy from the encircling movements of the Union forces did not entail abandonment by the German Commander of the whole of the Protectorate, but merely occupation of a reduced part of it.

It was far different after KARIBIB and WINDHOEK had been taken.

The Campaign in German South West Africa, 1914-1915

The sole remaining objective was the enemy force—the soundest in war—and unless it could be destroyed or captured it would remain a fighting body and a menace.

On the last occasion of advance therefore no chance which could be eliminated should be taken.

On the two former occasions many chances were taken, as has been shown, and, though much was achieved, the bulk of the German force remained intact.

The discussions between the two Generals had been most useful and enabled one undivided direction to be given to the operations for the first time.

The detailed measures—more or less in agreement with the memorandum already quoted—which were decided upon will be given later.

CHAPTER X

ON THE AFTERNOON of May 10 General Botha left KARIBIB to arrange the surrender of WINDHOEK.

Some measures of military precaution were necessary.

It was also desirable that the occupation of the capital should be made the occasion of some demonstration of strength and display, particularly to a population containing many good judges of military efficiency.

Accordingly Mentz's force at OKAHANDJA, the left wing of the 3rd Mounted Brigade, was ordered to OTJIHAVERA, roughly half-way to WINDHOEK, and Alberts was instructed to move a portion of his brigade from GREAT BARMEN to OTJISENA, 20 miles to the west of Mentz.

Camping by the road for the night of May 10-11, General Botha reached OKAHANDJA the following morning, and there, after a telephone conversation with the Burgomaster of WINDHOEK, arranged to take the surrender of that place at noon on the next day.

Staying the next night at OTJIHAVERA—a roadside waterhole—the Commander-in-Chief reached the outskirts of WINDHOEK at 11 a.m. on May 12. Here he met the Burgomaster, a dapper little man who—as was perhaps natural—betrayed symptoms of considerable nervousness.

On the assurance of the Burgomaster that he had full power to hand over the town without resistance, the formal entry was arranged for an hour later, and at 12 noon the burghers of Alberts and Mentz took possession of the enemy capital.

The town, situated in the midst of hills and in good grass country, contained some fine buildings—notably the Public Buildings and the Governor's residence—but, as was found to be the case at SWAKOPMUND and elsewhere, the sanitary arrangements were primitive to a degree; a curious fact when the thoroughness of the Germans in most essentials is remembered.

It was not surprising to learn that enteric fever and diphtheria were familiar inflictions.

The huge masts of the wireless station were visible from a distance.

The Campaign in German South West Africa, 1914-1915

Though essential parts had been removed, and the station could not be worked, the whole concern was in perfect condition and scrupulously well kept. It was as spotless as many places in the adjacent town were the reverse.

The firm conviction that Union occupation was merely a temporary inconvenience, tinged perhaps with a reluctance to destroy so fine a fabric of their own, was no doubt a powerful incentive to the Germans to refrain from any destruction.

After the entry into the town the Union troops were formed up in front of the Rathaus, and General Botha's proclamation was read to the assembled inhabitants in English, Dutch and German.

The behaviour of the population here, as elsewhere, was quiet and orderly, and, it is fair to add, remained so throughout the campaign.

Colonel Mentz was installed as Military Governor, and the Commander-in-Chief returned to G.H.Q. at KARIBIB, there to become at once immersed in the difficulties incidental to feeding a large force destitute of many essential supplies and to begin the preparations for the final advance.

Though the occupation of WINDHOEK marked the conclusion of the main phase of the campaign with the attainment of all its original objectives, it had been clear, since the escape of the enemy forces to the north, that what would amount to a second campaign had become inevitable.

During General Botha's return journey to KARIBIB he had been met by a dispatch rider carrying a letter from the German Imperial Governor, Dr. Seitz, asking that an armistice should be arranged to allow of a meeting " to discuss terms ".

A cessation of hostilities from 12 noon on May 20 was mutually agreed to, and it was arranged that the meeting should take place at GIFTKUPPE, a kopje on the eastern side of the main road about mid-way between KARIBIB and OMARURU, on May 21.

On this date, at 11 a.m., the two principals, accompanied by small staffs, met.

The proceedings were, of course, full of interest to those present, who took the opportunity of sizing up their opponents.

The conversations covered many topics, and were conducted virtually entirely by the Governor who was vehement, and even aggressive, in his bearing.

He was a small man, but made up for his lack of inches by

The Campaign in German South West Africa, 1914-1915

occasionally impressive utterances, and once or twice threatened his auditors with the displeasure of " sixty millions of Germans ".

Here, however, it is enough to record those points in the long and sometimes aimless discussion which were of military interest. The latter were few, and Colonel Franke, the German Commander, a soldierly-looking man, hardly spoke on this occasion of meeting his opponent.

Dr. Seitz assured his listeners that " the local fighting would now become much more sanguinary ", and proposed the establishment of a neutral zone between the contending forces in which order was to be re-established and maintained and that the settlement elsewhere of the whole dispute should be awaited.

This suggestion did not appeal to the Union Commander-in-Chief who, after long discussion, due mainly to his own reluctance to wound the feelings of Dr. Seitz, stated his inability to accept it.

On General Botha's final statement that unconditional surrender was all he could accept, the conference terminated, and following an arrangement that the armistice should conclude at 12 noon on the following day, each party returned to its own lines.

The conference at GIFTKUPPE has been recorded out of its chronological order to avoid interrupting the continuity of events in connection with preparations for the final advance to which it is necessary now to return.

For the first time in the campaign one undivided command was to direct the operations of the Union forces in the field, for it should be realised that hitherto General Botha—though styled Commander-in-Chief—had only commanded his own, Northern, force, and, to some extent and for a limited period only, that of McKenzie.

Up to this point there had been no single control of the operations as a whole.

The general plan decided upon after the meeting between Generals Botha and Smuts early in May underwent considerable modification in detail when the situation had cleared up after the occupation of KARIBIB.

For instance, the Lines of Communication were confined to the actual route of supply to the Field Force, and the police work and control of the lines in the occupied portion of the country were assigned to special commanders and troops.

This was made possible by the withdrawal of the enemy to an extent which placed any point off the actual line of supply to the Field Force practically beyond striking distance.

The reorganisation was as follows:—

The country south of WINDHOEK was placed under police control by Colonel Berrangé with his (5th) regiment of South African Mounted Riflemen, and other forces in the south were reduced to the small strength required for purely local purposes.

Two infantry regiments from the Central Force under Beves, the 1st Transvaal Scottish and the Pretoria Regiment, were ordered to join the Northern Force.

The 1st, 2nd, 3rd and 5th Mounted Brigades were each reduced to 1,500 rifles (each containing 2 wings of 750 rifles).

The artillery for future operations consisted of the five Field Artillery Batteries, one 4-in. Battery, one 6-in. Howitzer Battery and one Naval 12-Pdr. Battery.

The left wing of the 3rd Mounted Brigade and 300 rifles, to come from the disbanded Eastern Force, the whole under Colonel Mentz, were allotted as the garrison of WINDHOEK.

The arrangements for the supervision of the civil population took some time, and various demands for medical attendance, protection for European women on farms, banking and school facilities and so on showed that the role of protector of enemy civilians which had been transferred to General Botha by the enemy was to be no sinecure.

So far as the native question—one of the greatest importance —was concerned, expert assistance was obtained from the Native Affairs Department in the Union.

Beyond patrol affairs, only one engagement with the enemy took place before the final advance, and this was to the east of WINDHOEK where Mentz's troops, who were constantly reconnoitring in that direction, took 157 of the enemy.

The German G.H.Q. were now ascertained to be at OTJIWARONGO.

On May 20 the distribution of the Northern Force was as follows:—

1st Mounted Brigade	KLEIN AUKAS.
2nd Mounted Brigade	OKASISE.
3rd Mounted Brigade—	
Right wing	WILHELMSTAL.
Left wing	WINDHOEK.
5th Mounted Brigade	JOHANN ALBRECHTS HOHE.
4th Infantry Brigade	KARIBIB.

The Campaign in German South West Africa, 1914-1915

3rd Infantry Brigade ⎫ On L. of C. from
(with 2/Durban Light ⎬ WALVIS
Infantry and Southern ⎨ to
Rifles) ⎭ USAKOS.

The 6th (S.A.M.R. Permanent) Brigade and the two infantry regiments with Beves from LUDERITZBUCHT were beginning to arrive at SWAKOPMUND.

OKAHANDJA was held and the units of the Mounted Brigades were distributed over a wide front for water, some detachments being pushed out 40 miles north of the railway line.

The front was thus well covered by patrols.

The Northern Force had been reduced to complete immobility after its arrival at KARIBIB and WINDHOEK, and 18 days later, on May 23, was unable to move though the local supply situation had improved.

The railway was little more serviceable than it had been a fortnight earlier.

The action of the water was proving destructive to the tubes and boilers of the engines, and the repair of the permanent way, which included the restoration of bridges and the preparation of deviations was only beginning to go slowly ahead.

From all information, including intelligence gleaned in the capital, a retirement to the far north was contemplated. Persistent rumours from different sources indicated the existence of boats and pontoons. As a matter of fact, the boats were found on trucks at OMARURU station when the place was occupied rather less than a month later. They were the lighters which had been used for shipping at SWAKOPMUND.

Franke, too, had conducted a vigorous reconnaissance in the extreme north in December and had become engaged with Portuguese troops.

Waters had been developed and a line of retirement reconnoitred from TSUMEB via NAMUTONI northward.

The reservists, the larger portion of the German forces, who were the owners of many farms, where they had been compelled to leave their wives and families, were reliably reported to be sick of the struggle. The regulars were said to be half-hearted.

A constant retreat where no action is taken to damage the pursuer quickly affects morale.

From the demeanour of the German Governor and those

The Campaign in German South West Africa, 1914-1915

with him at GIFTKUPPE it was judged that they were uneasy, and the attitude of the former gave a clear impression of bluff.

While the escape of a small and determined body of regulars through Portuguese East Africa eventually to German East Africa was a possibility, such action by the reservists seemed improbable.

The enemy, with a long retirement in view, could not afford to become engaged for any length of time with superior forces for whose mobility they had conceived an immense respect.

The Governor had asserted that the German troops were concentrated and unshaken and promised his advancing opponent " much bloodshed ". This did not impress his auditors who regarded it as bluff and designed to impose a useful caution upon them.

In all the circumstances it seemed quite likely that the enemy forces could be surrounded before leaving the country and early movement was recognised as desirable.

In view of the distance which would have to be covered—it proved to be 200 miles as the crow flies—the movement once started would have to be carried through without pause if it were to be successful.

General Botha accordingly decided that far better supply arrangements were an imperative necessity before committing his troops to such an undertaking.

Once more the whole question of what could be done hinged on the amount of transport which could be obtained.

That which was in the country, though increased, was still far short of the amount which would justify an advance, but the disbandment of the Southern Army had released a large number of wagons and animals.

These were now available for use in the north, and the date of the advance depended upon the time that it would take to transfer the fresh transport to the scene of operations, and upon the railway reaching a state when a regular and sufficient flow of supplies from the coast to the advanced base could be relied upon.

The switch from the river route to the railway, and the constant passage of troops, material and supplies had produced grave congestion on the new Lines of Communication and steps were taken to investigate and improve matters.

A close inspection showed clearly the need for detailed instructions and afforded a reminder of the trouble which had existed since the outbreak of the Rebellion as a consequence of lack of foresight in the supervision of lines of communication.

Two instances of delay will suffice. There were many others.

At one railway station the officer who should have been superintending the whole business of railway work was found at the points doing shunting duty. A truck overloaded by a unit, in spite of remonstrance by a railway construction officer who said "he had no power" was holding up all the traffic while no one could be found to order the unit to comply with instructions and lighten the load.

At SWAKOPMUND a steamer, which had carried animals and been thoroughly cleansed and altered to take large numbers of burghers from the commando back to the Union was detained because the Naval Transport officer had been forbidden from PRETORIA to allow it to proceed.

At the base were observed "natives idling, doing nothing, working slackly, without white supervision" and "a total absence of ordered activity".

At SWAKOPMUND comfortable quarters had proved an attraction to people who in the absence of constant supervision and impulse were apt to remain longer than was necessary.

The clearing out of bases was an experience by no means new. Many will remember the periodical "purges" at the coast in the Anglo-Boer War.

These difficulties at all events could be solved, and a strict and competent Base Commandant at the coast was appointed and a general clearance effected at SWAKOPMUND which was eliminated except as an ordinary station on the railway line.

Skinner—now Brigadier-General—was appointed G.O.C., Lines of Communication, in which capacity he exercised the functions usually divided between an Inspector-General and a Commander of L. of C.

Railway Staff Officers, selected from the Permanent Force, were appointed under an Inspector of Communications responsible to the G.O.C., L. of C.

The Inspector was charged with the duty of keeping his G.O.C. posted as to the situation in respect of the conveyance of troops, stores and animals.

Henceforward the Lines of Communication functioned smoothly.

So far as the Northern Force was concerned, staffs were brought down to the minimum, but the many administrative staff officers from D.H.Q. continued to flit about on nebulous missions.

Some forward movements, preparatory to the advance, were now effected (see map facing page 128).

It had been decided that the 1st Infantry Brigade reconstituted in the north under Beves (now also Brigadier-General) was to accompany the Field Force, and on May 31 the 1/Durban Light Infantry, which was to join Beves as soon as the forward general movement should begin, was ordered to ERONGO.

The hard work of the railway personnel under the energetic direction of Colonel Hoy now began to show tangible results and the transport position became daily more secure. For the first time since General Botha had landed in the country, the supply question ceased to be an apparently insoluble riddle.

On June 1 Skinner arrived at KARIBIB and assumed command of the L. of C. To the latter were allotted the 3rd and 4th Infantry Brigades together with the Capetown Highlanders (relieving the 2/Durban Light Infantry demobilised) and the Southern Rifles.

With these troops the occupation and defence of the existing lines as well as of those which would call for attention as the coming advance developed were to be secured.

Each brigade was ordered to organise 200 mounted men for its protective reconnaissance work.

The Imperial Light Horse severed its connection with the 3rd Infantry Brigade and was transferred to Lukin's (6th Mounted Brigade).

Arrangements which called for much reshuffling of units and the reduction of the Mounted Brigades went on daily without unusual incident, the enemy remaining inactive.

Regular aerial reconnaissance was carried out from May 26 when the first aeroplane to be employed with the Union Forces arrived at KARIBIB.

General Botha had by this time decided the outline of his plans for the next move. Though the general scheme held good, minor alterations in detail were, as usual, found necessary before the forces advanced.

Brits with the 1st Mounted Brigade was to trek west of the OTAVI railway line via OKAMBAHE on OUTJO, thence west of OTAVI to NAMUTONI on the ETOSHA PAN, and, having there released the prisoners of war—an intercepted wire-

The Campaign in German South West Africa, 1914-1915

less message had indicated their whereabouts—he would move east and head off the enemy retreat.

This project of a wide turning movement by the west had been in General Botha's mind from the first. It appealed to him as taking the utmost advantage of his mobility and the release of the prisoners was an object which he kept constantly before him. He had even discussed the possibility of such a venture against FRANZFONTEIN, when the prisoners were there, from SWAKOPMUND but kept the execution of the plan until the time should prove ripe for it.

The centre of the advance, directly under the Commander-in-Chief, was to be formed of the 6th Mounted Brigade (Lukin) and the 1st Infantry Brigade (Beves) and was intended to follow the main road along the railway line.

Far to the east Myburgh, with the 2nd Mounted Brigade (Alberts), and the Right Wing (Jordaan) of the 3rd Mounted Brigade was to be entrusted with the capture of GROOTFONTEIN by way of the two big roads to WATERBERG.

Between Myburgh and the centre the 5th Mounted Brigade (Manie Botha, now also Brigadier-General) would travel east of the railway via OMBURO maintaining touch with the forces on either side of him.

It was intended that Brits and Myburgh, having attained their respective first objectives, should act in concert with the Commander-in-Chief in an envelopment of the enemy force.

On June 3 General Botha visited WINDHOEK to examine the situation there and to assure himself that all the arrangements were working smoothly on the lines of his instructions.

The movement of the 6th Mounted Brigade across the desert along the railway line required careful arrangement in view of the need for conserving the water. The method adopted is worth attention. Water had to be arranged for at ARANDIS and EBONY and was all carried by rail from NONIDAS and stored at the two points. The Brigade moved in three detachments at intervals of 48 hours to USAKOS where the water question presented no difficulty.

The 1st Infantry Brigade moved by rail, effecting certain exchanges of battalions with the L. of C. en route.

The whole of the infantry transport was sent round by the old SWAKOP River route, which for the last time proved a valuable ally.

The concentration of the 1st Infantry Brigade was to be

The Campaign in German South West Africa, 1914-1915

completed at ERONGO on the railway line and the Royal Naval armoured cars were sent to it. This concentration began on June 9 and proceeded steadily for the next ten days.

There were now enough wagons to enable each force to carry with it supplies for two to three weeks.

The rations carried were restricted to mealie meal, coffee, sugar, salt, biscuit, soap, tobacco and matches. For meat and most of the horse food commanders were to rely upon the country.

The distribution of the wagons was as follows:—

1st Mounted Brigade	100
2nd Mounted Brigade	100
5th Mounted Brigade	105
6th Mounted Brigade	120
Right Wing 3rd Mounted Brigade	57
1st Infantry Brigade	50

For the first time in the campaign, transport which would allow of anything more than two days' supply accompanying the fighting formations was to hand.

The forces moved on June 18. Twelve days later, though the distance covered was twice as far as the greater of the two earlier advances, the last shot in the campaign was fired and the enemy sued for terms.

Unhampered by incessant supply difficulties, full use could be made of the mobility of the South African mounted troops directed by a master of the art of rapid movement.

Each detached force was directed to use a line of supply immediately behind its line of advance, and the main road was reserved for the main body in the centre. Until the forces should have met, after having converged in the final movement, the supply of their commands and the protection of their trains were definitely assigned as responsibilities of the detached commanders.

The waters at ERONGO, ONGUATI and KANONA were developed and increased to allow of systematic use by the units advancing to OMARURU.

The repair of the railway line south of WINDHOEK was now nearing completion and, to relieve congestion on the SWAKOPMUND-USAKOS line, the latter was indicated as the main line of supply for the Field Force and all troops west of KARIBIB; the line from the south to WINDHOEK was to be used for all other purposes as far as possible.

The Campaign in German South West Africa, 1914-1915

In the week preceding the start, General Botha, as was his invariable rule, visited all parts of the forces and supplemented their written instructions by personal discussion and explanation.

On June 11 a record march of 90 miles without water was made by Claassens' Standerton Commando from NONIDAS to USAKOS.

The commando had been recuperating at the coast after a severe turn of duty at HUSAB on very short rations.

Meanwhile information had come to hand which entailed some alteration in the general plan.

The intention of the enemy to hold KALKFELD was indicated. His dispositions here were fairly well known and if the German Commander intended to make any stand anywhere, nature had furnished him with a position at KALKFELD ideal for the purpose.

This exceptionally strong place, formed of high hills surrounding the main road which passed below through thick bush, lent itself to a protracted delaying action and the " ambush " which was foreshadowed as the enemy's design.

Though the report from " escaped " natives was probably sent to the Union lines purposely, it could not be ignored.

Accordingly Brits' departure from the main body originally contemplated as starting from OMARURU was to be deferred until the situation at KALKFELD should have been cleared up, and the 6th Mounted and 1st Infantry Brigades were combined as a command under Lukin to the same point.

An enemy body—which proved to be von Kleist—was reported in the vicinity of WATERBERG. A smaller detachment was understood to be at NAMUTONI, and intercepted wireless messages contained orders for water reconnaissances towards ONDONGA, rather more than half-way between NAMUTONI and the Portuguese border.

The first objective of the advance was the OMARURU River line, and Brits was ordered to occupy OMARURU in advance of the centre by a direct march along the main road combined with a flank movement by a strong commando west of the ERONGO mountains. To this commando was assigned the task of clearing up the left flank and OKAMBAHE before the initiation of the general advance from the river line.

Mentz from WINDHOEK was ordered to secure the right rear by constant patrolling eastwards and to the north-east in the direction of OTJISASU, OWIKERERO, OTJOSONDO.

The Campaign in German South West Africa, 1914-1915

By June 17 the concentration of the Field Force was complete, and its formations stood in the following order:—

Brits.
    1st Mounted Brigade (Lemmer) (less Hall's Commando en route OKAMBAHE) KLEIN AUKAS.

Lukin.
    { 6th Mounted Brigade USAKOS.
    { 1st Infantry Brigade ERONGO. (Beves.)

Myburgh.
    { 2nd Mounted Brigade (Alberts).
    { Right Wing 3rd Mounted Brigade (Jordaan).
    WILHELMSTAL and OKASISE.

Manie Botha.
    5th Mounted Brigade.
    JOHANN ALBRECHTS HOHE.

Preparations for the final advance were complete.

CHAPTER XI

THE FIGHTING STRENGTHS of the Union forces now about to move forward were:—

Brits:	1,500 rifles; four 13-Pdr. Q.F. guns.
Lukin:	2,200 rifles; four 13-Pdr. Q.F. guns.
Beves:	2,550 rifles; four 13-Pdr. Q.F. guns.
	four 6-in. howitzers.
	two 5-in. howitzers.
	four 4 in. howitzers.
M. Botha:	1,500 rifles; four 13-Pdr. Q.F. guns.
Myburgh:	2,350 rifles; four 13-Pdr. Q.F. guns.
	two 12-Pdr. Naval guns.

The enemy was still greatly superior in artillery, and the disparity in rifle strength was not so much in favour of the attack as figures might suggest.

The retiring German force was concentrated, moving back on well-known routes to prepared positions on familiar terrain, and the strategy of the Union Commander compelled him to separate his forces widely and over long distances.

The field force in all amounted to some 13,000 men and 20,000 animals; in regard to personnel the strength was much the same as that which had moved against KARIBIB and WINDHOEK from RIET and JAKALSWATER, though the quantity of animals was considerably greater.

On June 18 General Botha left KARIBIB and bivouacked for the night at ETIRO.

The nights were now very cold and there was heavy frost after darkness fell but the climate was wonderfully healthy. The complete absence of tents was therefore not a matter of any importance.

Orders had been issued to the detached forces to reach the OMARURU River line on their respective lines of advance by the evening of June 20.

Brits was instructed to be at ONGUATI on the evening of the 17th, at KANONA on the following evening, and in OMARURU early on the morning of June 19.

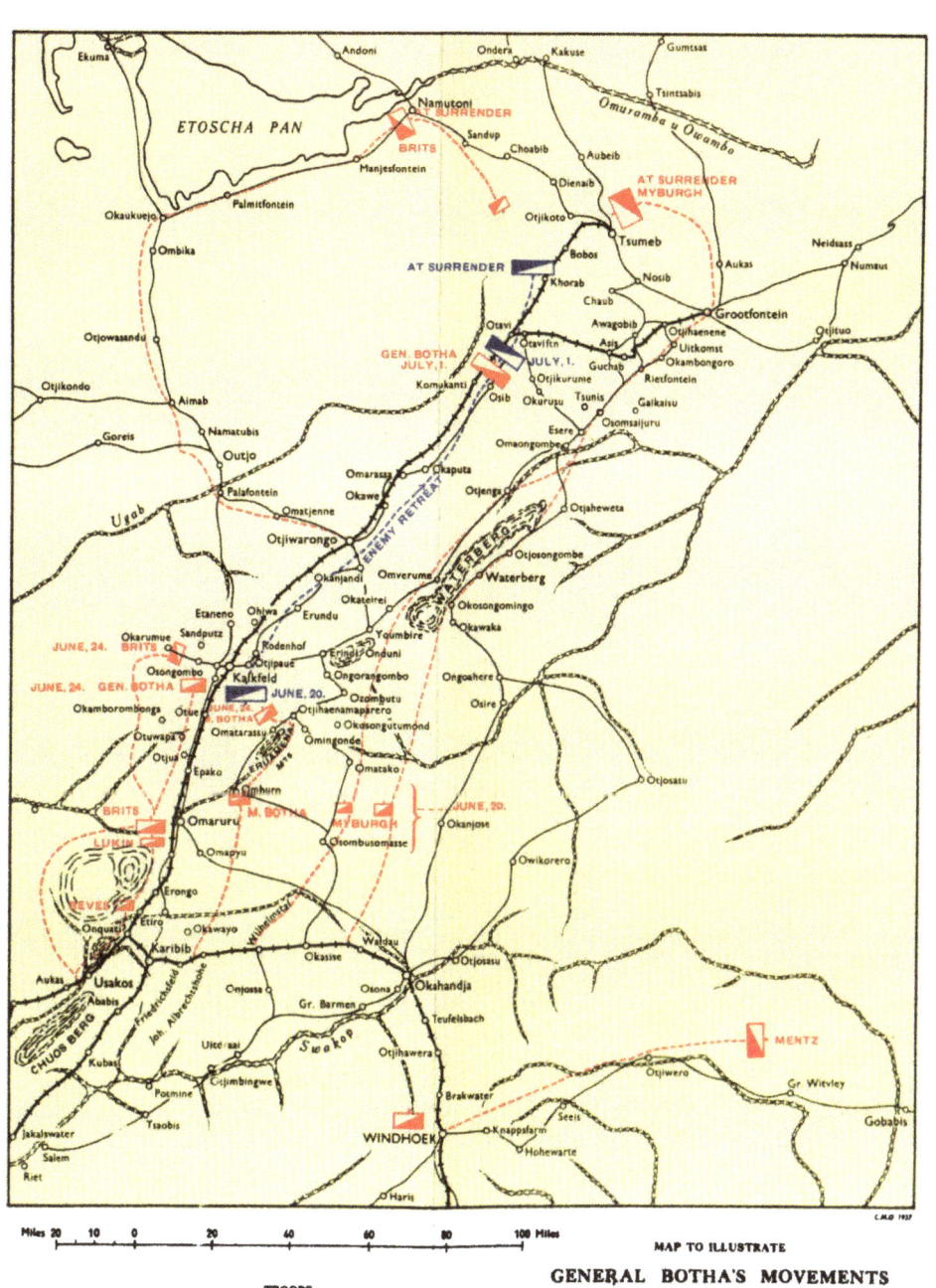

MAP TO ILLUSTRATE
GENERAL BOTHA'S MOVEMENTS
IN THE
FINAL ADVANCE

The Campaign in German South West Africa, 1914-1915

Lukin was to move from USAKOS on June 18, watering his force, suitably divided, at ONGUATI and ETIRO siding, and to reach ERONGO early on the morning of the 19th. Taking half water at ERONGO, he was to make OMARURU in the evening of the 19th, some twelve hours after Brits.

First line transport accompanied the troops; the remainder followed in order of the units' march.

Beves with his infantry—now concentrated and augmented by addition from Skinner's command to five battalions—was ordered to march to ERONGO, and, after allowing all mounted troops to pass him there, to reach OMARURU at daybreak on June 20.

This brigade was genuinely representative of Southern Africa, containing units from the Cape, Natal, Transvaal and Rhodesia.

At OMARURU Beves would place himself under the command of Lukin for the advance on KALKFELD.

On June 19 General Botha, once more following in the track of Brits, found the latter occupying OMARURU which he had entered without opposition.

A further addition to the families already on his hands was found here.

Lying on the bank of the river, which showed some considerable quantity of surface water and yielded an ample supply on digging, OMARURU is a pretty little village with pleasant gardens alongside the river-bed and well wooded. It stretched along the main road in one long street.

The usual hotels were here open and their proprietors wasted no time in furnishing meals to those who were prepared to pay for them.

During the native wars Colonel Franke had led an expedition by forced marches with much skill and determination to the relief of OMARURU, and a cairn to the south of the village commemorates the action.

Myburgh and Manie Botha reported having been engaged; each had lost one killed and sustained some casualties in wounded.

M. Botha had reached UMBURU.

Some destruction had been wrought to the bridges, and the large bridge across the river at OMARURU had been seriously damaged.

June 20 was spent in resting and adjusting the forces and arranging for the move on KALKFELD.

The Campaign in German South West Africa, 1914-1915

The remaining units of the Centre arrived on time.

The German aerodrome—a small and tricky landing place much affected by certain winds—was occupied by the Union planes, of which one sustained damage and was put out of action.

General Botha rode out to OMARURU FELSEN, a high rocky eminence to the east of the town, and spent the whole afternoon in examining the country to the north which lay open to view far and wide.

Personal reconnaissance, whenever a chance offered, was an unvarying practice of the Commander-in-Chief who used to sit for hours at a time closely watching the country before him through his glasses. He expected all round him to do the same and to be ready to give him information or answer the questions which he often put.

On the evening of June 20 the advance was resumed.

Brits, leaving at 6 p.m., was directed on OKAMBOROMBONGA, and was told at the same time to investigate conditions at the water-holes of OTUWAPA.

Beves, to whom were added 300 rifles of the 2nd S.A.M.R., was ordered to occupy EPAKO at daybreak on June 21.

At 8 o'clock in the evening the infantry started on their 200-mile march which they were to accomplish in a time which, when told to the Germand Commander and staff in answer to their inquiries at the surrender, they quite politely, but none the less firmly, declined to believe!

As these fine soldiers marched past G.H.Q. in the light of a half moon, almost noiselessly and enveloped in a dusty haze, they gave an impression of force and determination. Many of them were to fight and give their lives in Europe where the infantry of South Africa gained a magnificent reputation.

From wireless messages, already mutilated and soon, as before, to fail altogether, Jordaan of Myburgh's force was placed as at OKOSONGUTUMUND, and it was assumed that Alberts was to the south-east of him.

Pushing on the following morning by car the Commander-in-Chief found EPAKO, where the railway bridge had been destroyed, in Beves' hands, the S.A.M.R. holding some water ahead where they had taken some prisoners.

Water was found below the surface at EPAKO—the high railway bridge here spanned a dry river course—and it was at once opened up and improved.

By the evening Brits had announced his occupation of

The Campaign in German South West Africa, 1914-1915

OKAMBOROMBONGA and M. Botha's patrols had reached OMINGONDE, OKOASOMBUKWE and OMATASA.

The latter advised G.H.Q. that he proposed sending 750 rifles and two guns to OKATASA. He was ordered to cancel this movement, in view of the nearness of the enemy and the latter's power of concentration against him in superior force.

Air reconnaissance confirmed the presence of the enemy at KALKFELD, but, as was always the case in bush country, his strength could not be determined from the air.

Several minor instances of tampering with the railway behind the advance now culminated in serious damage to the bridge at OTJIHAVERA, midway between OKAHANDJA and WINDHOEK, which was blown up on the evening of June 20. OTJIHAVERA was an important point and the time had come to put an end to activity of this kind. The inexpert methods which had been adopted justified strong suspicion that civilians were taking a hand, and all enemy males near the railway line were removed into the towns, and the chief inhabitants were instructed to warn all the townspeople that serious punishment and reprisals would follow any repetition of such action.

The measures had a salutary effect and there were no more attempts at anything of the kind. General Botha's conciliatory and lenient attitude had evidently been misinterpreted.

The northward railway had been rapidly repaired and on the evening of June 21 railhead was on the south bank of the river just outside OMARURU.

Repairs to the railway and telegraph lines to the north were effected with remarkable rapidity throughout the operations, and the work spoke volumes for the efficiency of the two public departments of the Union concerned.

For June 22 the following movements were ordered:—

The 2nd S.A.M.R., moving ahead of Beves, to occupy the water at OKOSONGORO so as to enable the infantry to arrive there the same evening.

Lukin with the 6th Mounted Brigade, less the regiment in advance, to be at OTUWAPA the same evening.

Early on the morning of the 23rd Lukin was to attack the KALKFELD position under his own arrangements, subject to the one condition that the 2nd S.A.M.R. was to operate towards M. Botha on the right flank of the infantry and east of the railway.

The latter, reaching OMATASU on the evening before the

The Campaign in German South West Africa, 1914-1915

attack, would co-operate in the movement against KALKFELD early on June 23, clearing the western side of the EHUAMENA mountains en route.

The eastern side of the EHUAMENA was left to Jordaan, who was to make OZUMBUTU or ONGORANGOMBO, as Myburgh might decide, before the night of June 22-23. On the following morning he too was expected to join in the attack.

On the left Brits was ordered to reach OSONGOMBO or OKARUME—whichever might prove to be the better for his watering—on the evening of the 22nd and to conform to the general plan.

Far on the right the enemy was reported to be before Alberts at OMVERUME and OKOSONGOMINGO, and Myburgh was enjoined to direct him in two columns, one towards OKATEITEI west of the KLEIN WATERBERG and the other east of it.

Generally, the necessity for a rapid and sustained pursuit of the enemy wherever found was impressed upon all commanders.

Myburgh's means of communication, however, seemed to have failed entirely, and, co-operation being desired, movement was delayed for 24 hours.

At 8 o'clock on the evening of the 22nd General Botha was still without tidings from, or of, Myburgh, and the plan was put into operation without definite orders being known to have reached Myburgh who was aware of the general intention.

Brits was now ordered to be in the vicinity of SANDPUTS in time to move in to the attack on KALKFELD on the morning of the 24th, while Lukin received instructions preparatory to the attack to reach OKOMBOROMBONGA overnight with his mounted men and OTUE with his infantry.

Air reconnaissance had shown a few mounted men still at KALKFELD and no movement northwards by rail or road could be detected.

Runaway natives, however, late on the evening of June 22 reported an enemy retirement as in progress from the evening before.

Trains were now working through from KEETMANSHOOP to WINDHOEK, and this meant a welcome additional 200-ton daily lift from the south.

General Botha finally left OMARURU behind his advancing troops at noon on June 23 and, halting for the night at OKOSONGORO, rode on the following morning to OTUE. Leaving his horses here he pushed on by car and at 11 a.m. (24th) met

Manie Botha at KALKFELD. The latter had occupied the place at 8.30 a.m., having come in from the east ahead of the centre to find that the enemy, to avoid envelopment, had once more declined an encounter and had slipped away.

Night marches could only be carried out along the roads, and concealment of the advance was out of the question. The heavy dust and the fact that all practicable routes—and they were few—were well known and under observation had made it so far impossible to surprise the enemy.

Far wider sweeps were to be taken before the German forces were to find themselves cornered at last.

The further advance had now to be arranged, and it was clear that the infantry could no longer keep up with the mounted troops, if the pursuit was to be carried out at the pace that General Botha intended.

The 6th Mounted and 1st Infantry Brigades were therefore again separated and under their respective Brigadiers reverted to the direct control of the Commander-in-Chief.

After considerable enlargement the local aerodrome was occupied by the Union machines.

General Botha remained at KALKFELD, which was only a wayside hotel, store and railway station, throughout the day and for the night of June 24-25 and arranged the following movements.

Jordaan to press on by ERINDI ONDUNE and YOUMBIRA towards OTJIWARONGO, moving well to the east; instructions were also sent to Myburgh to clear the WATERBERG range and move rapidly on GROOTFONTEIN.

One hundred rifles, detached from M. Botha, were sent to try to get touch with Jordaan to deliver the orders. They failed, however, to reach him and it is clear, in the light of after-knowledge, that he was now rapidly forging ahead in touch with, and under the direction of, Myburgh.

The probability of losing contact with the latter had always been present to General Botha's mind and the present situation caused no uneasiness.

Myburgh was a sound and dependable leader and might be relied on to back up the chief command implicitly and to the best of his ability. How well he and Brits co-operated will be seen when the final operations are described.

The patrol from the 5th Brigade was not easily discouraged in its quest, for 8 days later—the day after the action at

OTAVIFONTEIN, it was discovered near ESERE by one of the aeroplanes, which was compelled to make a forced landing, still on trek over 100 miles from its starting point.

Brits was ordered to continue his advance to the west of the railway, and, moving by OHIWE, to reach OMATJENNE by the early morning of June 26.

M. Botha, who had arrived at OTJIPANE, was directed on OKANJANDE as was Lukin immediately behind him.

By 9.30 a.m. on June 26 General Botha had again come up with the mounted troops and found M. Botha at OKANJANDE and Lukin's leading units just short of that small village.

Two hundred and fifty political prisoners were released here and sent to the south by the first opportunity. They could give little or no information.

OKANJANDE had not enough water for animals, so the advance was pressed to OTJIWARONGO, which was occupied by a patrol from the 6th Mounted Brigade which turned an enemy party out of the village.

Abundant water was reported to be at OTJITASU, a farm a few miles west of OTJIWARONGO, and thither the 6th Mounted Brigade was at once sent.

Here was the first surface water which had been seen by the Northern Force and a large vlei contained an ample supply for the time being.

The 5th Mounted Brigade was divided between OTJIWARONGO and OKANJANDE.

The right wing of the 1st Mounted Brigade was also brought to OTJITASU, the left remaining at OMATJENNE.

A halt was called for June 27.

Information—though rather belated—now came from Myburgh which established his distribution at the time of sending his message.

He was occupying WATERBERG. The right wing of the 2nd Mounted Brigade at GROOT WATERBERG (shown on the map to the east of the mountains as WATERBERG); the left wing of the brigade at OKOSONGOMINGO; and Jordaan at OTJOSONGOMBE.

It was now apparent why patrols looking for the latter towards the railway had failed to pick him up.

All the information went to show that the German forces were retiring north 24 hours ahead of the advance.

The Campaign in German South West Africa, 1914-1915

The time had now come for Brits' enterprise against NAMUTONI and the enemy line of retreat, and General Botha gave his orders for the great march of the 1st Mounted Brigade.

Brits with this brigade—under the command of Colonel Lemmer and Colonels-Commandant (Wing Commanders) Piet de la Rey and A. P. Visser—was ordered to move at 6 p.m. on June 27 to OUTJO; thence by rapid marches to OKAKUEJO and NAMUTONI.

When he had arrived at NAMUTONI, the released South African prisoners of war were to be sent back by the route of his advance while he remained at, or near, NAMUTONI, watching the situation, reconnoitring towards TSUMEB, and, in due course, co-operating to the best advantage in the concentric advance from the east and south.

All motor transport which could be collected and every available means of communication were handed to him.

In this instance it was accepted that, at all events before the movement had gone far, all communication with G.H.Q. would cease until, if the operations went favourably, actual contact with the other forces should be regained. Before this could occur, Brits would in all probability have to cover not less than 200 miles.

By nightfall on June 27 he was well on his way.

The country was proving very difficult and broken, and, covered with bush, was quite unsuitable for motor transport off the roads. It was therefore decided to offer to return the Royal Naval Armoured Cars that they might be used to advantage in some theatre which would give them a fair opportunity for tactical action which local conditions now denied to them.

The unit had borne a useful share in the TREKKOPPIES engagement, and had a desperately trying time getting its cars over the country between SWAKOPMUND and the north. Under disappointing and discouraging conditions its personnel had shown resource, cheerfulness and ready obedience. The Ministers of the Union summed up the reputation of the detachment in the statement that " the conduct of the officers and other ratings of the squadron under all conditions and in all circumstances maintained the high traditions of the Royal Navy ".

After 24 hours' halt the movement in the centre was resumed —the discomforts of the advance had made the break, near plenty of good water, exceptionally grateful.

The 5th Mounted Brigade set out in the evening from OTJIWARONGO for OMARASSA followed two hours later by the 6th from OTJITASU.

By 10 o'clock on the morning of June 28 General Botha had overtaken the 6th Mounted Brigade at OMARASSA and later in the day found the Free Staters halted at OKAPUTA.

Air reconnaissances now reported the enemy in force at OTAVI and OTAVIFONTEIN and that trains were going northwards from OTAVI station.

After leaving OMARASSA the country was absolutely waterless as far as OTAVIFONTEIN—a distance of 40 miles—and, assuming that the enemy were found holding the water at OTAVIFONTEIN, unless he could be dislodged and the water seized and held, a retirement over the 40 miles would be inevitable.

It was impossible to think that the German Commander was not well aware of his opponent's difficulties at this stage and of the possibilities which the situation held for himself, and the importance of taking no avoidable chance was clear.

The centre was now presumably well ahead of the two flank movements in their general relation to the position of the enemy concentration, and the infantry were not as close up as they should be in view of possible eventualities connected with an encounter with the enemy at OTAVIFONTEIN.

The two mounted brigades represented no more than 3,500 rifles at full strength, considerably less than the enemy could bring into action in a prepared position with a heavy preponderance in artillery and machine-guns.

A retirement on OMARASSA unsupported was a risk which it would be highly injudicious to run, and, as will be seen later, was an event for which the German Commander hoped and was prepared.

Accordingly, the two brigades were halted at OMARASSA and OKAPUTA for two days, from midday on June 28 to the evening of June 30, with the twofold object of allowing Brits and Myburgh to make some further progress and to give time for the infantry to come nearer.

Beves was ordered to press on to OMARASSA and OKAPUTA and distribute his brigade between the two places.

Several parties of escaped prisoners of war joined the Union lines at the two last-named places.

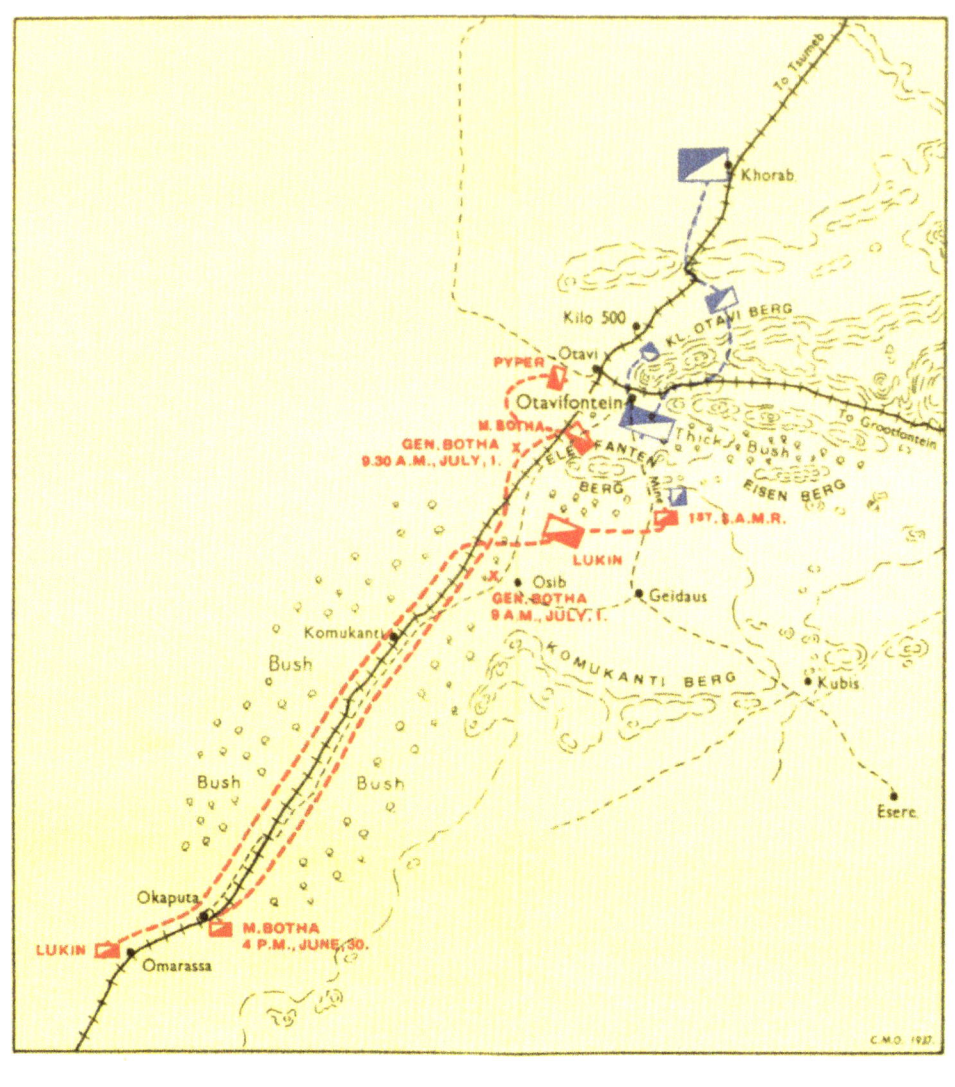

SKETCH MAP TO ILLUSTRATE MOVEMENTS
OF NIGHT JUNE 30 - JULY 1, 1915.
AND ACTION AT OTAVIFONTEIN 1 JULY 1915.

The Campaign in German South West Africa, 1914-1915

They were in rags and looked very fine drawn and had evidently had hard fare and none too much of that.

The relation of their experiences bore out the impression given by their appearance.

Neither Brits nor Myburgh was heard of during the halt and an aeroplane was sent to ESERE to try to locate the latter.

Reconnaissance and bombing raids were continued daily to the north.

The forces on the evening of June 29 were distributed as follows:—

G.H.Q. ...	OKAPUTA.
5th Mounted Brigade ...	OKAPUTA.
6th Mounted Brigade ...	OMARASSA.

Brits en route to NAMUTONI (via OKAKUEJO).

Myburgh en route to GROOTFONTEIN (via WATERBERG).

Aviation Corps ...	BRAKPAN.
1st Infantry Brigade ...	
Brigade H.Q. ...	3 miles south of
1/Durban Light Infantry ...	OTJIWARONGO.
2/Kimberley Regiment ...	
1/Transvaal Scottish ...	
Pretoria Regiment ...	6 miles south of
Heavy Artillery less 6-in. Howitzers ...	OKANSANDE.
6-in. Howitzers ...	ERUNDU.

The Rhodesian Regiment was dropped to garrison OTJIWARONGO.

On June 30 Manie Botha with his brigade moved at 4 p.m. from OKAPUTA on OTJIKURUME, north of OKURUSU on the OKURUSU–ELEFANTEN BERG road, while, half an hour later, Lukin, directed on GEIDAUS, left his bivouac at OMARASSA.

Intelligence of the enemy's intention to escape towards the north came without a contradiction, and prompt measures were now needed to bring him to action and divert his attention from Brits.

Forced marches were sustained, without any off-saddles,

throughout the night of June 30–July 1, General Botha riding with the columns which forged ahead in clouds of dust.

Daybreak found the 5th Brigade about opposite Kilo 475 on the railway, the 6th near Kilo 455 (12½ miles behind) and the Commander-in-Chief with G.H.Q. at KOMUKANTI close up behind the leading troops with the advance in full swing.

An encounter with an enemy outpost resulted in two casualties to a point of the covering troops of the 5th Brigade, and General Botha paused to learn the name and condition of a young Free Stater lying mortally wounded by the roadside.

Touch once established the pursuit was taken up and the regiments of the 5th Brigade passed rapidly out of sight.

The enemy stood for a short exchange of shots at OSIB and then continued their retirement to the western end of the ELEFANTEN BERG where M. Botha's artillery—the 2nd Permanent Battery (S.A.M.R.)—came into action and the enemy, after causing a few more casualties to the advancing troops, again turned and retired.

Into the thickly bushed country between the ELEFANTEN BERG and the OTAVI BERG pursued and pursuers now plunged.

It was about 9 a.m. when General Botha reached OSIB.

Here he found an officer and a few men from the 5th Brigade who, however, were only able to say that their main body had gone rapidly forward. The sounds of an action some miles ahead were audible.

Leaving his horse, General Botha now got into his car and followed the Free State troops.

G.H.Q. had become aware of the position of all mines laid by the enemy north as far as OTAVI and the information had proved so far absolutely correct.

The plan showed that the roads to the east and west of the ELEFANTEN BERG were heavily mined where they entered the defile at either extremity of the range.

It was over the western road that the Commander-in-Chief now followed the advance, and the knowledge that the route was one of the two chosen for mine-laying provided any element of excitement that the situation may have lacked before the defile was reached.

The eastern road contained the heaviest and most extensive mine laid by the enemy, as will be seen, but it was learned later from the officer who supervised all the mine-laying in the

The Campaign in German South West Africa, 1914-1915

campaign that the western approach, though it had been the intention to treat it similarly, had been left intact, owing either to lack of material or want of time.

Just after passing the end of the range, a motor-cyclist was met and he reported that, after an ambush, a short engagement had taken place and that he was on his way for ambulances.

Now that the scene of the fighting had been reached it was possible to size up the situation, and the danger of the enemy debouching from the eastern defile, holding off Lukin and isolating Manie Botha in the thick bush was clear and instant.

The map facing page 137 will show the position.

The cyclist was ordered to take a message to Lukin which instructed the latter at once to send a strong detachment to the eastern end of the ELEFANTEN BERG supporting it with his brigade with which he was to prevent a movement by the enemy such as that indicated above.

He was also told to send the bodyguard and a squadron of his S.A.M.R. to General Botha. Two hundred disciplined men might prove to be of the greatest value.

General Botha now went on, meeting Manie Botha a few minutes later.

It is now necessary to describe the terrain which was the scene of these events.

The map will help to form an idea of the country.

This, for many miles before reaching OTAVIFONTEIN, had presented the same features. It was slightly undulating and covered with bush which, though negotiable by mounted troops, albeit at a restricted pace, was thick enough to confine the view to the immediate vicinity.

The scene of the fighting was a stretch of ground bounded on the south by the ELEFANTEN BERG and a series of hills running due east until, meeting a high range extending from OTAVIFONTEIN to the south-east, they formed, with the latter range, an angle. Thus, on the north, east and south, this stretch of ground—about 17 miles at its broadest part from west to east and 4 or 5 miles at its greatest extent south to north—was completely shut in and commanded by high hills on three sides. The western side alone was comparatively level. Extensive observation was only possible by those who held the hills.

The enclosed space was thickly covered with bush—here considerably denser than it had been to the south—and the advantages possessed by a defending force with full power of observation and in selected positions over an attacking force restricted to a very limited view is manifest.

It was into this bushy enclosure that the 5th Brigade had pushed its advance and where it had become engaged.

The troops, engaged with and pursuing the enemy, had taken little heed of their actual progress, and Manie Botha had been compelled to abandon the caution which had hitherto marked his advance. Though the forward movement had not slackened for nearly 24 hours, all the ground had so far been cleared up by the advanced troops.

To recall his units in such circumstances was impossible, so the Brigadier of the 5th Brigade decided to push the attack with his whole force supporting his advanced parties engaged in front and directing all his efforts to securing his objective, the water.

The paramount importance of the latter, if a retirement was to be avoided, was the deciding factor in his decision.

His prompt action certainly saved the situation and proof of this was obtained from the opposite side, for the German Chief of Staff declared at the interview a few days later that, " if they (the Germans) had had only one hour's time to occupy their carefully selected positions, General Louis Botha and his two brigades would never have got back to OKAPUTA ".

If the strength of the two forces and the preponderance of four to one in field guns in favour of the enemy is borne in mind, it will be realised that there is much to be said for this opinion.

The 5th Mounted Brigade had become committed to their tactical enterprise in the manner in which commando units often entered a fight induced by the instinct of the individual to take a sudden line of action, as we have seen in a review of the actions at RIET and PFORTE, and there was no choice between trying to get out or seeing the business through.

Manie Botha's resolve—which had to be come to rapidly—to adopt the second course must be adjudged soldierly and sound.

The rapidity of the advance over the last 10 miles, however, had upset the German Commander's calculations, for his outposts came back into their positions with their pursuers on their heels, and he was thus prevented from disposing his main force as he had proposed to do, though why he had not done so long before is, in the circumstances, most difficult to understand.

Of several lost opportunities surely this was by far the most striking.

The Campaign in German South West Africa, 1914-1915

Only one of the two Union brigades had become seriously engaged. Lukin had been designedly kept just behind and in support of M. Botha, ready for rapid movement and such action as the course of events should suggest.

The situation at OTAVIFONTEIN having become more or less clear, the whole of Lukin's brigade was directed on OTAVI station except the 1st S.A.M.R. (the old Cape Mounted Riflemen) which had been sent to the eastern end of the ELEFANTEN BERG and continued its march on OTAVI by that route.

Previous warning had been given to its commander of the supposed existence of mines in the defile, and the regiment was enabled to avoid the danger by cutting the wires and took the enemy detachment at the spot prisoners.

There was no doubt as to the value of the information here for the road had been heavily and most elaborately mined for 150 yards in its whole breadth and subsidiary mines had been so placed as to divert troops from the veld into the main road. These mines were exploded by the Union engineers two days later, and the warning, which it was possible to give, saved the 1st S.A.M.R. very severe casualties.

A movement by a regiment of the 5th Brigade under Lieut.-Colonel Pijper by the left had accelerated the retreat of a portion of the enemy force with some casualties round the western end of KLEIN OTAVI BERG, but the German main body effected its withdrawal by way of the gap south of that mountain through which the railway ran to GROOTFONTEIN.

From the south the KLEIN OTAVI BERG and the hills running to OKOMBAHJINENE appear to be an unbroken range, and the omission to think of a gap for the railway was, in the hurried sequence of events, natural, and in any case, the pursuit of a force so superior in strength was not to be undertaken lightly.

The retirement of the enemy was therefore effected without further molestation.

In the running fight from OSIB to the water at OTAVIFONTEIN prisoners were taken from the 1st, 2nd and 5th regular companies and the 2nd, 3th and 4th reserve companies.

The force disposable by the enemy at OTAVIFONTEIN was 3,372 rifles with 36 guns and 22 machine-guns against some 1,200 rifles of the 5th and 2,000 of the 6th Mounted Brigades with 8 guns between them.

In his selected positions the German Commander was equal

to the attack in rifles and far better found in field and machine-guns on a terrain where the latter were ideal weapons.

The action had cost the Union troops only 4 killed and 7 wounded, all in the Free State Brigade.

The two brigades were now collected and disposed round OTAVI and OTAVIFONTEIN.

Running water, the first seen by the Northern Force since leaving their own country, passed through the enclosure in which the German barracks—where General Botha established his headquarters—were situated, and the appearance of the vegetation, a pleasant relief to eyes wearied by sand, stone and incessant glare, gave indication of approach to tropical conditions.

CHAPTER XII

NO NEWS HAD come from Brits or Myburgh and the situation called for some caution.

The enemy had been jockeyed out of a very strong position which he had clearly to his interest to retain for the water.

The German Commander was, as has been shown, stronger than the South African force immediately facing him, and he was intimately acquainted with every feature of the country over which any engagement would be fought, a knowledge which his opponent did not possess.

In these circumstances, apart from the exhausted condition of men and animals, an attack by the centre Union force was out of the question.

The enemy had once more shown a singular want of energy and enterprise, but this very fact suggested the unsoundness of too ready an assumption that this attitude of inactivity would not be abandoned, as it might be with advantage at any suitable moment.

Some liberty had been taken from time to time in consequence of the German Commander's lack of venturesomeness, but the present was essentially an occasion for watchfulness against an attack which would gain enhanced effect from being perhaps unlooked for.

The loss of the water would entail a long and dangerous retirement, for the infantry were not up yet.

An order by Colonel Franke too had been picked up on the field at OTAVIFONTEIN which indicated a resolve to put the situation to a test. The following was its purport. It is given in full as it makes it quite clear that, apart from the immediate position, the enemy had no intention of seeking any kind of decision in the south at any time:—

"The time to retire and avoid the enemy is now past. We have arrived at a stage where we must and will fight. Up to the present it was a question of saving and preserving the forces and material at my disposal in order to be as strong as possible for the decisive fight. We have been able to do that.

The Protectorate troops are assembled. By our retirement we have deprived our opponent of the chance of destroying our troops which were necessarily distributed over a colossal front detachment by detachment.

Considering his tremendous superiority he would have been able to do so.

For the benefit of those of little faith let us state once again that it would have been a mad enterprise to defend the greater part of this country permanently against this opponent of tenfold superiority who has all modern means of waging war at his disposal.

At the latest the small Protectorate troops would have bled to death in a fight near WINDHUK.

We can consider it an achievement that we have held the strong opposing forces and caused the enemy enormous expenditure.

Now everything depends upon it that we preserve ourselves till the conclusion of peace in Europe and for this require the greatest exertion and self-sacrifice of everyone.

Every personal interest must be pushed into the background; no other wish is to inspire us than unconditionally to remain the victors, confident in the strength of our position, in the firm resolve of the here gathered German men who to their last drop of blood will defend their homeland, and, lastly, with our faith in God who will grant the victory to our righteous cause."

This seemed to indicate an intention at last to submit to the test of a serious action. If such was the purpose of the enemy, now, if ever, was his opportunity.

If General Botha sustained a reverse, his opponent could deal with the forces on his flank one by one.

The Commander-in-Chief therefore for the present held his hand, and during July 2, the day after the action, the two mounted brigades remained in their positions at OTAVI and OTAVIFONTEIN.

Reconnaissances to clear up the country and search for prisoners were sent to ASIS and the north-west.

Air reconnaissance established the presence of the enemy in force at KHORAB, though some evidence of a contemplated retirement to TSUMEB was not wanting.

The aeroplane sent to pick up Myburgh's force had returned after a forced landing without news except of the patrol from the 5th Mounted Brigade still looking for Jordaan.

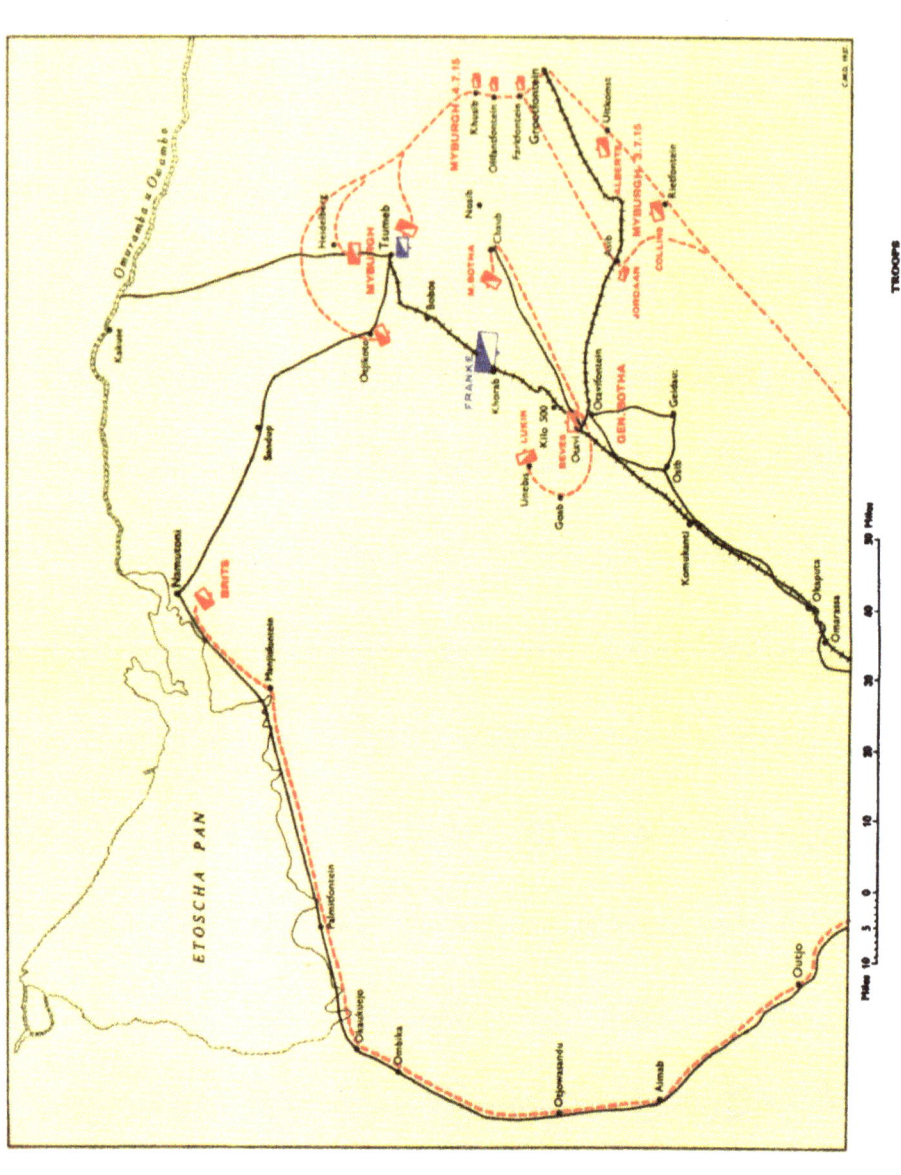

SKETCH MAP ILLUSTRATING
FINAL MOVEMENTS LEADING TO SURRENDER

The Campaign in German South West Africa, 1914-1915

A small party under Captain Louis Esselen was therefore sent out in motor-cars to endeavour to obtain touch.

While it was realized that contact with, or news from, Brits was highly improbable at this juncture, it seemed that Myburgh might very likely be within reach.

It was now decided that an advance on TSUMEB would have to be carried out by the centre force and orders were sent to Beves to press on with the infantry.

The Field Force now undertook the protection and control of the Lines of Communication as far back as OTJIWARONGO.

It seemed unlikely that the campaign could be much prolonged and it was desired to save the waste of a long march by L. of C. troops from the south.

The railway had been repaired and was working to KALKFELD where a large supply depot was formed.

Assuming that Brits' movement had developed to plan—as in fact it had—it appeared likely that a hard fought action at KHORAB was imminent.

The latter was another instance of an exceedingly strong position and was shown on the plan as heavily mined on all lines of approach.

Late on the afternoon of July 3, Esselen returned having reached Myburgh who sent the following information of his position.

He himself with Collins' left wing of the 2nd Mounted Brigade was at RIETFONTEIN; Alberts with the other wing of his brigade (Badenhorst) at UITKOMST. Jordaan was at ASIS.

At this time the known positions of the forces were as follows:—

General Botha.
G.H.Q.
5th Mounted Brigade (M. Botha)   OTAVI and
6th Mounted Brigade (Lukin) ......   OTAVIFONTEIN.

Myburgh.
Left Wing 2nd Mounted Brigade
   (Collins)   ....   RIETFONTEIN.
Alberts with Right 2nd Mounted
   Brigade (Badenhorst) ....   UITKOMST.
Jordaan Right Wing 3rd Mounted
   Brigade ....   ASIS.

The Campaign in German South West Africa, 1914-1915

Beves with

1/Durban Light Infantry	OKAPUTA.
1/Transvaal Scottish ⎫	
Pretoria Regiment ⎬	OMARASSA.
2/Kimberley Regiment ⎭	

Brits was placed as at NAMUTONI.

General Beves undertook to be at OTAVIFONTEIN with the Heavy Artillery and his four battalions on the morning of July 6.

At sundown on July 3 a parlementaire arrived at OTAVI station from Dr. Seitz, the Imperial Governor, bearing a letter suggesting the termination of hostilities on the basis of the internment of the German force, with all its arms and war material, till the end of the war.

The Governor laid stress upon the fact that reconnaissance would have made the Union Commander aware that the German troops were concentrated in a position of unusual strength, and invited attention to the accounts from Europe which indicated the strong position of Germany.

To this proposal an answer of refusal was returned and the preparations for the advance went on.

The desire of the enemy to treat and his continued presence in the KHORAB position foreshadowed the end, and it was not expected that the refusal which had been conveyed to KHORAB would terminate negotiations.

Orders were sent early on July 4 to Myburgh to move, after securing GROOTFONTEIN, so as to arrive at KHUSIB, OLIFANTFONTEIN and FARKFONTEIN on the morning of the following day where he would await orders in connection with a general advance.

As a matter of fact GROOTFONTEIN had already been taken over single-handed by a signalling officer—Captain Poole—who throughout the campaign had been well ahead of the advance to the great advantage of the communication arrangements.

On July 5 Captain Esselen was sent again to instruct Myburgh to move against TSUMEB, approaching it from the north and with his forces so disposed as to intercept any movement of the enemy by OTJIKOTO and HEIDELBERG.

Brits, from whom no news had come, was isolated and out of touch, but in view of his great mobility and the ease with which he could avoid becoming seriously engaged was left unsupported.

Air reconnaissances were continued over the enemy position and the presence of the German main body was constantly verified.

In the afternoon of July 4 another parlementaire arrived and Dr. Seitz asked for a formulation of terms by General Botha upon which a cessation of hostilities might be arranged.

The reply to this brought a further communication in which an interview was definitely asked for, and a meeting was arranged for the following day at kilo 500 on the railway.

A local armistice between the enemy at KHORAB and the Union forces at OTAVI was agreed upon, special care being taken to exclude Brits and Myburgh from its operation.

The scope of the armistice was definitely and purposely restricted so as not to interfere with Myburgh's movements and to avoid embarrassing Brits, the circumstances of whose position were quite unknown at G.H.Q.

That there might be no mistake about this condition, General Botha sent his Chief of Staff to explain it verbally to the German General Staff Officer in confirmation of his written letter.

Beves was now nearing OTAVIFONTEIN; the 1/Durban Light Infantry and 1/Transvaal Scottish were close up and the Pretoria Regiment and 2/Kimberley Regiment were halted two miles behind them.

On the morning of July 6 the 1st Infantry Brigade, with the Heavy Artillery, marched into OTAVIFONTEIN in fulfilment of their Brigadier's undertaking.

Anxiety as to the local situation was now at an end, and General Botha left for kilo 500 confident in his power to deal with the enemy at once should the conference prove abortive.

Once more Esselen was sent to Myburgh with full information as to the situation.

General Botha had communicated tentative terms as a basis of discussion to Dr. Seitz making it, however, quite clear that nothing could be regarded as final without the sanction of the Union Government, to which all proposals would have to be referred.

General Botha laid stress upon his desire to terminate hostilities on any terms which might prove acceptable to his Government and drew attention to the fact that the German forces were composed of two main classes—regular soldiers and reservists.

Holding the opinion that it was to the interest of all concerned that the territory should revert to a condition when business and farming work might be resumed, he was prepared to recommend to the Union Government that the reservists should be allowed to resume their civil occupations and continue them, provided their behaviour was orderly and in agreement with such conditions as the Union Government might see fit to impose for the proper government of the country.

The regular troops " must accept the fortune of war and remain as prisoners of war ".

The Governor on meeting General Botha, while recognising that the suggested terms for the reservists were " arrived at from a humane and economic point of view ", urged the claims of the regular soldiers to treatment which should not " infringe on their honour " and once more, as at GIFTKUPPE, resisted the idea of unconditional surrender.

His Excellency, however, bore traces of anxiety and worry on his face, and no longer exhibited the pungency of comment and self-confident air which had been observable on the first occasion of meeting.

It was clear that the enemy was quite incapable of continuing the struggle and that whatever terms were imposed would have to be accepted in the end, even if that end were delayed for a final test of arms.

The helplessness of an adversary was a sure passport to General Botha's sympathy and he endeavoured, while making the position absolutely secure, to mitigate the soreness of defeat.

" We are in a position where we can afford to be generous " he telegraphed to his Government.

He undertook to recommend that the regular troops should retain their rifles, but in reply to a suggestion that the regular artillery should keep their guns—the reserve batteries the German Commander at once agreed to hand over—as the equivalent of the rifles of the mounted troops, said he saw much difficulty in agreeing to this.

The regular troops were to be interned at some place selected by General Botha till the end of the war.

The conference came to an end after provisional terms had been drawn up for submission to the Union Cabinet.

These terms, though going some way towards satisfying the

The Campaign in German South West Africa, 1914-1915

amour propre of the enemy, could, in the opinion of General Botha, be accepted with absolute safety. At this stage he conceived it to be his duty to place any suggestion which was not unreasonable before the Government, and the first proposals—which he realised would have to undergo modification—were duly communicated to the Union.

An interesting feature of this first discussion was that the Union Commander-in-Chief went to it in ignorance of what had happened to Brits and not knowing how nearly the task of attacking TSUMEB which had been given to Myburgh had approached completion.

Information on both these points was obtained by guarded questions in the course of conversation, and this process of gaining intelligence from the enemy gave some added zest to a situation already full of interest.

After arranging for the general application of the armistice and a total suspension of hostilities from noon on this date, July 6, General Botha returned to his headquarters to await the decision of his colleagues in the Union.

He came back from kilo 500 wiser by the knowledge that Brits had seized NAMUTONI and released the prisoners there and that TSUMEB was in the hands of Myburgh who had also released the South African prisoners at that place, armed them, and had handed over to their charge their late custodians, the garrison of TSUMEB.

He had previously engaged and defeated von Kleist at GHAUB.

He had, of course, been in touch with the latter all through his advance which was known to the enemy, but Brits' sudden appearance at NAMUTONI across the prepared German line of retreat explained the abandonment of any idea of " the decisive fight " and the resort to parleying.

Accustomed though they had become to General Botha's flanking movements, it was obvious at the conference that Brits' march had made a deep impression on the German officers.

Myburgh's occupation of TSUMEB was challenged by Colonel Franke as a breach of the conditions of the first armistice arranged on July 5. As, however, the written agreement was on record and clearly established the limited application of the armistice, which left Brits and Myburgh beyond its scope, and a careful verbal arrangement between the two Chiefs of Staff had removed all possibility of misconception, the protest was unavailing.

Incidentally, the action of the local German Commander at TSUMEB, who, during a lull in the fighting opened fire on a group surrounding his own parlementaire and wounded a Union soldier, placed the argument of the German Commander-in-Chief still further out of court.

At the succeeding conference on July 9 Colonel Franke acknowledged the correctness of General Botha's attitude in insisting on retaining possession of TSUMEB and expressed his " deep regret " at the incident described above.

An officer was now sent by rail through the enemy lines to acquaint Myburgh and Brits with the situation and the terms of the general armistice.

All telephonic and rail communication with the Union troops to the north was henceforward through the German position at KHORAB and Zulu was the medium adopted once or twice for important conversations.

The reference to, and exchanges with, the Union resulted in the evolution of terms which, based on the proposals submitted on the 6th, had undergone some alteration when they reached General Botha in their final form at 3 a.m. on July 8.

The terms were dispatched to the enemy lines on the same day with a request for acceptance by 5 p.m., extended at the request of the Imperial Governor by two hours.

At 7 p.m. the latter sent a reply saying the letter was not clear but that Dr. Seitz would meet General Botha to discuss it.

To this General Botha replied that no ambiguity could be discovered in the proposals and that, failing an acceptance by 2 a.m. on July 9, hostilities would recommence.

On the evening of July 8 the distribution of the Field Force was as follows:—

G.H.Q.   ⎫
M. Botha   ⎬ OTAVIFONTEIN.
Lukin   ⎪
Beves   ⎭

Brits   NAMUTONI.
Myburgh   TSUMEB.
Alberts   ASIS.
Fouche   (from M. Botha)
    moving from   ASIS to OTAVIFONTEIN.

The Campaign in German South West Africa, 1914-1915

The enemy concentrated at KHORAB held the hills south of that place between kilos 510 and 520.

The Union forces, warned to be ready to move at once, remained at their positions from 9 p.m. disposed for the following movements:—

> Lukin to GOAB and UNEBIS, thence on KHORAB.
> M. Botha on the OTAVIFONTEIN–GAUB road, thence from the east on KHORAB.
> Beves by the road along the railway on KHORAB from the south.

The arrival of a letter from Dr. Seitz at 2.30 a.m. on July 9 accepting the terms of the Union Government made the advance, timed to begin half an hour later, unnecessary, and the troops dispersed to their bivouacs.

A meeting for the formal conclusion of the surrender was arranged for 10 a.m., and at the appointed hour General Botha and Dr. Seitz met for the last time.

The former was accompanied by five officers, while with Dr. Seitz were Colonel Franke, commanding the Protectorate Troops, Lieut.-Colonel Bethe, commanding the Protectorate Police (who spoke English fluently), and four or five junior officers.

The Governor seemed to take defeat far more to heart than did any of the military officers who surrounded him. He was a very different person from the alert, brusque individual who had talked at length at GIFTKUPPE, and now concerned himself mainly with indicating some directions in which more exact definition appeared, to his mind, to be necessary. They were very insignificant points and the military commander was understood, in an audible aside, to express annoyance at trifling about " bricks and mortar ".

Colonel Franke endeavoured to maintain that the tentative proposals of the 6th, which General Botha undertook to recommend, had been regarded by himself as final, and for some reason held that the use of the German telephone by General Botha to communicate with TSUMEB had some vaguely confirmatory effect upon the suggestions.

To the last point General Botha drily replied that he very much appreciated the use of the telephone, and all the more as it enabled him to " keep quiet commandos which would otherwise have been on the move all the time ".

No real or valid objection, however, was raised and the

The Campaign in German South West Africa, 1914-1915

conference soon became occupied in arriving at the final form of the terms of surrender; General Botha stating his readiness to change the form of the conditions in a way acceptable to the other side, so long as principles were not interfered with.

When the document had assumed a mutually acceptable tone it was signed by General Botha, Dr. Seitz and Colonel Franke and the conference broke up.

A German version of the terms of surrender was also signed with the stipulation that, in the event of any interpretation of meaning becoming necessary, the English version alone should be employed.

Thus terminated the campaign of the Union forces in German South West Africa.

The casualties to the Union forces of all ranks had been as follows:—

Killed in action 88
Died of wounds 25
Died of disease and accident 153
Wounded 263

Four thousand seven hundred and forty prisoners of all ranks of the German forces were captured and surrendered in the final operations; 37 field-guns, 22 machine-guns and a large quantity of ammunition and warlike stores also fell into the hands of the Union forces at KHORAB and TSUMEB.

Loyally responsive to the brilliant leading of their Chief, all ranks of the South African troops, English- and Afrikaans-speaking, mounted and foot, had supported his operations with the greatest physical effort of which they were capable.

The campaign had been, above all, one of rapid movement. The enemy was deeply impressed by the constant reaching out of the tentacles which finally caught them, and those who were present must remember well the vivid description by the German Chief of Staff of the effect produced by the widely directed movements on either flank of the main advance, especially that of Brits.

Some facts about the marches will be of interest.

When the campaign ended the 1st Mounted Brigade had moved 460 miles from its base; the 2nd Mounted Brigade 480; the Right Wing of the 3rd Mounted Brigade (with Myburgh) 480; the 5th Mounted Brigade 420; the 6th Mounted Brigade 350; and the 1st Infantry Brigade 330.

The Campaign in German South West Africa, 1914-1915

On the last advance the 1st Mounted Brigade covered 340 miles from AUKAS to NAMUTONI in 20 days, an average over the entire period—there were of course several days' halts—of 17 miles a day; the 2nd Mounted Brigade went from WILHELMSTAL to TSUMEB, 280 miles, in 20 days, averaging 14 miles a day; the 5th and 6th Mounted Brigades from KARIBIB to OTAVI, 230 miles in 13 days, an average of 17·7 miles a day.

The 1st Infantry Brigade performed a magnificent feat of marching, covering the same distance as the two last-mentioned mounted brigades, 230 miles, in 16 days with an average daily march of 14 miles, arriving at OTAVIFONTEIN only four days behind their mounted comrades.

Colonel Franke and his officers found it impossible to believe that this performance had been achieved without considerable assistance from the railway, whereas every yard of the distance had been covered on foot.

In the early operations up to KARIBIB food, as has been stated, was extremely scarce. Though rations were none too plentiful on the last advance, they were known to be on the way behind the troops, and the healthy climate and dry weather were very helpful factors.

There was some fine marching too in the south. McKenzie's rapid movements which culminated in his successful action at GIBEON have been described, and the Southern Force also had fine records.

The central column of the Southern Force covered the 100 miles from KARUS to WARMBAKKIES in 10 days, and Colonel Dirk van Deventer's column went from NEU KHAIS to KABUS, 120 miles, in 6 days.

In estimating these performances it should be remembered that in every case the advance was through the most difficult country which made careful reconnaissance imperative.

To the fine work of his soldiers General Botha paid tribute in the following words of his final order:—

> " Peace having been arranged in German South West Africa, all ranks in the Union forces in that territory are reminded that self-restraint, courtesy and consideration for the feelings of others on the part of the troops whose good fortune it is to be the victors are essential.
>
> The General Officer Commanding-in-Chief relies confidently on the support of the troops who have assisted him

so loyally in the campaign to maintain the good reputation which the Union forces in the field have won."

After arranging that General Lukin, with the S.A.M.R. Brigade, should superintend all details of the actual surrender, General Botha bade farewell to his troops on different parades and left OTAVIFONTEIN for the coast on July 13 in the evening and reached OMARURU late on the following day.

KARIBIB was reached at midday on July 15 and General Botha, after a visit to WINDHOEK, sailed in the hospital ship " EBANI " for CAPETOWN.

In rather less than six months from the date of his departure from the Union, he had in the face of difficulties, which can perhaps only be realised by those who faced them on the spot, compelled the surrender of an enemy force and acquired possession of a territory of 322,000 square miles, rather more than half as large again as the German Empire in Europe in 1914.

CHAPTER XIII

THE LESSONS OF a campaign may be divided broadly into those which indicate faults which should in future be avoided, and those which afford a basis for constructive improvement.

In this chapter it is proposed to deal with the former and to examine the mistakes which came to light in 1914-15 in the prosecution of the campaign which has been described in the foregoing pages.

The reader is asked to bear three points in mind.

First. It is the system or lack of it, which is blamed, and, in no case, any individual, for, whatever else may have been lacking in the forces, at Headquarters or in the field, it was certainly not zeal nor a desire on the part of all concerned to do the best of which they were capable.

Second. As has been explained in the preface, elementary as the mistakes may have been, they *did* occur, and will recur in similar circumstances, unless recorded and borne in mind. Their effect was often disproportionate to their actual magnitude.

Such record is the work of the General Staff which is responsible for the collection of data which go to compose it, and for the teaching for which it furnishes the material.

There was no such General Staff in the Union Defence Forces in 1914, just as there was no such staff in the British Army before the Anglo-Boer War of 1899-1902, to the grave detriment of that army.

Third. The Union Defence Forces had only come into existence as a combined national force in 1912, less than two years before it was called upon to face an emergency which had been neither considered, nor of course provided for, by Defence Headquarters.

In all the circumstances the reaction of the forces to this severe test presents features—especially as regards the fighting troops—full of encouragement for the future. If, however, their experiences are to be—as they should be—of use to their successors, the attitude of us who examine those experiences should be not " how well we did! " but " how much better we should have done, and, incidentally, how much might have been

The Campaign in German South West Africa, 1914-1915

saved in the way of sacrifice and energy in 1914, had we known what we know now!"

Strategy has been defined as "the art of bringing the enemy to battle" and, it might be added, "in circumstances best calculated to ensure his defeat", while tactics are described as "the methods by which a commander seeks to overwhelm his opponent when battle is joined".

The campaign in German South West Africa in 1914 was essentially strategic, one of wide and rapid movements planned to bring the enemy to battle in circumstances favourable to his defeat or capture.

The engagements which took place have been described and such comments on tactical points as have seemed apposite have been made.

We will, therefore, proceed to a consideration of the campaign as a whole.

General Botha's strategy in the north will be dealt with in the next and final chapter.

The system obtaining at Defence Headquarters in 1914 has already been described in Chapter II, and here it is enough to repeat that such co-ordination as was effected at that centre was attempted by the Civil Head of the Department and there was no trained soldier in the capacity of a Chief of the Staff.

There is no need to labour this point, the unsoundness of the arrangement was recognised later, and it may be assumed that such an experiment will not be repeated. It, however, held good for some time after the campaign which is dealt with here.

Though means and methods of waging war change constantly and rapidly, certain basic principles which affect its conduct will remain while war may continue to be a method of settling disputes.

Most of these principles are to be found in the military maxims of Napoleon, of which the following is one:—
> "Nothing in war is so important as an undivided command."

History affords abundant examples of the truth of this statement and yet it was not until the end of March, 1918, that its implication was accepted on the Western Front in Europe.

General Botha, though styled Commander-in-Chief, only exercised command over his own (Northern) Force and a limited and temporary direction of McKenzie's (Central Force) movements.

The Campaign in German South West Africa, 1914-1915

If to some extent the intimacy of Generals Botha and Smuts and intercourse between them gave each of them an idea of the views of the other, this meant no close combination of effort, and the dual command was a cause of dissipation of resources and strength.

Defence Headquarters, where such co-ordination as was ever attempted was effected, was in no position to give orders on its own responsibility while the two generals were in the field.

Only at D.H.Q., where all information was collected and all supply of men and material arranged, could a continuous general survey of the operation as a whole be carried out.

To consider the actual strategy.

The first plan evolved by the meeting of senior officers which has been described in detail (in Chapter III) arranged for an advance into enemy territory by three widely separated forces —each far inferior to the strength which the enemy could rapidly concentrate. (See Plan A opposite.)

The country was of a nature which would enable the German Commander to hold off with much smaller strength any two of the three forces while he brought far superior strength to deal with the third.

An indication of what this meant is afforded by the affair at SANDFONTEIN.

Under the most favourable circumstances the three forces, moving without one command co-ordinating their advance and timing their movements, would have faced a most difficult task, but the conditions were far from favourable.

An advance from LUDERITZBUCHT would have entailed most unjustifiable risk, while Maritz's defection became early apparent as a highly probable event.

In these circumstances a decision to advance must be regarded as quite unsound.

As a preliminary defensive disposition to watch the enemy, the arrangement of " A ", " B " and " C " forces was good, but it should never have been regarded as anything but *strictly* defensive.

The decision to send a force to WALVIS to threaten the decisive point at WINDHOEK was in agreement with the soundest strategic principles. The effect of the capture of WINDHOEK has already been fully discussed, and the threat to the capital, as has been seen, compelled the enemy immediately

The Campaign in German South West Africa, 1914-1915

to concentrate in the north, and leave small detachments only in observation in the south.

A second instance of faulty strategy was the decision to concentrate strong Union forces in the south against enemy detachments amounting in the aggregate to some 700 rifles. (See plan B facing page 160.)

The direct effect of this was to prolong the decisive operations in the north and cause unnecessary delay and expenditure.

The following is a record of the actual movement of General Botha's Northern Force.

The force was in the field for 133 days, and of these only 24 were occupied in the movements which took it from the coast to WINDHOEK and thence 200 miles north to TSUMEB where the enemy surrendered.

The details of these movements are as follows:—

The advance which resulted in the occupation of RIET and JAKALSWATER was carried out in ...... 3 days.

The second and successful attempt to reach WINDHOEK occupied ...... 8 days.

OTAVIFONTEIN was reached from the KARIBIB line in ...... 13 days.

The sole reason for the failure to reach WINDHOEK at the first attempt was lack of transport. Had it been successful, the campaign would have been shortened by 40 days and the six weeks' wait at KARIBIB would have been sensibly curtailed.

The transport was not, however, forthcoming, for the large concentration in the south needed it.

In addition to the Central Force, a portion of which was of course required for the occupation of LUDERITZBUCHT, the combined strength of the Southern and Eastern Forces amounted to 11,662 (O.H., p. 60).

Only if such a strength was absolutely essential can justification be found for the omission to concentrate every means of ensuring a quick decision in the north.

If the circumstances be carefully considered no such justification can be found.

The enemy gave not the slightest indication of intending to

The Campaign in German South West Africa, 1914-1915

adopt the suicidal plan of invading the Union. If his circumstances are taken into account, at any time such an effort would have been extremely ill-advised, and after the failure of the Rebellion altogether out of question. Such an intention can alone have justified the retention of large Union forces in the south after a force had landed at WALVIS.

The strategy which contemplated an advance by some 3,000 troops into the country of the enemy in September, 1914, when the German Commander possessed his full capacity for concentration, and decided six months later on the concentration of nearly 12,000 to deal with less than 1,000 of the enemy when the latter had lost all his railways in the theatre of actual operations, was at least inconsistent. Both the decisions must be regarded as unsound.

The dispositions which have been criticised aided the enemy strategy.

To quote Napoleon again:—

"It is an approved maxim in war, never to do what the enemy wishes you to do for this reason alone, that he desires it."

In the order quoted on page 144 Colonel Franke considered it an "achievement" to have "held the strong opposing forces and caused the enemy enormous expenditure". The period of his resistance was not due to any tactical resistance on his own part, for he consistently declined any engagement after the affair at RIET and PFORTE, but to the employment of large Union forces remote from the decisive point and the consequent serious shortage of transport at that point. The very heavy additional expenditure, and it was very large if not perhaps "enormous", followed as a matter of course, and the Union strategy in this respect aided the German Commander to a very great extent.

Three important conclusions may be drawn from an examination of this strategy.

1. Undivided command is an essential condition of a full measure of success in war, and the introduction of any element, political, personal or of any other nature, tending to prevent this single command is bound to affect the conduct of military operations adversely.

2. There must be competent military advice available to a

Government at the centre where operations are to be ordered and co-ordinated.

The Union was not alone in experiencing the ill-effect of insufficient staff at the centre of activity in 1914.

It is recorded that at the beginning of the Great War there was a general exodus from the British War Office of staff officers who had worked upon and were familiar with all the plans for the employment of the British Expeditionary Force. They accompanied the formations to the front, and we read in 1920 in an obviously officially inspired article:—

"The first and perhaps the greatest mistake was the weakening of the Central Body at the beginning of the war.

The staff at the War Office to which the Empire looked at that critical time for direction was dangerously weakened, not only by the sudden withdrawal of most of its best officers, but also by being filled up with others of inferior quality brought in from by-ways and hedges to fill their place."

It would seem necessary that in the event of war a competent military officer shall be available at D.H.Q. as an adviser to the Government and to co-ordinate all military staff work there. Perhaps a Deputy Chief of Staff might fill this appointment.

Generally, great expansions of the forces will prove necessary in time of war and if occupants of *all* staff appointments are selected and allotted in time of peace an enormous advance on the condition of affairs in 1914 will have been made.

3. Preparation of plans, at leisure in time of peace, for war is of the utmost importance.

It is impossible to think that if plans for the probable employment of the forces of the Union had been worked out before 1914 many of the mistakes (certainly those of a strategic nature) would have been made.

The alternative to plans carefully considered and arranged beforehand to meet an emergency, is hurried measures in which a compromise between different views usually features largely. There is little doubt that some such compromise vitiated the decision of the meeting of senior officers at PRETORIA in August, 1914, arrived at " after prolonged discussion ".

Neither the composition, training nor employment of military

STRATEGICAL POSITIONS

26 SEPTEMBER 1914

Union Forces .... | German Forces ....
Lukin .... A | Relative strength .... D
Maritz .... B | of Potential Enemy
Beves .... C | Concentration against ... A. B. OR C.

NOTE:— This takes no consideration of additional great preponderance of Field Artillery in enemy's favour.

50 0 50 100 150 200 250
Scale of Miles

END OF MARCH 1915

Union Forces ....
Southern Army ..... A
Berrangé .... B
Central Force C
Northern Force ..... D

German Forces ....
von Kleist } E
Enemy detachments ....
Franke } F
Enemy concentration ...

NOTE:— Comparison of Field Artillery not included.

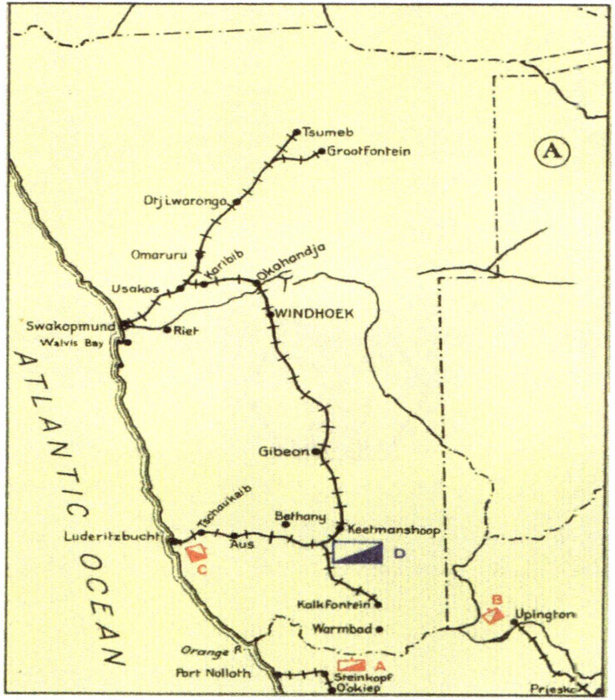

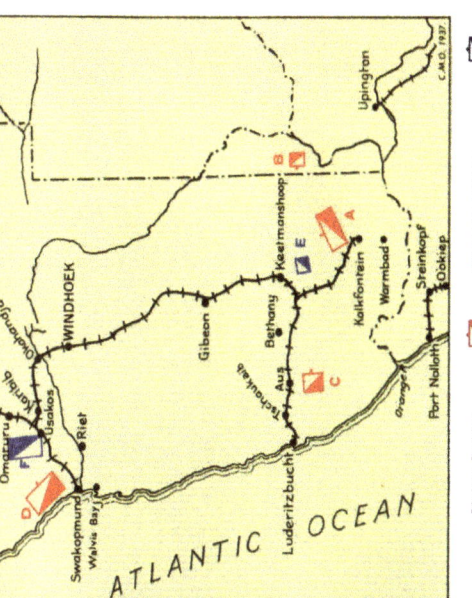

The Campaign in German South West Africa, 1914-1915

forces can be properly provided for without a clear conception of the purposes for which they are maintained and for this conception careful investigation is required.

We may now turn to the work of the different departments and services in the campaign.

Lines of Communication.

The forward bases of the forces were as follows:—

Northern Force	WALVIS.
Central Force	LUDERITZBUCHT.
Eastern Force	KIMBERLEY.
Southern Force	{ UPINGTON and STEINKOPF.

WALVIS was supplied from CAPETOWN 850 miles and LUDERITZBUCHT from the same place 550 miles by sea.

All the forces were really served by Lines of Communication which stretched back to PRETORIA.

A deficiency in the organisation was the absence of supervision from the forward bases back to the Union. The absence of control of the different lines in the Union had proved a drawback in the Rebellion. The lack of an authority which would decide the priority to be granted to troops and supplies of all kinds was a great handicap.

As an instance of what occurred it may be mentioned that the General Manager of Railways on one occasion reported that wagons of a similar type were being sent at the same time from PRETORIA to CAPETOWN and from CAPETOWN to PRETORIA, as were supplies of lucerne.

Supervision of the loads on the railway, from a strictly military point of view, would undoubtedly have prevented considerable waste of effort and material, but it was never carried out within the Union. Want of staff may have prevented it, but the point is worth attention.

Water on all lines of advance was a problem calling for solution in many different ways. The line of the Eastern Force was especially difficult in this respect. It was over 500 miles in length and included waterless stretches of over 100 miles (O.H., p.57).

" Tank stations were established that were filled by motorcars carrying 60 gallons each; these cars, of which about 40 were allotted to each station, worked in pairs, the drivers having to fill and empty the drums themselves."

The Campaign in German South West Africa, 1914-1915

Valuable help was given by the Irrigation Department of the Union on all lines of advance.

All the railway work was carried out by the staff of the South African Railways and many notable feats were performed.

In addition to the work from WALVIS and SWAKOPMUND to KARIBIB and the north, which has already been mentioned, between August 31 and November 20, 1914, the 3·6 in. railway line, which had ended at PRIESKA, was extended 153 miles to the south bank of the Orange River opposite UPINGTON.

On June 25, 1915, the German WINDHOEK–KALKFONTEIN line was joined up with the Union. This work, over a distance of 170 miles, included the bridging of the Orange River at UPINGTON, and a record in railway work in South Africa was established by laying $5\frac{1}{4}$ miles of line in one day.

Telegraphic and telephonic communication was attended to by personnel from the Post and Telegraph Department of the Union which also performed efficient and rapid work.

Sea communication and protection was looked to by the Royal Navy which, in addition to examining and sweeping the waters of LUDERITZBUCHT, SWAKOPMUND and WALVIS BAY and removing the mines, escorted, conveyed and disembarked the Union Forces from CAPETOWN to their various destinations on the coast without the loss of a life or a vessel. Animals, heavy railway and other stores and thousands of troops and natives were conveyed and disembarked with the loss of one locomotive tender which was subsequently salved.

The Naval Armoured Cars have already been mentioned.

Intelligence.

The Union intelligence staff was aided to some extent by the enemy who maintained little—or a very ineffective—censorship over letters, telegrams or wireless messages. The latter were particularly productive of information, supplies for one company, grass for another, and other requests or orders in connection with other named units gave material for estimating the strength of the forces and many other important factors were unconsciously presented to the Union staff.

Orders in cypher from German G.H.Q. compared with the information collected from the first-named sources sometimes resulted in the key word being soon discovered.

A habit of sending messages partly in cypher and partly

The Campaign in German South West Africa, 1914-1915

in clear was an additional help. The Union staffs were not guiltless in this respect, nor was D.H.Q.

The interception of the message ordering water reconnaissances to the north from NAMUTONI, which has been mentioned, indicated the direction of a contemplated retirement frustrated in the end by Brits' final march.

The method of commando "close" reconnaissance was such as to interfere with the regular transmission of information collected by the troops.

In any case, the intelligence staff, keenly anxious for such details as the troops can gather from contact with the enemy, has to wait long for such help in rapid mobile warfare.

The advanced scouts ahead of the commandos made good long stretches of country at a time and, unless information was of obvious and immediate importance to the actual movements of the main bodies behind, it was rarely communicated.

That those accustomed to the comparatively small bodies in which they operated in the Anglo-Boer War should not appreciate the value of every item of information which they might collect to the General controlling the whole operations was natural, and, to the end of the campaign, General Botha's repeated injunctions on the subject did not bear much fruit.

A great defect throughout the operations was an altogether inadequate supply of maps.

The need for good maps was not appreciated at D.H.Q., and perhaps the fact that the previous experience of many of those who were connected with the arrangement of the campaign had been gained in country with which they were entirely familiar may have had some influence.

The original supply of maps was so small and the maps were so indifferent as to be of little use.

A topographical section for field work—already collected and available—was applied for in the Northern Force during its organisation at PRETORIA.

To reinforce the recommendation, the place and utility of such a section was explained at length, and it was added that, in view of the lost opportunities of the past in the way of recording the country's experience in war, full topographical records would be of much value for the purposes of instruction.

The request was refused on the ground that, while sympathy was accorded with the views as to future instructional value, the first consideration was to reduce transport to the smallest limits!

The personnel numbered four and the transport needed was one scotch cart.

On a second urgent request from the scene of operations the section was sent up, but late, and as a consequence even mapping material was lacking to an extent which limited the issue of maps throughout the campaign to senior officers only, and valuable data remained unrecorded.

As was observed in the *Times* History of the Anglo-Boer War, at the outset of which the British Army suffered from the same defect, " accurate mapping is not a very expensive operation: at any rate its cost bears a very small proportion to the total cost of preparing for or conducting a campaign ".

The action at Headquarters in this instance argued a want of perception of essentials.

Transport.

The influence of the question of supply and transport in the campaign has been very fully discussed, and it is enough to observe that the mule wagons all required 12 animals to the wagon in the deep sand and heavy going.

In 1915 the use of any motor transport off the beaten track was impossible and even on the roads, such as they were, the water in the radiators often boiled every quarter of an hour or so and water tins had to be carried on all the running boards and frequently filled up.

The armoured cars were eventually sent back because their chassis were so twisted and bent as to make their further progress impracticable.

Medical Services.

The country in which the campaign was fought was very healthy and the casualties were relatively small and the demands on the medical services were not heavy.

Like all the other services, however, accompanying the troops, they were compelled to accommodate themselves to a rate of marching to which none of them had before been accustomed.

Hospitals were found in SWAKOPMUND, LUDERITZ-BUCHT, KARIBIB and WINDHOEK and were made use of by the Union Medical Staff.

Three cases of enteric fever occurred at WALVIS, and in each instance the victim had failed to submit himself, for some reason or other, to inoculation and became infected from a tank of water.

CHAPTER XIV

AS HAS BEEN stated in the last chapter, only 24 days of actual movement by the forces under General Botha were necessary to carry them from SWAKOPMUND to RIET and WINDHOEK, and thence to TSUMEB and OTAVIFONTEIN, a distance in no instance less than 400 miles.

If halts are allowed for and the nature of the country calling for careful close reconnaissance is borne in mind, these figures indicate an unusual degree of mobility.

It was this mobility directed by a master hand that cornered the enemy at last. The leadership and the response to it constituted a formidable combination.

And first to give an estimate of General Botha as a soldier.

Clausewitz says: " However pre-eminently a great commander does things, there is always something subjective in the way he does them; and if he has a certain manner, a large share of his individuality is contained in it which does not always accord with the individuality of the person who copies his manner."

The personality of General Botha was a factor of outstanding importance in all his public life and his military work was part of that life.

He was blessed with Solomon's gift of " an understanding heart " and was an intensely sympathetic and human man, and he possessed as a leader of men, which he essentially was, all the advantages, and what sometimes appeared to be the weaknesses, of his keenly sympathetic nature.

His personal charm, which so quickly won men's hearts, derived its main strength from the kindly attitude which he adopted towards those who served him. A complete stranger would fall instantly under the spell of General Botha's humanity.

Such a gift enables its possessor to call upon his subordinates for effort beyond the point where human endurance seems to have reached its limit without some powerful stimulus and discipline has ceased to have its full effect.

This, in a military commander, is a priceless possession.

If sometimes his reluctance to wound gave the impression

of a dislike to act strongly, it was really deceptive, for, once his mind had been made up as to the right course, he adopted it and rigidly adhered to it.

It follows that the path of duty was often bitter to him involving, as it did from time to time, misunderstanding on the part of old and proved friends, and separation from them, and in the Rebellion the death in arms against him of staunch comrades of earlier years.

The injustice which comes from a wrong conception of motives and sooner or later is meted out to every man of eminence in public life, wounded him deeply, and often roused him to anger.

Added to his great personal charm and power of inspiring affection were abundant common sense and a capacity to recognise and estimate the realities of any situation which might confront him and, perhaps the most striking of all his personal characteristics from a military point of view, an extraordinary sense of confidence and security which emanated from him and reassured those round him in any difficult circumstances.

He was also a good judge of character and human nature, and if, occasionally, he used men in positions where their qualifications were short of those required, it must be remembered that the political situation often complicated matters.

It would be idle to pretend that many military appointments in German South West Africa were not largely determined by political considerations, but, so far as General Botha was concerned, he was well aware of the limitations of those appointed and did his best so to employ them that their military shortcomings should not affect results.

Those who, in the course of military operations, had to refer to General Botha constantly, when things were going smoothly and often when matters were far from smooth, militarily or politically, never met with anything but courtesy, sympathy, help and generous appreciation.

Reports, suggestions, difficulties, all received careful attention and, if the suggestions were not always adopted, whoever made them felt that the Commander-in-Chief appreciated his work.

General Botha added to his personal attributes military skill of a high order.

He had a keen appreciation of good staff work and evinced a very clear perception of the relations which should exist between

The Campaign in German South West Africa, 1914-1915

a commander and his staff to whom, once his confidence had been gained, he left all detail.

As the result of constant free intercourse with his Chief of Staff, while he never delegated a vestige of responsibility which he regarded as his own and exercised command in every sense of the word, the performance of staff duties was enormously lightened in a campaign in which staff work for many reasons was unusually heavy and trying.

It soon became apparent to anyone who had the opportunity of frequent conversation with General Botha that he had carefully observed the methods of his opponents in the Anglo-Boer War, and had noted their mistakes. Granting his great natural military talent, he could not have displayed the often surprising knowledge he possessed of details which as a rule are only familiar to professional soldiers after study and experience, unless he had gained it by shrewd observation.

He recognised, for example, the necessarily limited mobility of infantry, an arm which he had never before handled strategically or tactically.

The very best of the commando leaders subconsciously thought, if they thought at all, of the marching rate of infantry as little less than that of their mounted men, and often expressed disappointment at the failure of the infantry to achieve some impossible rate of marching.

General Botha's plans were always based on a reasonable calculation so far as the infantry rate of marching was concerned, and he constantly expressed his unstinted admiration for their fine conduct during their wearisome halts and splendid marching when they were on the move.

Such an injunction as the following indicates his recognition of the need for combination of all tactical means of offence.

Speaking to a gathering of his senior officers explaining a forthcoming operation, he said: " I should advise you to consult these machine-gun people and see what is the best manner in which they may be employed."

He was intimately acquainted with the military worth of his rapidly moving mounted men, but was also alive to their defects as such orders as the following will indicate.

" Another point I wish to emphasise is the necessity of your men keeping together. Let them stay with their field-cornet and let them follow their field-cornet but do not let them rush in

The Campaign in German South West Africa, 1914-1915

in small numbers and get separated from the others. The field-cornet must go with his men. Let me impress upon you that we are not fighting natives now, and therefore I want you to take all necessary measures to deal with a properly armed and properly trained enemy."

And again: " Do not bring all your 1,100 men into the fighting line at once. Of course bring in sufficient men, but keep the rest in reserve, because you may want them."

We have already noted the tendency of the commando to adopt an early aggressive attitude, and the manner in which the 5th Brigade went into action at OTAVIFONTEIN, and the instructions of their Commander-in-Chief show clearly that he recognised the danger of too ready a commitment of large bodies in an attack.

Another military characteristic of General Botha was an invariable practice of personal reconnaissance whenever opportunity offered.

The sense of the value of ground and of direction possessed by so many of his countrymen was his in a marked degree, and on many occasions he would sit for hours at a time continually watching the country before him through his glasses with the result that he obviously came away with the terrain over which his operations were to be conducted imprinted in his memory.

He would often arrange to meet Brits or some other commander at a given hour at a certain locality in country which neither knew from previous experience and the meeting invariably came off at the time and spot arranged.

Strategists abound. " Military strategy ", wrote General Maurice in " Forty Days in 1914 ", " is to the amateur more fascinating than a chess problem and in appearance not more difficult to grasp "; there are many tacticians skilled in their own and other arms; there is no inconsiderable number of able soldiers who are capable strategists and sound tacticians; there is a comparatively small body of great leaders in whom strategic insight and tactical ability are joined to great personal gifts and General Louis Botha was one of these.

The success of his strategy in German South West Africa was of course due, after the boldness and sagacity with which he adopted it, to the mobility of his troops which he gauged to a nicety and of which he took full advantage.

It is important to emphasise that the tactics of the mounted riflemen of the Union in 1914 and 1915 were national in the

The Campaign in German South West Africa, 1914-1915

strictest sense of the term. They were the outcome of the environment and circumstances of the every-day life of the forbears of those who fought in German South West Africa and in essential respects these circumstances had undergone little practical change. The English-speaking South Africans were as adept in these tactics as were their Afrikaans-speaking comrades, though perhaps in the first instance some acquaintance with military discipline had tended to affect the marked individualism of the man in the ranks.

Many men of British descent served in the commandos under General Botha and General Smuts, and the work of McKenzie's mounted men was as remarkable as that of those in the north or the south. McKenzie's Natal regiments were preponderantly English-speaking.

The fact that the tactics employed were of a national character is of great interest, for the mode of fighting which gave the Union the advantage over their opponents in 1914 when the latter were numerically inferior to them enabled the same mounted riflemen in the two South African republics, when relatively far inferior in strength to their opponents, to keep at bay for two and a half years the military strength of the British Empire and to compel the use of 256,340 regular troops and a number of Colonial forces against them.

For offence or defence then, a national military system employed in country suitable for its use is of the greatest value.

Before going further in a consideration of General Botha's strategy, it may be well to attempt to visualise the conditions which the military forces of the Union may have to face in future, for it is clear that any feature of a national system which has served the country well in the past should not be abandoned unless, after careful reflection, the course appears to be unavoidable in view of modern changes.

The position for which the General Staff of the military forces of South Africa should prepare would seem to be the practicable mean between the most satisfactory condition in which the Union may face an invasion of her territory and the most unfavourable circumstances which can attend such an event.

The most satisfactory condition possible is that at present obtaining, viz.: partnership in the British Empire with common measures for mutual protection by all partners in that alliance and the best measure of protection which can be afforded for the ocean trade routes between all parts of that Commonwealth.

The Campaign in German South West Africa, 1914-1915

The most unfavourable circumstances in which the territorial integrity of the Union could be threatened would be a denial of all trade routes over the seas to the Union, in which event South Africa would find herself in the position of the two Republics in 1899, cut off entirely from every kind of supply or means of waging war that she could not produce within her borders.

Invasion in the last event would be by a direct descent on the seaboard of the Union from oversea.

Between these two sets of circumstances lies the possibility of invasion from the north overland by any Power with a base in Africa which could be maintained from oversea. Such a situation would postulate the ability of the invader to keep his armies in Africa supplied from oversea to an extent which would make the success of his attempt possible, and would not entail the entire loss of sea communications to the Union.

In other words, each combatant could look to some degree of assistance by means of ocean transport.

Resistance to such an attack would have to be initiated as far north of the borders of the Union as possible, and would mean fighting on terrain which in itself would be an aid to a stubborn defence, if properly turned to account.

Great mountains, huge tracts of heavily-bushed country, lengthening communications, unhealthy climate, extreme difficulty of ground transport in certain seasons are all obstacles to any European force in an advance from the north towards the south and in almost all the respects mentioned to any force depending upon modern means of warfare.

Napoleon said that the " secret of war lies in the communications ". The introduction of mechanisation and aircraft has increased the significance of this statement.

Spare parts for repairs, workshops, oil and petrol are all indispensable to the maintenance of modern machines of war, and their importance and the difficulty of providing them increases as an advance progresses over difficult roads or perhaps no roads at all.

South Africa produces neither the machines, the material for their maintenance or repair, nor the fuel to keep them mobile, and if she relies upon modern methods alone her resistance to an enemy capable of initiating an overland invasion of her territory must be strictly limited as to effect and duration alike.

It would seem therefore that the Union military system, while

The Campaign in German South West Africa, 1914-1915

taking advantage of modern implements and methods of war to the full extent which the resources of the country may allow and the probable conditions of the employment of its military forces may suggest, must seek to adjust a probable inferiority in respect of modern material and supplies.

This can be best done by a national system of training for the personnel which will not be needed for the air arm and mechanised and other special units. Such a system will develop to the full any natural aptitude for war which the South African may possess with the object of fitting him for campaigning in the country which will be the probable scene of operations.

The question of training is of much importance.

It is quite clear that, as has always been the case in South Africa, any considerable emergency will call for immediate and rapid expansion of the normal military forces of the country.

In 1914 on expansion, though it was impossible to provide an adequate number of staff officers, the extra forces mobilised were practically all trained to the tactics which were to be employed and had had the inestimable advantage of two and a half years' practical experience in the shape of hard fighting twelve years earlier.

For the special form of campaign in which they were engaged they were literally first-class soldiers.

These men are no longer available, even if the tactics of which they were such striking exponents are allowed to be still practical. Any strength over and above the establishments of the Permanent and Active Citizen Forces is untrained.

It is highly important that some form of training should be laid down for the relatively large numbers of additional men who will have to be made available in time of war.

It will be war of movement, and leaders and men need far more training for this form of warfare than that for which men were trained in Europe in a comparatively short time.

What is this training to be?

Admitting that in certain possible scenes of operations by the South African Forces the employment of mounted riflemen is, if not impossible, at all events too wasteful to be considered, has the mounted rifleman of 1899 to 1915 served his day and become obsolete? In that day he was probably as fine a representative of his particular arm as ever served in war.

Such questions as these must exercise the ingenuity and engage the attention of the General Staff.

The Campaign in German South West Africa, 1914-1915

It may be admitted that as the conditions of country life in South Africa tend to recede from pioneer conditions, and, with the introduction of the motor-car, become more comfortable, several of the circumstances which contributed to the strategical and tactical value of the mounted soldiers of South Africa have ceased to exercise such influence as they did.

Successors to the men who fought against each other 35 years ago and side by side 12 years later can still be found, however, if their employment in war on the same lines is considered worth while.

While it is General Botha's strategy that is dealt with, it must be remembered that the troops he directed were the counterpart of those who served under General Smuts and General McKenzie.

Of General Botha's three advances two failed of their full possible effect and the third and last was completely successful.

While the enemy force remained in the country as an objective General Botha took the chance of failure to gain that objective, but when, after the fall of WINDHOEK, the intention of the enemy to escape to the north was thought likely and was eventually shown to be actually in contemplation, he took no risk.

Until he was sure that his movements, so far as preparation could ensure it, would suffer no interruption before the object of those movements should have been achieved, he declined to advance.

The proper use of mobility connotes surprise of the enemy against whom it is employed.

Any check, not reckoned with in plans for movements intended to end in the surprise of the enemy, at once lessens the chance of that surprise and if protracted renders it impossible.

General Botha's last movements in the campaign show clear recognition of this.

There is no doubt that it was the appearance of Brits at NAMUTONI which compelled the enemy to abandon his intention to fight " collected " and sue for terms instead.

By fixing the German Commander's attention on his own and Myburgh's advances and throwing Brits wide to the west on the decisive point at NAMUTONI, General Botha again employed the soundest strategy and whether infantry, mounted men or mechanised units are employed, mobility, and the result

The Campaign in German South West Africa, 1914-1915

of its correct use, surprise, will remain factors of success in war tactically or strategically.

The mobility of the mounted men in German South West Africa was due to their horsemanship, horsemastership and ability to live on hard fare and endure fatigue.

Judged by one of the greatest masters of the art of war who laid it down that: " The first qualification of a soldier is fortitude under fatigue and privation ", the soldiers of South Africa who served in German South West Africa in the Great War displayed military qualities of a high order.

Their tactics were, to risk undue repetition, the outcome of their ordinary life which, in addition to the advantages mentioned above, made them self-reliant and good marksmen.

The campaign clearly shows that military training is much simplified if it takes full cognisance of national aptitude for war.

In mobile warfare extended and close reconnaissance, gathering information, operations against the enemy communications (nowadays more vulnerable and vital than ever) are among many important tasks which have hitherto fallen to the lot of the mounted soldier in South Africa.

These tasks will all have to be carried out in future and in much of the country south of the equator they must be carried out by ground troops often moving as individuals.

The campaign in German South West Africa in 1914-15 was a brilliant success at a time when success was badly needed and at the time was hailed as such.

Its casualties paled into insignificance in comparison with the tremendous loss of life which the Great War caused.

As a small " side-show " in the world-wide upheaval it was soon forgotten.

To the Union of South Africa it must always be of much interest, for the chief command was exercised by the greatest of South African soldiers under whom the men of the two races, whose differences have loomed so large in the history of their country, faced a common danger side by side.

Whatever may be the future of the military forces of the Union, the successors of these men will find much to inspire them and will derive instruction from the first campaign which the Union of South Africa conducted solely on its own responsibility.

INDEX

"A" Force (Lukin), composition of, 28.
Adler, Lieutenant, at Sandfontein, 41.
Alberts, Colonel J. J., 57; 64; in command at Pforte, 69; 71; moves on Otjimbingwe, 103; 108; 116; 124; 132; 145; 150.
Armistice, local, arranged, 147; terms purposely restricted, 147.
Artillery, 4th Permanent Field Battery at Pforte, 70; 12th Citizen Field Battery at Gibeon, 91; allotment of, 112; on last advance, 119; German superiority in, 128; 2nd Permanent Field Battery at Otavifontein, 138; German superiority in, at Otavifontein, 140; Heavy, marches into Otavifontein, 147.
Aus, German position at, 52; Germans evacuate, 80.

"B" Force (Maritz), composition of, 28.
Badenhorst, Colonel-Commandant, 63.
Berrangé, Colonel C. A. L., commands Eastern Force, 55; 80; 119.
Beves, Colonel P. S., at conference, D.H.Q., 27; occupies Luderitzbucht, 30; 119; 123; 128; 129; starts record infantry march, 130; occupies Epako, 130; 136; 145; marches into Otavifontein, 147; 151.
Beyers, Brig.-General C. F., at conference, D.H.Q., 27.
Bezuidenhout, Commandant, 65; 68; 69.
Boer, military forces in 1899, 11; the, a fighting man, 11; tactics consequence of life and environment, 12; defects of military system, 13.
Botha, Brig.-General H. W. N. (Manie), 97; 101; 104; 124; 127; 128; ordered to cancel movement, 131; occupies Kalkfeld, 132; 133; occupies Okanjande, 134; 137; fights action at Otavifontein, 138; his decision, 140; 150.
Botha, General Louis, first Premier of Union, 4; experience of command, 17; confers with McKenzie, 52; assumes command at Swakopmund, 54; clears front at Swakopmund, 57; decides plan of first advance, 58, 59; dispositions for Riet and Pforte operations, 65; keeps in close touch with fighting troops, 74; withdraws bulk of forces to coast, 78; confers again with McKenzie, 79; instructs Bastard Chief, 83; decides plan of second advance, 84; decides to advance, 86; orders second advance, 95; instructions prior to advance, 99; again advises Bastard Chief, 100; leaves Riet with second advance, 100; final instructions for advance on Windhoek, 102; meets General Smuts at Pot Mine, 103; occupies Karibib, 104; results of strategy of, 105; confers with General Smuts at Karibib, 114; objective of third advance, 115; leaves for Windhoek, 116; occupies Windhoek, 116; meets Governor Seitz, 117; in sole command, 118; insists on sound supply arrangements, 121; decides moves in final advance, 123; visits all forces, 126; leaves Karibib on final advance, 128; habit of personal reconnaissance, 130; threatens reprisals, 131; orders Brits' flank march, 135; at action of Otavifontein, 138; situation after action of Otavifontein, 143; refuses Governor Seitz's proposals, 146; asked by Governor Seitz to formulate terms, 147; communicates tentative terms to Governor Seitz, 147; purposely restricts terms of armistice, 147; meets Governor Seitz, 148; communicates provisional terms to Union Ministers, 149; learns of success of own plans from the enemy, 149; sends Governor Seitz final terms, 150; leaves G.S.W. Africa, 154; his achievement, 154; his military talent and character, 165; his use of mobility, 172.

The Campaign in German South West Africa, 1914-1915

Botha, Commandant Piet, at Pforte, 71.
Brink, Major A. J., 68; 77.
British Army, in 1899, 9; defects of, 10; reform of, 1904, 10.
British Government, early action of, in S.W. Africa, 2; annexes Walvis Bay, 3; enlists aid of Union Government, 6.
Brits, Brig.-General C. J., 64; his character, 64; commands at Riet, 66; 67; 68; commands a force in second advance, 96; moves from Riet, 99; occupies Kubas, 103; rôle in final advance, 123; 126; 127; 128; occupies Omaruru, 129; 130; 132; 134; leaves on flank march, 135; out of touch, 137; force excluded from terms of armistice, 147; occupies Namutoni, 149; enemy impeded by march of, 149; informed of final situation, 150; 172.

Cape Colony, military forces at Union, 14.
Casualties, German, at Riet and Pforte, 76; at Gibeon, 91; at Trekkoppies, 94; at Otavifontein, 141; at Surrender, 152.
Casualties, Union, at Sandfontein, 43; at Riet and Pforte, 76; at Gibeon, 91; at Trekkoppies, 94; at Otavifontein, 142; total, 152.
Central Force (McKenzie), composition of, 55; line of advance of, 56; removed from control of General Botha, 85; moves from Aus, 88; in action at Gibeon, 90; marching of, 153.
Claassens, Commandant, 126.
Collins, Colonel-Commandant W. R., 58; 64; at Pforte, 71; 73; 96; 145.
Commando Brigades, their composition, 56; tactics, 73; leaders personality in, 74.
Commandos, Bloemhof at Riet, 65; Ermelo at Pforte, 69; Standerton B at Pforte, 69; Bloemhof, 108; record march by Standerton, 126.
Communication, Lines of, on second advance, 98; after second advance, 108; Swakop route abandoned, 109; on occupation of Windhoek, 111; 112; congestion on, 121; reorganisation of, 122; 161; sea, 162.

Defence Headquarters, constitution of and system at, 1914, 19; its defects, 19; conference at, to decide initial plan, 27; urges Lukin to press on to Sandfontein, 32; unsound strategy, 47; fails to advise Lukin in time of enemy concentration, 48; dissipation of effort by, 52.
de la Rey, Colonel-Commandant Piet, 63; 96; 135.
Desert, feeding armies in, 24.
Deventer, Colonel Dirk van, in south, 80; 81.
Deventer, Brig.-General J. L. van, commands Southern Force, 55; 80.

Eastern Force (Berrangé), composition of, 55; line of advance of, 56; 80.
Eighth Mounted Brigade, at Gibeon, 89.
Esselen, Captain L., 145; 146; 147.

Field Forces, Union, disposition of, prior to occupation of Windhoek, 108; reorganisation after fall of Windhoek, 119; initiate last advance, 125; concentrated for final advance, 127; strength on final advance, 128.

Fifth Mounted Brigade, 97; 99; 101; 105; 119; 124; 133; 134; 136; 138; 140; at Otavifontein, 140; marching of, 153.

First Infantry Brigade, reconstituted, 123; 124; 125; temporarily under Lukin, 126; starts record march, 130; 133; marches into Otavifontein, 147; marching of, 153.

First Mounted Brigade, 65; 96; 99; 119; 123; 134; marching of, 153.

First Mounted Rifles, at Gibeon, 91.

Fouché, Colonel-Commandant W., 97; 150.

Fourth Infantry Brigade, 82; in field force, 98; 119.

Franke, Colonel (German Commander-in-Chief), reconnoitres to north, 120; indicates intention to defend Kalkfeld, 126; dispositions before final Union advance, 129; order by, at Otavifontein, 143; statement of strategy of, 144; complains of breach of armistice, 149; 151.

German Imperial Government, relies on Boer co-operation against England, 5.

German Press, on South African soldiers, 107.

German Protectorate Forces, establishment and strength, 1914, 20; organisation of, 21; advantages possessed by, 21; power of concentration, 26; portion of, surrenders at Pforte, 71; bulk of, withdraws to north, 80; defeated at Gibeon, 91; repulsed at Trekkoppies, 94; dispositions of, on second Union advance, 99; concentrated before General Botha, 99; retirement to north completed, 106; dispositions of, before final Union advance, 126; surprised at Otavifontein, 140; retire from Otavifontein, 141; strength at Otavifontein, 141.

German South West Africa, earliest exploration of, 1; early history of, 2; extent and physical features of, 7.

Gibeon, action at, 89; comments on action at, 92.

Giftkuppe, abortive conference at, 117.

Grant, Lt.-Colonel R. C., assumes command at Sandfontein, 40; wounded, 41; surrenders to von Heydebreck, 43.

Heydebreck, Colonel von (German Commander-in-Chief), attacks Grant at Sandfontein, 40; captures Union force, 43; death of, 61.

Hoy, Sir William, at conference at D.H.Q., 27, at Karibib re railway, 109; improves railway position, 123.

Husab, supply base, first advance, 62.

Imperial Light Horse, at Gibeon, 90.

Intelligence, 162.

Jordaan, Colonel-Commandant, 97; 124; 130; 133; 145.

Kalkfeld, advance for attack on, 131; occupied, 132.

Karibib, direct movement on, begun, 103; occupied, 104; description of, 105; Germans formally surrender, 106.

Kilo 500, venue of final peace discussions, 147.

The Campaign in German South West Africa, 1914-1915

Kleist, Major von, defeated at Gibeon, 91; withdraws to north, 92; 99; 126; defeated by Myburgh, 149.

Kühnest, Justice, surrenders Karibib, 106.

Lemmer, Colonel-Commandant L. A. S., 63; 96; on march to Namutoni, 135.

Lessons of Campaign, 155-161.

Lüderitzbucht, occupied, 30.

Lukin, Brig.-General H. T., at conference at D.H.Q., 27; commands "A" force, 28; disembarks force at Port Nolloth, 30; occupies Sandfontein, 31; his character, 32; responsibility in connection with Sandfontein affair, 45; leaves with force for Union, 49; 124; 126; 127; 128; 129; 131; 132; 134; 137; at Otavifontein, 139; 141; 150; 151; 154.

Maps, shortage and inadequacy of, 163.

Marches, details of, notable, 152.

Maritz, Lt.-Colonel S. F., commands "B" Force, 28; his character, 33; refuses to enter G.S.W. Africa, 34; goes into rebellion, 34.

McKenzie, Brig.-General Sir Duncan, at conference at D.H.Q., 27; assumes command at Lüderitzbucht, 52; moves from Aus, 88; fights action at Gibeon, 89; defeats von Kleist, 91; returns to Union, 93; 99.

Medical Services, 164.

Mentz, Colonel H. S., 97; 101; 103; 108; 116; military governor, Windhoek, 117; secures right rear of final advance, 126.

Mines, Explosive land, 77; 101; at Otavifontein, 138; 141; 145.

Missionaries, Moravian, first settlers in S.W. Africa, 1.

Mobility, of Union forces under-estimated by Germans, 18; German commander surprised by, 103; full use of, possible, 125; of Union forces at Otavifontein, 140; proper use of, 172; causes of South African, in 1914, 173.

Mounted Riflemen, efficiency of South African, in 1914, 171; future value, 172.

Myburgh, Brig.-General M. W., his character, 95; commands a force in second advance, 97; moves from Riet, 99; 101; moves against railway, 102; 103; 104; 108; 124; 127; 128; out of touch, 132; 133; 134; 137; 145; ordered to move on Tsumeb, 146; excluded from terms of armistice, 147; defeats von Kleist and occupies Tsumeb, 149; informed of final situation, 150, 172.

Nakob, affair of, 22.

Natal, military forces at Union, 14; forces in south return to Union, 93.

Natal Light Horse, at Gibeon, 90.

Naval Armoured Cars, Royal, arrive at Swakopmund, 87; at Trekkoppies, 94; to First Infantry Brigade, 125; returned to Union, 135.

Ninth Mounted Brigade, at Gibeon, 89.

Northern Force (Botha), composition of, 54; line of advance of, 56; first advance, 65; second advance, 99.

Nussey, Colonel-Commandant, 97.

The Campaign in German South West Africa, 1914-1915

Omaruru, description of, 129; occupied, 129.
Operations, factors in Union plan of, 26; first Union plan of, 27.
Orange Free State, military forces at Union, 14; burghers, 16.
Otavifontein, action at, 138; terrain at, 139.

Pforte, action at, 69; comments on action at, 75.
Pijper, Lt.-Colonel, at Otavifontein, 141.
Poole, Captain, at Grootfontein, 146.

Railways (German), strategic arrangement of, 24; confer mobility on German forces, 50.
Railways (Union), rapid work by personnel of, 162.
Reconnaissance, lax at Sandfontein, 46.
Rehoboth Bastards, Chief interviews General Botha, 83; collision with German forces, 100.
Riet, action at, 66; comments on action at, 74; held after action, 79; reinforced, 82; supply base, second advance, 85; concentration at, for second advance, 99.
Ritter, Major, in south, 80.
Rodger, Colonel, 93.
Royston, Colonel, at Gibeon, 89; casualties at Gibeon, 91.

Sandfontein, occupied by Lukin, 31; position described, 38; Grant assumes command at, 40; attacked by von Heydebreck, 40; Union force surrenders at, 43.
Schuit Drift, affair of, 22.
Scouts, Swart's at Pforte, 70; feature of commando system, 72.
Second Mounted Brigade, 65; 78; 96; 100; 119; 124; marching of, 152.
Second Mounted Rifles, at Gibeon, 91.
Seitz, Governor, disclaims intention to invade Union, 23; on arming of natives, 100; seeks armistice, 117; meets General Botha, 117; conference with, 118; suggests terms, 146; asks General Botha to formulate terms, 147; meets General Botha again, 148; receives final terms, 150; accepts terms, 151; final meeting with General Botha, 151.
Signalling, proposed arrangements, 112.
Sixth (Permanent) Mounted Brigade, 86; 120; 124; crosses desert, 124; 127; 133; 134; 136; 138; marching of, 152.
Skinner, Brig.-General P. C. B., at conference at D.H.Q., 27; lands at Walvis Bay, 52; occupies Swakopmund, 52; commands in action at Trekkoppies, 93; moves on Aukas, 103; commands L. of C., 123.
Smith, Major, in south, 80.
Smuts, General J. C., presides over conference at D.H.Q., 27; keeps in close touch with fighting troops, 74; commands Southern Army, 80; meets General Botha at Pot Mine, 103; returns to south, 103; 110; arrives at Karibib, 114; confers with General Botha, 114.

Third Infantry Brigade, 120.
Third Mounted Brigade, 97; 99; 101; 105; 119.
Third Mounted Brigade (Right Wing), 124; marching of, 152.
Transport, great importance of, 24; difficulties in connection with, 25; serious shortage of, 60; lack of, interferes with campaign, 84; position in detail, 85; urgently asked for, 86; exhaustion of, animals, 113; again vital factor, 121; available from south, 121; allocation of, in final advance, 125;164.
Transvaal, military forces at Union, 14; burghers, 16.
Transvaal Horse Artillery, at Sandfontein, 41.
Trekkoppies, action at, 93.

Umvoti Mounted Rifles, at Gibeon, 90.
Union Defence Act, 1912, provisions of, 15.
Union Defence Forces, available for war in 1914, 17; inadequate staff, 17; in 1914 national, 168; value of national defence system to, 169.
Union Field Forces, disposition prior to occupation of Windhoek, 108; reorganisation of, after fall of Windhoek, 119; initiate final advance, 125; concentrated for final advance, 127; strength of, on final advance, 128; distribution of, after action at Otavifontein, 145.
Union Government, undertakes military obligations, 1914, 6; military situation facing, in 1914, 22; receives General Botha's provisional terms of surrender for German forces, 148.

van Deventer, Colonel Dirk, in south, 80; 81.
van Deventer, Bir.-General J. L., commands Southern Force, 55; 80.
van Tonder, Colonel-Commandant, 97.
van Vuuren, Captain, in south, 81.
van Wijk, Chief, see Rehoboth Bastards.
Visser, Colonel-Commandant A. P., 96; 135.
von Heydebreck, Colonel, attacks Grant at Sandfontein, 40; captures Union Force, 43; death of, 61.
von Kleist, Major, defeated at Gibeon, 91; withdraws to north, 92; 99; 126; defeated by Myburgh, 149.

Walvis Bay, Union troops land at, 52.
Water, first surface, found, 134; importance of, at Otavifontein, 136; first running, found, 142.
Windhoek, its value to German Commander, 50; situation after occupation of, 110; occupied, 116.
Wylie, Colonel J. S., commands at Riet, 79; reaches Kubas, 103.